Stop the Presses!
I Want to Get Off!

T0307906

VOICES FROM THE UNDERGROUND SERIES, EDITED BY KEN WACHSBERGER

Insider Histories of the Vietnam Era Underground Press, Part 1

Insider Histories of the Vietnam Era Underground Press, Part 2

My Odyssey through the Underground Press, by Michael "Mica" Kindman

Stop the Presses! I Want to Get Off! A Brief History of the Prisoners'
Digest International, by Joseph W. Grant

Voices
from the
Underground
*

Stop the Presses!
I Want to Get Off!

A Brief History of the
Prisoners' Digest International

JOSEPH W. GRANT

EDITED BY KEN WACHSBERGER

Michigan State University Press • East Lansing

♾ The paper used in this publication meets the minimum requirements of ANSI/NISO Z39.48-1992 (R 1997) (Permanence of Paper).

 Michigan State University Press
East Lansing, Michigan 48823-5245

Printed and bound in the United States of America.

18 17 16 15 14 13 12   1 2 3 4 5 6 7 8 9 10

LIBRARY OF CONGRESS CATALOGING-IN-PUBLICATION DATA
Grant, Joseph W.
Stop the presses! I want to get off! : a brief history of the Prisoners' digest international / Joseph W.
Grant ; edited by Ken Wachsberger.
p. cm. — (Voices from the underground)
Includes bibliographical references and index.
ISBN 978-1-61186-061-0 (pbk. : alk. paper) 1. Grant, Joseph W. 2. Prisoners' digest international.
3. Prisoners—United States—Biography. 4. Prison periodicals—United States—History—20th century.
5. Prison journalism—United States—History—20th century. 6. Prisoners—United States—Periodicals—
History—20th century. I. Wachsberger, Ken. II. Title.
HV9468.G7325A3 2012
365'.6092—dc23
[B]
2011050531

ISBN 978-1-61186-061-0 (paper) / ⓔ ISBN 978-1-60917-346-3 (e-book)

Cover design by Erin Kirk New
Book design by Sharp Des!gns, Lansing, Michigan

OPPOSITE PAGE: Prisoner giving peace sign, Graterford Prison, Graterford, Pennsylvania. Photo by Joe Grant. Courtesy of PDI Archives.

g green Michigan State University Press is a member of the Green Press Initiative and is committed
press to developing and encouraging ecologically responsible publishing practices. For more
INITIATIVE information about the Green Press Initiative and the use of recycled paper in book publishing, please
visit *www.greenpressinitiative.org.*

Visit Michigan State University Press at *www.msupress.org*

AUTHOR JOE GRANT DEDICATES THIS BOOK . . .

To S. T. and Chi Chi
and
in loving memory of
"Peggy" Magda Christine (Folwick) Grant
(December 24, 1904–January 5, 2002)
born in Trondheim, Norway;
died in Milaca, Minnesota

SERIES EDITOR KEN WACHSBERGER DEDICATES THIS BOOK . . .

To Emily, David, and Carrie,
who still make me laugh

Contents

Into the Future: Rambling Thoughts as I Bring This Story Up to Date

Afterword by Paul Wright   213

Sidebars

About the Authors   217

Index   219

Foreword

MUMIA ABU-JAMAL

t would be sheer understatement for me to praise Joe Grant's prison bio as "groundbreaking," "moving," or "eye-opening." It is all these things, but certainly much more.

It is history, as told by a talented raconteur, to be sure. But it is more.

It is *journalism.*

Joseph W. Grant (or, the man formerly known as prisoner #84219, FCI Leavenworth) has completed a work of history, first-person, of the days when the imprisoned were known as "prisoners," not "inmates." Notably, the latter term rarely enters his narrative. He writes sparely, with a sense of humor that is both understated and delightful—a kind of "gallows humor" used by cons and cops. Smiling in the midst of madness. And horror.

Remarkably, Grant resisted repeated urgings for him to pen his memoirs. All the more remarkable in that he is quite a talented writer, with an eye for detail, an ear for dialogue, and a memory scarred as only a prisoner's can be.

He has also lived through and seen some of the most memorable times of the twentieth century.

Want to know the inside story of how the Cuban Revolution got armed—*and the role American sailors had in arming the rebels*? Look no further than between these pages.

Imagine, if you will, that you are in a maximum security prison (well, some of us ain't got to imagine), and you want to put out a newspaper.

No, you don't get it. Not an administratively approved, guard-censored newspaper. *An underground newspaper.*

Grant, writing like it's a script from a Stephen King science-fiction series, pens how he and his homies did it—under the nose of the guards, chaplain, and administrators—and then got it distributed throughout the joint!

This is journalism, of a kind that never made it into the curriculum of J-School. This ain't your grandmama's *New York Times.* This is the real stuff.

Grant gives us all a bird's-eye view of how prisons ran during the sixties and seventies, and gives us a glimpse of what might have been, before the prison reform movement fell into the black hole of the corrections industry, and the culture of mass fear emerged.

His recollections of the broad movements of the sixties and seventies will give young readers history lessons about what was once possible in the U.S. This is especially important as these words are written, and we witness the emergence of the Occupy Wall Street movement.

Grant's heart-work, or that which quickens his blood and fevers his imagination, was the launching of the *Prisoners' Digest International*, a radical journal that swam into prisons across the country and inspired poets, artists, journalists, and readers to join the effort and make it a success.

I admit, cleanly and fully, the following: Before reading this work, I had never heard of Joseph W. Grant, nor the PDI. Although we've certainly lived through much of the same era, and undoubtedly crossed some of the same streets, I wasn't aware of this remarkable story when it was being written on hope and a dream.

I am therefore doubly grateful to have read this work, and learned of corners of the U.S. Incarceral Empire.

I, like you, am grateful to have this opportunity to do so now.

Don't do it because I say so.

Do it because it's a great story. Do it because it's great first-person history. Do it because the dreams of yesterday must once again take wing, to bring new days to live in the vast prison house that we all inhabit today.

Editor's Preface

KEN WACHSBERGER

I f you believe in predestination, and there are definitely times when I do—although at other times I call it vibes, karma, luck, a major coincidence, going with the flow, and the Yiddish *b'shert* (It was meant to be)—I'm the guy about whom God said, probably somewhere between Day 6 and Day 7, "He'll cover the underground press for me." I just seemed to be in the right place at the right time often where the underground press was concerned.

Certainly that's how I came to meet the folks who lived and worked at 505 South Lucas in Iowa City, the *Penal Digest International* collective. It started with a woman. I know that's a cliché. It's corny. Looking back, I'm a little embarrassed. But there's no way around it. I broke up with a woman, got depressed, fell into my "woe is me" state of mind, and did what I always did in the early seventies when I was depressed or restless: I hit the road. It was May 1972.

My first stop was Madison, Wisconsin—one of the Midwestern countercultural hotbeds of the sixties and seventies. My next stop was Boulder, Colorado—not as much of a radical hotbed, but current residence of my all-time oldest friend. I traveled by my usual mode of transportation, my thumb. And so on this particular afternoon I was hitching west on I-80 from Madison to Boulder. I got let off in Iowa City, Iowa. Before I had time to recharge my thumb, a car pulled up alongside me. Two guys sat in the front seat. "Where ya headed?" one asked.

"Boulder," I said.

"Hungry?"

I was, although I didn't pay much attention to hunger in those days until someone called my attention to it. I fed off the exhilaration of being on the road, being as one with the universe, waving the shopping bag that displayed my destination so seductively that drivers wanting to pretend they didn't see me were nonetheless forced to make eye contact and thus either stop and offer me a lift, or pass me anyhow but now be immersed in guilt. And if all that wasn't enough to assuage or hide my hunger, I always had a bag of raisins in my knapsack—they never went bad and you could squish them into any open bubble of space.

The passenger swung open the back door, I got in, and they drove me to 505 South Lucas. On the way to 505, as they called it, they explained to me that they were ex-cons and that they worked on a paper called *Penal Digest International*, or PDI. I had never heard of the paper, in part because it wasn't a member of Underground Press Syndicate, the first nationwide network of underground papers, including *Joint Issue*, the paper I worked on in East Lansing/Lansing, Michigan. But I sure as hell was intrigued by the idea of a paper that was published by ex-cons, and whose reporters were all prisoners covering their respective "beats" in Folsom, Leavenworth, Soledad, Attica, and other prisons all over the country. My two drivers radiated excitement as they talked about the paper, but became even more passionate as they shared news of the recent addition to their collective, a girl who had been born less than a month before in an in-home ceremony that featured music in the background and residents passing around the hash pipe in the foreground.

I was greeted warmly by everyone I met at 505 and shared a scrumptious vegetarian dinner. While waiting for the meal to begin, I happened to notice a light table in the layout room and went over to take a look. A partially laid-out page was on the table, and I started to read it to get a preview of the upcoming issue. Lo and behold, I discovered a typographical error. Being the compulsive spelling fanatic that I was then and still am, I typed the word correctly on a piece of paper that was already in the typewriter that was stationed next to the table, and I cut it out, leaving as little white space around the word as possible. Then with a tweezers I picked up the tiny piece of paper, lightly covered the back of it with Glue Stick, and carefully positioned the correctly spelled word over the incorrectly spelled word, using the light that shone through the page from underneath for guidance. Naturally I found another misspelled word, and another, and corrected them as well.

In my memory, I can't remember if I spent the night at 505 or had them take me back to the highway right away. I suspect I did spend the night; their hospitality would have demanded it. What I do remember for sure is that the visit left a major impression on me. I sent a letter back to the folks at *Joint Issue* that I know they published.

Sixteen years later, when I was beginning to conceptualize what would become the first edition of *Voices from the Underground*, I knew I wanted PDI—whose collective members somewhere along the way had changed its name to *Prisoners' Digest International*—to be included. I was fortunate that the Special Collections section of the library at Michigan State University, only seventy miles northwest of Ann Arbor, where I was now living, had copies of PDI, and the general library had an impressive phone book collection that included Iowa City. Perusing issues of PDI, I found a few complete names—not just first names, nicknames, or pseudonyms—in some of the staff boxes. I then looked them up in the Iowa City phone book to see if any of them still lived in town.

I found a name in the phone book that corresponded with the name of one of the women who had worked on PDI, and I called her. Yes, she responded to my first question, she had been a staff member of *Penal Digest International*. Pleased that I had finally made contact, I described the project that I was conceptualizing and then, to burnish my PDI credentials, told her about how I had been picked up by two staff members while hitching on I-80, and about the baby that had recently been born and the hash celebration that had welcomed her.

Unfortunately she answered no to my second question; she was not a key person who could write an authoritative history of the paper. "Who would you suggest and how could I reach him or her?" I asked.

"You would have to talk to Joe Grant," she said.

But, alas, Joe was out of town, and, no, she wouldn't give me his phone number. But, she said, "If you give me your phone number, I'll tell him to call you." I graciously did. As I hung up the phone, I lamented the unfavorable odds of his ever actually contacting me.

Two weeks later—he did! As it turns out, Joe wasn't even there the day I visited the house. But I had made a memorable enough impression on those who were there that they told him all about me when he returned. "Ken," he said, "a lot of people stopped by 505 when we were publishing PDI. They smoked our dope, ate our food, slept in our beds, and had a great time with us. But no one but you ever voluntarily helped on the paper without being asked."

Many writers and scholars over the years had asked him to tell them his story, he told me, and he had always turned down their offer. To me, he said he would. All because I had corrected a typo.

Over the next year and a half, we formed a precious bond and a warm friendship as he dove into writing what became one of the two longest stories in the first edition. It should have been its own book, I thought at the time. And now it is—updated, expanded, and with some earlier errors corrected.

And what a great story Joe tells. Joe had a few years on the rest of us who contributed to the Voices from the Underground Series. While the rest of us came of age during the Vietnam era, Joe's story starts in pre-revolutionary Cuba during the Korean War, at a time when most of us were still in grade school. It takes us through his years as publisher of a rank-and-file newspaper, then into Leavenworth.

"Back then," Joe writes, the feds "used Leavenworth for the truly incorrigible."

Leavenworth was where they sent the prisoners when they closed Alcatraz.

Stepping into that prison and becoming part of it reminded me of the opening paragraph of *Tale of Two Cities*. It was the best and the worst place to do time. The best place to be if you wanted to serve your prison sentence and not be bothered by anyone—prisoner or guard. The worst place to be if you were hoping to make parole. The best place for quiet in the cell blocks. The worst place for informers. The best place for food. The worst place for library books. The best place if you could learn by observing and be silent until spoken to. The worst place if you had a big mouth.

It was in this atmosphere that the idea began to take shape for *Prisoners' Digest International*, a newspaper with two purposes: to provide prisoners with a voice that prison authorities could not silence, and to establish lines of communication between prisoners and people in the free world.

From there, soon after his release, his story brings us to 505 South Lucas and the PDI, the vehicle that gave voice and hope to prisoners and their families all over the country.

That voice was important in the seventies, and it is more so now, when prison conditions have gotten worse than they were even then. Witness contemporary examples of cruelty for cruelty's sake:

- A new law in Arizona requires that all adult visitors to their fifteen prison complexes pay a $25 fee, an added burden to low-income families who often have to travel long distances already to visit their loved ones.

- In Wisconsin, Governor Scott Walker combined union busting and prisoner bashing by allowing inmate labor to perform maintenance work that public employees have traditionally performed, such as landscaping and shoveling.
- Mass hunger strikes, involving over 12,000 California prisoners, took place in September and October 2011 in a dozen prisons in California, plus out-of-state prisons in Arizona, Mississippi, and Oklahoma; attorneys involved in mediation efforts were harassed and denied entry into the state institutions, and family members of striking prisoners were denied visitation rights.
- Meanwhile, the Republicans, who never fail to find a reason to be punitive instead of rational, religion-filled instead of religious, are waging a war on the right to vote, and prisoners are among the key targets. As Joe wrote to me, "Recently passed laws are removing ex-felons' rights to vote. Iowa Governor [Terry] Branstad overturned old Iowa law allowing ex-felons to vote — will deny 100,000 Iowans from voting in 2012. In Florida, thirty minutes after taking office, Rick Scott overturned his predecessor's decision and instantly denied 97,491 ex-cons the vote and prohibited another 1.1 million from voting. If I were living in Iowa I would not be allowed to vote and my parole ended over 35 years ago. Ditto for AZ."

We need a voice for prisoners today.

Fortunately we have some important voices. The most famous is that of Mumia Abu-Jamal.

Mumia Abu-Jamal is an award-winning journalist and former member of the Black Panther Party, as well as a founding member of the Philadelphia chapter of BPP. He is a brilliant philosopher and historian whose words often read like poetry, but whose message can only be terrifying to the white and nonwhite power structure. I might add that he is an honorary member of the National Writers Union, in part due to my yes vote while I was a member of the national executive board. (If my memory is correct, the vote was unanimous.)

In *We Want Freedom: A Life in the Black Panther Party*, his analytic history and personal reflection on the Black Panther Party, he traces the BPP's call for self-defense back to the earliest slaves in the 1600s, and reminds readers that to incoming Blacks, pre–Civil War America was not the immigrants' "land of the free":

> To Blacks cognizant of history, what remains unforgotten is the unending war that has lasted for five centuries, a war against Black life by the merchant princes of Europe. Unforgotten is the man-theft, the wrenching torture, the unremitting bondage — bondage that occurred for centuries to ensure that the Americans could sell cotton to the British, or that the British could sweeten their tea, or that the French could sweeten their cocoa, or that the Dutch could add great sums to their bank accounts.
>
> This "past" is written in the many-hued faces in the average Black family, which may easily range from darkest ebony, to toffee, to café au lait, each a reflection of white rape of African women or of the tradition of concubinage exemplified by the New Orleans *les gens de couleur libres*. For many Blacks, the past is as present as one's mirror.
> It is in this sense that history lives in the minds of Black folk.

Mumia has been on death row in Philadelphia since 1982 for allegedly killing a police officer. *We Want Freedom* emerged from his master's thesis, which he researched and wrote while in solitary confinement. On October 11, 2011, the Free Mumia Web site reported, the United States Supreme Court rejected a request from Mumia's prosecutors to reinstitute the death sentence that the federal appeals court had declared unconstitutional. What was a death sentence now becomes life in prison without the possibility of parole, unless the district attorney elects to seek another death sentence from a new jury.

I don't know for a fact if Mumia is innocent or guilty of pulling the trigger, or what the circumstances were that led up to the officer's death. What I do know is that Philadelphia's city government, including its police force, under Police Commissioner and Mayor Frank Rizzo in the 1970s and beyond was known universally as an incredibly racist, cruel institution that itself should be standing trial for crimes against humanity. It isn't. Therefore, Mumia shouldn't be. I also know that I am against the death penalty, with the possible exception of mass murderers. If George Bush II, Dick Cheney, and their peers—who invaded Iraq based on a well-calculated lie, and are responsible for more American deaths than al-Qaeda, plus countless Iraqi civilian deaths—are not facing the death penalty, nor are the Wall Street criminals who guided their businesses into bankruptcy while stealing the futures of their loyal employees and investors and reaping huge bonuses for their deeds, then Mumia shouldn't be.

My invitation to Mumia to write the foreword for this volume is my declaration to Free Mumia! I am deeply honored that he accepted.

Personally connecting to anyone on death row is a logistical challenge because of the barriers to communication that are set in place to prevent communication. After obtaining his mailing address from my friend, fellow National Writers Union member Susan Davis, I sent him volume 1 of the Voices from the Underground Series and a cover letter of introduction. It was returned. A second attempt yielded the same result and led me to discover that a book to a prisoner on death row can only come from the publisher. My friends at Michigan State University Press complied with my request to send a book from their inventory. Meanwhile, I sent my cover letter for the third time, this time without the book.

While still trying to get through to Mumia, I read his book *Jailhouse Lawyers.* One day I was at Panera Bread in Farmington Hills, Michigan, doing my e-mail. The book was lying on the inside corner of the table along with my notebook and appointment book. A regular member of the morning Panera crowd, whom I recognized but had never talked to, stopped by the table and inquired about my interest in Mumia. I was surprised that anyone there even knew of Mumia, let alone would stop and introduce himself. I explained my interest, as well as my failed attempts thus far to reach him. The man introduced himself as Michael Fox, director of the Japan Innocence and Death Penalty Information Center. He said he knew Mumia, had met him before, and was the very next week going to be visiting him again. He invited me to send him the cover letter that I had written for Mumia so he could relay my request personally! I did it that evening. When I next heard from Michael, it was in the form of an e-mail: "I had a good meeting with Mumia yesterday. We talked for close to three hours. Unfortunately, he didn't seem to know anything about your project. A weird thing indeed."

In *Jailhouse Lawyers,* Mumia mentions a prison paper called *Prison Legal News,* which was founded in 1990 by Paul Wright when he was a prisoner in a Washington state prison, and which Paul has continued to publish since his release in 2003. By the time Michael introduced himself to me, Paul had already accepted my invitation to write an afterword to this volume. When I told him about my failed attempts to reach Mumia, he told me that he was in regular contact with him and promised to pass along my cover letter and get an update. The next time I spoke to Paul, he told me that he had spoken to Heidi Boghosian, executive director of the National Lawyers Guild, and had given her the letter. Further, she was going to be meeting with Mumia that very day and had promised to report back to us. When she did, she explained that she had spoken to Mumia and mailed him my cover letter. She promised to get back to us again when she heard back.

Five days later she wrote to Paul and me again: "Good news: I received a letter from Mumia today with the enclosed note to Ken."

Dear Ken W.:

I have rec'd Vol. I of the Underground Press series. As you know, your other books, etc., were returned for some reason.

This very day, Prof. Fox (the American fellow whom you met in a coffee shop . . .) mentioned your name to me, and while I wasn't sure, I told him it sounded like the guy who edited a book I was riffling through this morning on the Underground Press.

I won't make this long, but I look forward to reading your MSS., and hopefully contributing to this project.

We have both had the honorable pleasure of having our work awarded the Choice award (mine for We Want Freedom: A Life in the Black Panther Party).

As you now know, I heard from Heidi this evening on your behalf.

I look forward to hearing from you—

Alla best—
Mumia

So, after all that time, after approaching him from so many directions, three separate routes—the book, Michael Fox, and Heidi Boghosian—all converged on the same day. Vibes, karma, *b'shert*. I'm a believer.

Finally, I am honored that Paul Wright, founder and publisher of *Prison Legal News*, in addition to helping me reach Mumia, also contributed his afterword. "PDI was one of the first independent prison publications to give voice to current and former prisoners," Paul writes. "Unlike the government-run prison publications, PDI and the free prison press were not the warden's press office and could, and did, tell it like it was. . . . PDI did not have a long life in terms of longevity or issues published. But it had a profound impact."

When *Prisoners' Digest International* folded, it left a void in the world of national prison newspapers. Others later attempted to fill the void, though most were local. In fact, there were many. As Paul continues, "When *Prison Legal News* started in 1990 it was a newsletter focused on Washington state, one of at least 40 other independent prisoner rights magazines that were publishing at that time. California alone had six!"

Today, "Prisoners are more restricted, surveiled, censored, and silenced than at any point in the past 40 years. It is little wonder that the prison press is a frail skeleton of what it once was. So, too, is American journalism as a whole."

Fortunately, *Prison Legal News* exists still to carry on the legacy of *Prisoners' Digest International.*

* * *

When I wrote this preface, Mumia was still on death row, even though the United States Supreme Court had rejected the prosecution's request to reinstitute the death penalty that the federal appeals court had declared unconstitutional. The ruling meant that Mumia should have been released to the general prison population for the first time since his arrest in 1981.

However, in violation of the court order, prison authorities moved Mumia, on December 7, 2011, into administrative custody (a.k.a., "the hole," or solitary confinement), where, according to his attorneys, his living conditions were more restrictive than when he was on death row. Only seven weeks later, on January 27, 2012, was Mumia officially transferred to the general prison population.

The treatment of Mumia by the Pennsylvania justice system is a continued indication of Pennsylvania's desire to silence him not because of his alleged guilt but because he is a powerful voice of truth about prison conditions today. His release first from death row and next from the hole was a major victory for the worldwide movement to free Mumia. The struggle will not be over until Mumia and all political prisoners have been freed and prison conditions nationwide are on the fast track to humane overhaul.

Introduction

JOSEPH W. GRANT

T he courage that the four-volume Voices from the Underground Series celebrates is ancient. That it details the times of our lives is happenstance. The writers included in this series fought the Vietnam-era war machine with an assault of words and actions that weakened the walls of exclusion and secrecy our own government had erected, and exposed its military machinations.

My time in the military, the U.S. Navy, was during the Korean War. It was then, during the early fifties, that Cuban revolutionaries, when referring to me and everyone in the U.S. military, introduced me to the term "Uniformed Assassins."

Many nights, with cold bottles of Hatuey beer to loosen tongues, I listened to the angry Cuban poor lash out at the U.S. support of the dictator Fulgencio Batista. These conversations changed my life.

My part in the traumatic period in our history called the Vietnam era was small. My contribution, as detailed in this final book in the series, concerns the *Prisoners' Digest International* (PDI). It is properly placed. Imprisonment and isolation are a last resort of the tyrant. My nobility was after the fact. I came late to the party, as a voice from the dungeon.

Twenty years later, back in 1990, Ken Wachsberger asked me to write the PDI's history for the first edition of *Voices from the Underground.*

I was a different person. The *Penal Digest International* had become the *Prisoners' Digest International* and had long since been passed on, in modern forms and under different names, to intensely ardent young women and men. I was by then suffering through other lonely efforts under the ever-watchful eyes of a wife, whose intellect and field of study I greatly admire, and grown daughter and sons. At first I thought the publication of my old voice might finally enable me to explain myself to them. It was ego. I felt the pain of this reconstructed dissonance in purely personal terms. I did not see myself as one small part of a larger portrait.

Ken, on the other hand, believed that the other contributors and I were sitting on information of immense social value, especially to the younger generation of scholars and creative dissidents he calls "our intergenerational peers," who have learned about the sixties and the Vietnam era from the people we opposed then—many of whom cheered as our heads were busted and we were thrown into jail for exercising our constitutional rights to free speech and assembly.

While the writing of the PDI's biography was occupying me obsessively, the original publisher withdrew from the project, citing a bad economy as one reason and the possibility of libel as another. By the time my lengthy article was finished—the last of many—Ken had found a New York agent, and the manuscript was making the rounds of major publishing houses.

Ken and I talked at night long-distance. With his usual energy and positive outlook, he read me the letters of rejection. The editors who wrote them were saying no in a wind of admiration: "an impressive piece of scholarship," said one; "much needed collection," said another; "couldn't put it down . . . extraordinary book . . . rave rejection," said a third.

They wrote with praise and turned-away eyes, as they said no, in the "I-can't-afford-it" voice of the meek who fear libel suits.

They were wrong, of course. For in the same way that we needed to hear history's voices from the underground that had witnessed against slavery and the Holocaust and the incidents at Wounded Knee, it was critically important that we heard, read these Vietnam-era *Voices from the Underground.*

One night, long after these books should already have been in libraries and bookstores, after another of those midnight conversations with Ken, it finally dawned on me that I could not limit my participation to that of contributor and observer. And so, again late to the party, and worried about the insidious forms censorship—including self-censorship—continues to take in the nineties, I became a publisher.

Many from the "underground" helped make this possible. I had no money, but my drive around the country enabled me to collect the donations necessary for the set to be published.

The voices you have been privileged to read in the first three volumes of the Voices from the Underground Series are those of my political sisters and brothers, brought together to share their dreams as well as their anger and frustration; their beatings, arrests, and deaths; their triumphs, failures, and the lessons they learned the hard way.

It was an unforgettable adventure and a challenge creating the foundation for that first edition of *Voices from the Underground.*

As this new, expanded, updated Voices from the Underground Series arrives in libraries and bookstores, I am confident that the past efforts by the biographers will do justice to the efforts and the determination of our editor Ken Wachsberger and of Michigan State University Press. The combined efforts of everyone exemplify the kind of sharing and acceptance that came of age within the underground movement of the Vietnam era.

Acknowledgments

The persistence of editor Ken Wachsberger is the primary reason these histories of "underground" newspapers, of which mine is the fourth volume, are seeing the light of day. Gloria Williams provided sound advice, as did my partner Sharlane and our daughter Charity.

Looking back at the history of the PDI, and the before and after of what I think of as *that* adventure, I know I didn't bring that much to the table. Right from the beginning, with only the idea of "tearing down the walls" that hid the brutality and hopelessness of an industry that is anchored to medieval thinking about what constitutes humane punishment, I was in over my head.

The PDI became one of the notable "underground" newspapers during the Vietnam era through the combined efforts of an ex-prisoner, his teenage assistant, and a free-world community of supporters in Iowa City and beyond. They were the force that generated the first tabloid edition of the PDI: 72 pages of information for and about prisoners, the families of prisoners, and the prisons. From that point on, the core group who worked for room and board during those years grew:

- Becky Evans, Merilea, Catherine Kelly, Warren Dearden, Bro. Richard Tanner, Bob Copeland, Rebecca Hensley, Jimmy "Mr. James" Crawford, Connie Klotz, Will Corrado, Randall Knoper, Warren Levicoff, Bro. John Price, Gordon Peterson, Jean Schneller, Jackie Ratchford, Mel Wildt, Rex Wilson Fletcher, Shirley Jones, Phyllis Lehrman, Al Cloud, and many more volunteers from the university, and all those eager, hungry kids who kept me anchored: Lester, Jeanne, Patrick, Brenda, Patty, Chris, Diane, et al.;
- Rights lawyers Duane Rohovitt, Clara Olsen, and Eddie Berkin locally; Bill Kunstler, Stan Bass, James Cleary, Steve Bergeson, S. Brian Willson, and others nationally;
- The Irwin Sweeney Miller Foundation, the Playboy Foundation, Teamsters Union International; David Braverman and August Bergenthal;
- Board members and advisors: Dick Myers, Jackie Blank, Myra Mezvinsky, Jessica Mitford, Vance Bourjaily, Miles Braverman, John C. Clark, Paul D. Burean, Sharm Sherman, Dick Richardson, Kitsi Burkhart, Dr. Magorah Maruyama, Julian Tepper, Diane Schulder, and many more;
- National Prison Center Board: Dr. Penny Baron, Robert D. Bartels, Edward Berkin, Joseph W. Grant, Major L. Clark, James M. Craft, J. Jane Fox, Dr. Steve Fox, Joseph C. Johnson, Donald Mazzioti, Jerry Nemnich, William J. McDonald, Thomas Renwick, Mark F. Schantz, William Simbro, and Richard Tanner;
- Prisoner Advisory Board and PDI Associate Editors: *State Prisons: AK*: Cummins Farm— Rick Hamil; *CA*: Fontera—Marguerita Ferrante; San Luis Obispo—J. R. Williamson; San Quentin—John Watson; Tracy—C.R. Riggs; Chino—James Fox Felix Jr.; Terminal Island—Celeste Clark; *CO*: Canon City—Jerry Nemnich; *CT*: Somers—Henry Rogers; *FL*: Raiford—Gene Jones; *GA*: Reidsville—James Bofiger; *ID*: Boise—Ernie White; *IA*: Ft. Madison—Al Ware and Gene Salazar; *IL*: Joliet—Dick Hayward; *IN*: Pendleton—Dave Edgell; *KY*: Eddyville—Chas DuRain and E. M. Matsko; *ME*: Tomaston—Joe Appleton; *MD*: Baltimore—Malcomb Christenson; *MN*: Stillwater—Norman Mastrian and Gordon Lee Peterson; *MO*: Jefferson City—James Caffey; *NJ*: Trenton—Anthony Puchalski; *NY*: Stormville—Raymond McNeill; *OH*: Columbus—Howard John Conte; Chillicothe—Lou Torok; *OK*: McAlester—Joe C. Aneston; *PA*: Allenwood—Frank Collochio; Pittsburgh—Lee Johnson; *SD*: Sioux Falls—Charles Spaulding; *TX*: Hunstville Unit—Bill White; Wynn Unit—Fred Cruz; *VA*: Lorton—William R. Davis and James "Q-Ball" Irby; *WI*: Waupon— S.L. Poulter and Augie Berganthal. *Federal Prisons*: Atlanta—Patrick O'Shea and SRM; El Reno—George Knox; Leavenworth—Arthur Rachel; Lewisburg—Maurice Schick; Marian FCI—John R. Glover; McNeil Island—E.E. Albaugh; Sandstone—Ray Shroll; Terre

Haute—John Mayberry; *PDI in Punitive Transit*: John Wagner and Edward Allen Mead; *England:* Leicestershire—S. J. Delany;

- For inspiration: Gabriela and Julio Guerrero, Meridel LeSueur, John Eastman, Craig Vetter, Jerry Dorrough, Shiloh: Bishop of Tellus (aka Harry Theriault), Clarence Carnes, Frankie Sepulveda, Eddie Sanchez, and the Green Lizard.

Stop the Presses!
I Want to Get Off!

A Brief History of the
Prisoners' Digest International

Prisons and Prisons, My Daughters and Sons

Penal Digest International. The PDI. A newspaper with two purposes: to provide prisoners with a voice that prison authorities could not silence, and to establish lines of communication between prisoners and people in the free world. At one point the staff chose to change "Penal" to "Prisoners" and we became the *Prisoners' Digest International.* But, *Penal* or *Prisoners*, we were the PDI.

Over forty years have passed since the idea for *Prisoners' Digest International* began to take shape. I was a prisoner in the federal penitentiary at Leavenworth, Kansas, at the time. You've heard of Leavenworth—one of the end-of-the-line prisons where feds, and even the states, send their "bad boys." At that time the federal prison at Marion, Illinois, was being used as a youth joint while the feds perfected what was to become the most repressive monument to absolute security that the U.S. government could design. Back then, they used Leavenworth for the truly incorrigible. Leavenworth was where they sent the prisoners when they closed Alcatraz.

Stepping into that prison and becoming part of it reminded me of the opening paragraph of *A Tale of Two Cities.* It was the best and the worst place to do time. The best place to be if you wanted to serve your prison sentence and not be bothered by anyone—prisoner or guard. The worst place to be if you were hoping to make parole. The best place for quiet in the cell blocks. The worst place for informers. The best place for food. The worst place for library books. The best place if you could learn by observing and be silent until spoken to. The worst place if you had a big mouth.

I was a first-timer, a fast learner, nonviolent, and, in many respects, lucky.

So what was I doing behind the walls at Leavenworth with guys who had averaged five previous incarcerations for violent crimes? It's a long story. I've never told it before. But the memories of that period are clear. My thoughts frequently turn to the injustices that surrounded me then. I internalize them. Sometimes, when I am alone, maybe sitting on the patio in Lawrence late at night, I doze off. I awake suddenly, look up, and everything seems new. Fresh. The shadows on the trees are a deeper, richer, more visible green. The air is clear. The sound of the cicadas is sharper, crisper, vibrating. The sound waves can be felt—almost seen. A raccoon is eating at our cats' food dish. As I watch, her eyes pick up the light from a full moon—a female, heavy with young and leading a good life. She ponders what to do and continues eating. In a reverie about the life around me, I shift and reach for a beer that has warmed as I dozed. She looks around at me, casually waddles off, and disappears into the wall of brush, trees, and tall grass that encloses us and provides a sanctuary for a variety of critters, including me.

In the joint, one afternoon. Very hot, the last week of July. I'm in the shade, in a slight breeze. Half asleep, thoughts freed, a child again daydreaming. My eyes skim along the ground, moving fast, observing, soaring over the factories, cell houses, walls. The factories are humming and the yard is almost empty. Flying as in a dream, yet even in a dream staying inside the walls. Constantly turning away and gliding back in. Flying lightning-like through clouds and around corners. Observing. Even the shades of gray are a miracle in the blinding Kansas sun, contrasted with dark shadows that turn into a phosphorescent, trippy darkroom green. A few black prisoners across the yard work with weights. From this distance, they reflect a deep, rich blue/black. Suddenly blood splatters black across bleached concrete as a face is smashed with a handheld barbell. Awake. Back on earth. I quickly stand and walk away. One sees death in the can, but there is never a warning of impending violence. Arguments? Never any warnings. Clueless, sudden, unseen death. No one has eyes in the back of his head.

I wondered when the war would ever end. I still do.

Godless Country Not the Worst Country

Today, when conversations turn to prisons and prisoners, I listen. I learned long ago that the moment the conversation turns serious, eyes (and minds) begin to glaze over. It was the same when the conversations turned to Cuba and Castro years earlier. I remind people of writer Dorothy Day's trip to Cuba after the Cuban revolution. She had gone down to see for herself if life was as oppressive for churchgoing Catholics in Cuba as the U.S. government was reporting. In one of the columns she wrote for the *Catholic Worker* she said, "Better a Godless country that takes care of its poor than a Christian country that doesn't."

Believe me, talking to the average citizen about injustice is like walking into a white Southern Baptist church in Danville, Virginia—the last headquarters of the Confederacy—and asking for donations to the Black Panther Legal Defense Fund or the American Civil Liberties Union. Anyone present who knew what you were talking about would think you were completely mad. Those who didn't would think you were an affront to their selective, lily-white God and attempt to do to you what the Romans did to the good carpenter. Not pretty.

When I began getting phone messages in the summer of 1989 that someone interested in *Prisoners' Digest International* was trying to contact me, I was only mildly interested. Over the years I have been contacted by an occasional law student or theology student who was doing research on, or volunteer work with, prisoners. Invariably they had gotten a taste of prison life, and had heard about the rise and fall of the PDI and/or the Church of the New Song, a prisoner religion whose philosophy had been successfully spread to prisoners internationally by the PDI.

These links to my PDI past show themselves unexpectedly. I'll notice someone staring at me. Usually I walk over and introduce myself. Not infrequently the person turns out to be a former PDI subscriber or a librarian. Occasionally, after I am steered away from the crowd and into a private space, the person confesses that he or she was once a prisoner. That confession is followed by a narrative of memorable moments. "Acid flashbacks," as the person says. "I remember the Sunday church service in Atlanta," or "The Terre Haute tour was a gas; whatever happened to John?," or "I was at Oklahoma Women's Penitentiary."

Sometimes it's a writer, someone with a clear enough understanding of what gets into print in these United States to know that to be well informed, a person has to set aside money to subscribe to a few progressive publications: *In These Times, The Progressive, The Nation, Mother Jones, Z Magazine, Utne Reader, Catholic Worker, Washington Monthly, Workers World, Dollars and Cents,* and *EXTRA* have been a few of my favorites. They are publications and organizations with staff who understand the insidious Rain Barrel theory of politics, the theory that best describes politics in the United States—the scum rises to the top. People whose names are anathema to the FBI, the Secret Service, the CIA, Nixon, Kissinger, Reagan, the Bush presidents—organizations and individuals whose existence personifies the Rain Barrel theory's validity.

(One of these days you will read that I have finally gotten enough prize money together to invite artists to submit works for the "Rain Barrel Art Classic." Artists can portray the scum in oils, watercolors, clay, whatever. And with five-dollar contributions from the folks who were ripped off by the Keatings, the Madoffs, the Wall Street financiers et al., we will have big money to hand out for prizes and purchases. We'll save enough to put all the submitted works together in a book so the scum will be given a permanent place in history. The artists will do a better job of exacting equity for the servant class than the justice department will ever do.)

This most recent contact was different. Ken Wachsberger not only knew about the PDI, he had been part of the day-to-day insanity we had all learned to love in a sadomasochistic way. Ken had been hitching west on I-80 one afternoon in May 1972 and was picked up by some PDI staff members who were returning from D.C. Like so many road-weary wanderers, he accepted an invitation to join us for dinner and a night's rest. While waiting for dinner, he wandered into the PDI offices—where the lights burned 24 hours a day—and Ken went to work.

Seventeen years later, he asked if I'd like to look back at those years and share some thoughts on the PDI, the times, and the people. I had doubts about whether I was the best person to do so. For many years, friends who were witness to those traumatic years had urged me to tell the story. I always assumed that someone else would. The PDI had staff members who were skilled writers—far better writers than I. But Ken wanted me to write the history because I was the founder. After calling around and finding the writers with the skills to do a professional job too busy, I agreed. My story was one part of his landmark *Voices from the Underground: Insider Histories of the Vietnam Era Underground Press*, which came out in 1993 and went out of print far too soon. Sixteen years later, he told me he wanted to see *Voices* back on the bookshelves and in the classrooms. So here I am, tweaking the first edition, and maybe even correcting a few errors that slipped in during that first writing, and elaborating on some stories that got shortchanged to meet deadlines.

In this brief memoir, I share pre- and post-prison experiences with the observations that convinced me that the PDI was desperately needed; I also include information on why

I thought it would succeed, and how, with the help of an unusually diverse group of people, we forced it to succeed.

The PDI came into existence in 1970 during politically painful times. We had caught the tail end of the Vietnam War both in and out of the can. Our detractors called us radical. We probably initiated as many lawsuits against agencies of the federal and state governments as any newspaper in history. The list of our reporters, sales agents, and prison representatives read like a Who's Who of jailhouse lawyers—those prisoners who became experts in the legal system because they were forced to defend themselves and others. Many were serving life terms with no hope of parole for committing acts that ranged from political crimes against the state to crimes for profit, revenge, you name it. In prison, they had turned to education and law as a means of self-fulfillment. Many became very adept at writing sophisticated briefs for other prisoners as a method of getting back at the system that traditionally screws other prisoners. They were our newspaper's strongest supporters and most committed advocates. They never gave up. They had nothing to lose. They were afraid of no one. They could be threatened, but they remained uncowed.

For over three years, with a staff that started with two and grew to twenty-five, the PDI operated out of a three-story house at 505 South Lucas in Iowa City, Iowa. At the time, 505 became synonymous with PDI. I bought the house at 505—with the help of sympathetic realtors and a no-down-payment GI loan—so the PDI and the staff would have a place to live. For three years, using a variety of means, I fed, clothed, and sheltered the staff, their friends, drifters, runaways, wanted men, women, and children, and paid the bills. Well . . . most of the bills.

A little over four years and a couple hundred thousand dollars later, I walked away from the PDI with exactly what I'd walked away from the slam with. Nothing. I wasn't totally without resources, however. I owned a home in Georgeville, Minnesota, in the west central part of the state that had been home to *Hundred Flowers*, the underground newspaper edited by Eddie Felien, the Marxist scholar from the University of Minnesota who ended up on the Minneapolis city council. My home there didn't have running water or electricity, but what do you expect for a real estate package of two houses and a 60' × 30' two-story brick office building for a total of $400. The house we lived in was once the town's post office. I also had a 1963 one-ton International pickup that looked like it had been abandoned in Watts during the riots. The pickup had been part of the junk pile out back of the house. It needed tires, a battery, and six weeks' worth of hard work to get it running. Along with everything else, I considered it a gift. Hell, the PDI was a gift that for a long time nourished prisoners and their families. And why not? It was their newspaper. They wrote for it, produced it, paid for it pennies at a time. We never refused a prisoner a subscription. We accepted whatever they could afford. Most could afford nothing. How they got it and why they got it is part of the story I will get to.

Witnessing and Experiencing Violence

Those PDI years were lean, hungry, tough, violent years. By that I mean we were witnesses to endless prison violence. Violence against men, women, and children in prison. Violence against the families of prisoners. Violence against the poor, many of whom were on their way to prison—even the poor in Iowa City, where there wasn't even a semblance of a ghetto. Year after year of never a payday; but we had a roof over our heads at 505, food stamps, and people committed to social change.

And finally, violence against the primary staff members of the PDI by the federal, state, and local police that culminated in murder—a murder that was committed by a man who was pushed over the edge by an undercover cop who sealed all of our futures by giving the man a gun and urging him to use it. Staff members were arrested for possessing drugs that were stashed by ex-prisoners who had been released from prison for the express purpose of destroying the PDI and the Church of the New Song. The seemingly unlimited power and resources of those three levels of government were more than a handful of overworked men, women, and children could withstand. Most took off trying to find a place to rest and restore themselves. Consequently, the PDI and a number of staff members were destroyed.

With the PDI's voice stilled, the prisoners lost their voice. By the time I began writing the first edition of my story in 1989, prison conditions had grown more repressive. As I begin again, over twenty years later, those conditions look comparatively good by comparison. Extreme overcrowding exists, mainly because of the longer prison sentences that are handed out today, frequently for victimless crimes. Increasing numbers of prisoners are being locked up for minor drug offenses—many are denied the opportunity to earn a parole. With more of the poor, uneducated members of society ending up in prison, the need for educational and vocational programs is greater than it has ever been. Yet, vindictive legislators continue to initiate legislation depriving prisoners of the means to return to society prepared to function in an increasingly difficult environment of fewer jobs and no access to the resources available to non-offenders. Today we live in a society that is more oriented to using endless punishment to show how committed they are to "law and order." Legislative commitments to cutbacks in correctional-department budgets mean that fewer of these programs are available.

And the PDI? Today it is a mass of notes, letters, papers, and subscription lists that are safely stashed in boxes in the State Historical Society of Iowa. And, of course, there are memories.

I look back, see the victories, and I'm reminded of a line by author Barry Hannah: "Not only does absence make the heart grow fonder, it makes history your own beautiful lie."

This gathering of relatively recent history will not become my "beautiful lie." Not with so many participants looking over my shoulder.

Cuba: Political Beginnings While Korea Cooks

The foundation for the government's intense rancor against me goes back to an incident that happened in Cuba, where I served in the navy in 1952. There, I had knowledge of a delivery of some Springfield rifles from our destroyer squadron—old rifles that were being replaced by the new M1s—to a group of remarkable people who showed me firsthand what Fulgencia Batista, the U.S.-supported Cuban military dictator, was doing to the Cuban people. It was a time of personal political awakening that took me far past the simple, pro-union childhood I enjoyed, surrounded by uncles who were Farm/Labor activists. It was my first serious political act.

My activities in Cuba might never have surfaced if I hadn't "lost it" one day in Cedar

Rapids, Iowa. It was twelve or thirteen years after Cuba, and I had too much to drink at a SERTOMA Club meeting. "SERTOMA" was an acronym for "SERvice TO MAnkind." One day a former resident of Cuba visited our local SERTOMA gathering to speak about the Cuba he had fled when Fidel Castro led the people's army into Havana. He was a banker and a *gusano* (Spanish for "worm"), one of the "haves" who skipped to the United States with enough gold and connections to "make a new begin in the land of the free." He managed to leave with enough to steer clear of the fast money from criminal activity in Miami and had opted for banking—another form of criminal activity. His new life began as a vice president in the bank that served eastern Iowa. Why settle in Miami and take the chance of being illegal when you could be a bank executive and steal with the blessing of the FDIC?

He talked about how he had fled the horrible Communists who nationalized industry, closed down the nightclubs, took over the hotels, and forced the doctors to practice the oath they took when graduating from medical school—that is, to provide medical care to people regardless of their ability to pay. His speech was perfect for this group of men, who were hanging on his every word. Applause constantly interrupted him every few sentences. He was living proof to these people that Castro was a Communist who had to be eliminated—living justification for programs of assassination by U.S. agents, programs that would work better during the sixties when J. Edgar Hoover infiltrated antiwar groups through his COINTELPRO activities.

Listening to him whine his way through a litany of greed was intolerable. I turned to my bottle of Old Style and was soon retreating into my memories. I could smell gun grease. My soul warmed as I left the dry, bone-chilling cold of Iowa and returned to the 98 percent humidity and nighttime temperatures of 110+ degrees that I had found in revolutionary Cuba previous to the people's victory.

When I arrived in Cuba in the early fifties, I was fresh out of high school and sincerely believed that the United States of America was the greatest country in the world. The land of opportunity. Anyone and everyone could make it. "We hold these truths to be self-evident . . ." etc., etc.

I was in the navy to protect the world from dictators—most of whom happened to be Commies at that point in history. The generation immediately before mine had taken care of the Nazis, Il Duce's Brown Shirts, and the Japanese. Frank Sinatra was singing, "I am an American, and proud of my liberty and my freedom to make derogatory remarks about Dorothy Kilgallen's chin." I was one of many young, tough Americans. I had my share of faults: no ambition, couldn't deal with routine, I bored easily, carried a book with me at all times to read as soon as the teacher (or boss) turned away. On the plus side, I didn't abuse people, was generous with what little money I had, and was loyal to my friends.

Korea was starting to cook and I was ready. Truman was paying big bucks to anyone who would extend his hitch for two years. The combination of patriotism and pay was all I needed. After my experiences in Cuba, those additional two years would become intolerable. But the bad times were yet to come. At this point, the navy was a perfect fit.

My passion during this period in my life was the Sixth Naval District boxing team. I relished it—not just the easy life and the lack of supervision, but the workouts, the sparring, and the actual fighting. At 165 pounds, I was a lanky middleweight, but I fought as a light heavyweight, and occasionally as a heavyweight because the spot was empty and my coach, a redheaded chief petty officer who had once been a featherweight contender, convinced me that I was faster and better than anyone bigger than me—with the exception of my shipmate from Wisconsin, Freddie Krueger, who, using an alias, was prowling around South and North Carolina picking up pro fights and winning them.

Staying in shape was simple. Freddie would shake me awake at 4:30 A.M. and we would jog the five or six miles to the main gate of the base, make disparaging remarks to the Marine guards, and jog back to the ship in time for steak and eggs. The boxing team had no work-detail assignments. As long as we worked out and won, every day was a vacation from the drudge work. Fighting wasn't work—as long as you could avoid getting kicked around in the ring. Plus, being able to take off for town every night was sweet.

Red's orders were simple: "Stay in shape and stay on the team. Get lazy and start working."

Not smoking was easy, and the second drink never tasted as good as the first, so I rarely consumed enough to adversely affect my timing. I was hell in a barroom fight simply because I was usually the sober fighter. I had an extraordinary appetite for anything that moderately altered my conscious state if it enhanced the party, the lovemaking, or the fighting. But as the man in the toga once said, "Moderation in all things." The enhancers I used in moderation; but as a middleweight in the ring with fighters who frequently outweighed me by 40 pounds, "moderation" was not a word I used or heard. It certainly wasn't part of Red's vocabulary.

If I had a reputation back then, it was that I had to be pushed long and hard before I could be provoked into a fight. My best friends required less pushing. One night, Nelson King, Jim Oler, Dean Bohy, Buck, and I went over to the canteen on the base in Guantanamo, Cuba. We sat and talked and drank beer until the place closed. As we were walking back to the pier to catch the launch, Buck walked over to one of the Marine barracks and ripped the thin wooden slats out of two windows. Then he leaned inside and asked if there were any Marines who wanted to get their asses kicked by a sailor from the coal mines of West Virginia. We grabbed Buck and started running. By the time thirty or forty Marines came piling out of the barracks, we were about a block and a half ahead of them.

Sand burs stopped the ones with no shoes. Three caught up with Nelson, which was like catching up with a tiger. Jim had turned around, and those two were like nitro and glycerine. Buck and I stopped and watched. Nelson and Jim were two shy young men, but in a fight they were frighteningly efficient.

The next morning, with all the men lined up for muster, the captain demanded to know which men had attacked the Marine barracks the night before. Fortunately, when Nelson's shirt was torn off, the Marines didn't get the piece with his name stenciled on it.

I loved Cuba.

Back in the present, the Cuban banker droned on and on. It was easy to shut myself off from the words of this fat, soft *gusano* and remain lost in memories. I could almost smell the island and feel the heavy, humid heat that made our white uniforms sag and our shoes squish with sweat.

I wondered what Bobby, Julio, and Gaby would think about this banker. I recalled the night in Cuba when I met them. Buck and I were on shore leave in Guantanamo. We had been ashore for almost 24 hours, and had 24 more ahead of us, thanks to his shifts in the galley and mine as a coxswain running liberty launches. It was midweek, the best time to be ashore. No military personnel were around, the shore-patrol units were few and far between, and the prices were fair. Even the general pace of the people slowed down during the week, as if they were storing up energy for the make-or-break hustle of the weekend.

We had closed a couple of small clubs and were walking around trying to decide where to crash. The heat was oppressive. The humidity steamed my glasses, softened even the landscape. You had to wade through it.

As we crossed a park, I saw a hose connected to a sprinkler. The thought of cool water was irresistible. I hung my wallet on the branch of a bush, took my shoes off, aimed the sprinkler at a nearby bench, turned it on, and sat down. Buck was more vocal about the cool water; his whoops and hollers attracted the attention of a young woman, who stepped out of a doorway just across a narrow street from us. She was so close, Buck recognized the profile of the one-eyed Indian on her bottle of Hatuey beer. Always the gentleman (and always thirsty), Buck stood up. As he introduced himself, water in his hat spilled down his face. She laughed so loud I could barely hear Buck when he asked her if she had a beer he could buy. She didn't, but she offered to get some if he had the money. Buck turned to me and mimicked Hank Williams with a whining, "If you've got the money, Honey, she's got the wine—Hatuey that is!" I pointed to my wallet hanging on the branch. Buck took it, tossed it to the woman, and said, "Take what you need. Bring us as much Hatuey as you can carry." She took a twenty, tossed the wallet back to Buck, and disappeared.

She returned with a half case of beer and a small block of ice in a burlap bag. I was surprised when she handed me change.

Then she went into her house with the beer. She looked so good walking away that I didn't say anything.

The house was a typical "crib" house. The door led into a long, narrow room, where a second door led into another narrow, but smaller room. The backyard had just enough space for a small vegetable garden. In this part of town, and in many others, the streets were lined with hundreds of these "crib" houses. Prostitutes, many with small children, sat on the steps in a never-ending hustle for enough money to live on. If she had been a hooker, twenty dollars was more than she would have made working hard on a Saturday night. But there she was, handing me my change with a bag of ice-cold beer. When she came out of the house for the second time, she had two guys with her. Each was drinking one of my cold beers. Oh well . . .

Robert "Bobby" Vaughn: Poet of the Revolution

The woman and one of the guys joined us in the sprinkler and introduced themselves as Gabriela and Julio. They were both into the humor of the situation. The other man sat on the ground. He was not amused. Gaby and Julio were sister and brother, but they looked like they could have come from different families. Gaby was a slim, dark-skinned young woman with strong African blood; Julio was blessed with a skin color George Hamilton would have killed for—the color of copper mixed with gold. He was also, like me, an amateur boxer. Unlike me his nose was still straight. The other guy, Bobby Vaughn, was a skinny little Anglo poet from Key West.

That first night we small-talked and drank beer. Before long, Buck and Bobby were asleep—Buck from the beer, and Bobby from washing down cough medicine with beer. It was a memorable evening. I had met my first poet and turpin-hydrate addict and had become friends with the first Cuban civilians I had met outside of a bar. Bobby also was the first American I met in Cuba who didn't work at the navy base.

Buck and I spent that night sleeping on pallets on the floor. After a night of listening to Bobby howling, crying, and cursing in his sleep, I arose at dawn to the sound of barking dogs. My uniform was wet and dirty and I had a headache. No one had any aspirins, but Bobby had some painkillers that worked better than anything I'd ever taken for a headache. Julio loaned Buck and me each a shirt and a pair of old pants that we wore until our whites could be washed.

I offered to buy breakfast, but Julio was already cutting up some fruit and making coffee. He said something about relaxing and enjoying the day. Buck had already had a beer and was launching into a long rambling tale about mining coal in West Virginia. His job had been to set the charges that blasted loose the coal. With each beer, the story got longer and the fuses attached to the charges got shorter. I'd heard the story many times, almost as many times as Dean Bohy's stories of Olympic wrestlers from Clarion, Iowa—stories I never tired of.

Life in Cuba had a mellow, low-pressure rhythm unlike any other place I had ever been. That first day, Bobby's painkiller had me humming songs and thinking about settling down in Guantanamo. I had enough "down-home country" in me to appreciate the simple life.

We sat around for most of the day talking. Later Julio and I walked to a nearby market for beans and rice, a couple of chickens, and some vegetables. Buck almost killed himself trying to ride a bike with a bent wheel.

That night, over beans and rice, I made an offhand remark about how nice it would be to sit down to a first-class meal some day. I was speaking facetiously, but it didn't come across as I intended. Bobby exploded in anger and called me an American pig. Julio told me to ignore him because he was high. Bobby started yelling poetry and cursing about a U.S. political system that was killing people in Cuba and all over the world. I thought he was nuts, but I was a guest and couldn't say anything. Fortunately, I kept my mouth shut. If I had said anything, it would have been some naive comment about loyalty and being a little more respectful about the United States of America. I didn't want to offend anyone. Bobby was beyond me, but I was eager to continue the friendship with Julio and Gaby—especially Gaby.

Interesting day.

The following Wednesday I was back. Bobby was there but said nothing. For two days and two nights, he listened to scratchy records by Chet Baker, Charlie Parker, Miles Davis, and Dave Brubeck. He seemed to know Chet Baker and Charlie Parker, but he wasn't in the mood to talk to me about them. During those two days, he became increasingly abusive to everyone. Gaby grabbed my hand, pulled me up to dance with her, and said, "You must excuse Bobby. I want to have fun, and Bobby's vocabulary doesn't include the word *fun.*" Chet Baker set the mood that afternoon, and hearing his music would return me to this day for the rest of my life.

Gaby and I rode bikes out into the country and up the coast. We went swimming, bought fresh fish for supper, and made plans to go fishing the following week.

It was on the third visit that I asked Julio about the revolution that was spoken about so disparagingly by our ship's officers. He asked me what I knew about Castro and the revolution. Not much, I told him. Castro was anti-American, and Americans were good for the island's economy. He was probably a socialist. The more I said, the sillier I sounded. Julio listened calmly, but Bobby turned and started yelling angrily, almost incoherently. He was spitting and sputtering: "You're a whore! Worse than Truman! Pigs!" Finally he lurched to his feet and stumbled off.

No Room in the Revolution for Druggies

I asked Julio and Gaby if I was as ignorant of what was going on as Bobby accused me of being.

"You have to understand that Bobby is going through a very bad time in his life," Gaby explained. She looked at Julio, seemingly for permission to continue. He shrugged his shoulders and she gave me a real shock.

"Try to understand Bobby. He has been rejected by people he admires very much. Don't take what he says personally. He was with the revolutionaries for a few months. He has been with Fidel and Che in the mountains."

I couldn't believe it. A real shocker. Not just Vaughn's involvement, but the casual manner in which Gaby spoke of Fidel and Che. Vaughn was the last person in the world I would picture as a revolutionary. He was small and skinny and as physically weak as any person I had ever known. I didn't know much about what was happening in Cuba, but I knew that Fidel Castro and Che Guevara were heading a small army that was involved in what officers on our destroyer described as a hopeless attempt to take over the island, and they weren't going to get much done with an army of Bobby Vaughns. "You mean he's been fighting with the people who are trying to overthrow the government that we support?"

"Yes and no. Bobby is a poet. He's in love with the idea of the revolution. He has a strong mind for words. The problem is that he's a drug user—an addict—and nobody trusts an addict. Plus, he is a physically weak man unable to even defend himself, much less his comrades."

It seems he had been given a choice: drugs or revolution—choose one or the other; the two didn't mix.

As she continued talking, I learned that Bobby was returning to New York City, and that she and her brother were all involved with the revolution.

We had reached a point where they spoke of the revolutionary army calmly and with some authority.

"Tell me more," I asked.

And they goddamn sure did exactly that.

Cuba Owned by the U.S.

They fed me statistics on how the Cuban people lived under Fulgencia Batista. They had no medical care, no schools, no wages, no futures to look forward to. The United States controlled 75 percent of the agriculture, all of the tourist trade, and all the gambling. Pay in the factories and on the plantations was so low, people died of malnutrition.

"You see hundreds and hundreds of women lining the streets selling themselves," Julio said. "You can buy any perversion you can imagine for a dollar or less. Do you think they enjoy being whores?"

At a loss for words, I responded to his questions with silence.

"If you go down the street and buy a woman, do you think she likes you because you are clean and pay cash?"

Silence. And a shake of my head.

"Do you think you are special because you have money and they do not? Can you even imagine what it is like to have no money, no resources of any kind, and need a doctor for a sick baby and know that the doctor will not treat the baby unless you have cash?"

Some questions have no answers.

"Can you imagine a doctor who will let babies die because the mother has no money?"

Julio was talking softly, but his hands were trembling. Gaby, with tears in her eyes, got up and left the room.

Bobby returned. He had calmed down and now added bits of information that must have been poetry, because I understood little of what he said. I did understand, though, that he idolized both Castro and Che: "Castro the fearless warrior/scholar" and "Che the fearless warrior/poet."

Bobby would look you in the eye and start with simple thoughts and ideas, then slowly lead you down an increasingly complex path of words and phrases and ideas. Just about the time you thought he was trying to make a fool of you, he would stop. Then he'd sit there looking through you, his mouth half open. After a long pause, he would recite a poem. A sonnet. He would recite it once, twice. Play with a word. Discuss a rhyme. Go over it. Explain a sestet. Finish a sonnet with—according to Julio—a perfect sestina. Most of the time I was completely lost, but Bobby was a hard person to dislike.

Bobby had a very serious attachment to two writers, Ezra Pound and Ernest Hemingway. I'd read all of Hemingway, and nothing by Pound. Bobby shared with me his Pound books, but Pound was beyond me. Gaby once asked him how he could admire Hemingway, who only wrote about fighting, fucking, and fishing. Bobby answered, "It's not what he writes about, but the way he writes what he writes about." When it came to discussing literature or poetry with Bobby Vaughn, I kept my mouth shut.

(Fifteen years later, Bobby, John Eastman, and I spent many days and nights together near Marion, Iowa. John was working on film scripts, and Bobby was working on getting high. By that time, Bobby had a patch covering the hole in his head where someone had beaten out one of his eyes late one night in Kansas City. He had been looking for Charlie Parker's mother. That search, in some circles, was legendary. Bobby was traveling with all of his belongings—mostly books—packed in four wooden boxes he was unable to lift. If someone stopped for him, they had to load the boxes into the vehicle for him. Bobby's strength was his mind, which contained a wealth of words, mostly in the form of poetry.)

Any Prostitutes in Your Family?

Julio never spoke about himself. Once when we were discussing how a poor woman survived in Cuba with only four square yards of garden to feed her family, he told me that his and Gaby's mother had been a prostitute on this very street. The two of them had grown up here. He would use the word "prostitute," but he never used the word "whore." "You must be careful about the words you use," he told me seriously. "Be careful how you categorize people. A Cuban woman sells her body. Batista sells our country."

Silence.

Then, "Think about who the prostitutes are. Maybe you have a prostitute in your own family. Tell me, Joe, who in your family are selling themselves and what price are they being paid?"

I didn't like talk about having whores in my family, but I understood the point he was making.

"Which is worse, Joe, a rapist or a prostitute?"

"The rapist, of course."

"Which is worse, Joe, a pimp or a prostitute?"

"The pimp, of course."

"Don't you understand that Cuba is a woman who is being abused by your country? Cuba is being used like a prostitute. Small countries all over the world are the prostitutes, and the United States is a rapist and a pimp."

Strong words. Perceptive words.

Why Do Poets Have to Carry Guns?

One night, Bobby announced that he was leaving and returning to New York City. He was sad that there was no place for him in Cuba—sadder still over his own drug habit. "Why does a poet have to carry a gun and be prepared to kill?" he asked.

"Because a poet of this revolution must be prepared to kill for this revolution, not just write poems about it," Julio answered.

For some reason Bobby turned to me and asked, "Who broke your nose, Joe?"

"A person who suffered far more pain doing it than I suffered having it done," I answered.

* * *

I flashed back to a serious ass-kicking by a Parris Island Marine one night in Charleston, South Carolina. Mine was a semifinal bout, and Red, my boxing coach when I was in the navy, had me fighting a light heavyweight. I was standing in my corner when the Marine entered the ring. As he crawled through the ropes, I could see he was big. I glanced at the referee, who happened to be a friend. He looked at the Marine, then back to me, and shook his head, indicating I was in trouble.

The first round was painful. The second round was much worse. Unfortunately for the Marine he became careless. When we were told to "break" by the ref, I dropped my hands, and he hit me so hard I was still seeing stars and walking with a wobble after the fight had been awarded to me for that illegal punch.

The next morning over steak and eggs, a teammate asked me how I felt. I told him I was miserable and added, "Those were two of the toughest rounds I have ever fought."

My friend looked surprised. "What do you mean 'two rounds?' You won in the third round."

I finished round one on my feet, fought round two on my feet, came out for round three, and won on that illegal hit—but I didn't remember the second round. I sat there, stunned. Suddenly others at the table began asking questions. When they understood what I was saying, a fellow fighter said, "Man, you are bad. The Marine hit you so many times I thought we'd be carrying you out of the ring."

I didn't say anything until I finished my breakfast. I went to the gym and told Coach he had to find himself another middleweight. Then I called Mom and told her I was through with the boxing. The dear soul said, "It's about time, Bud."

* * *

Bobby was grinning, and he didn't grin much. "A poet with a broken nose?"

Julio asked me if I would fight for the revolution. "If this was my country I would be in the mountains. But it's not my country," I answered. Then I added, "I think that I would fight for the three of you. I love you all. I even love your revolution, but I don't even know the language of your revolution—at least not yet."

Julio looked at me. "Do you know any more or any less about the Cuban people than you know about the Korean people?"

The question jolted me. I had come to know these people. I knew they were right in what they were doing—that it was the only way their lives would ever have any meaning. I was in the U.S. military, but I could never take action against them. Now Julio had made me realize that people just like Gaby and him were sitting in houses just like this one halfway around the world in small towns in Korea. And I was soon to be heading over there. If we were wrong in Cuba, were we wrong in Korea also?

I didn't even have to ask.

As for Cuba's revolution, I knew at least enough of the language to understand what was happening. I learned that many other military personnel also understood. Julio worked hard at smuggling. He made regular trips into the Sierra Maestras with weapons and spare parts that came from the naval base.

The talks always went on late into the night. Bobby would be high on turpin hydrate or thorazine, and occasionally heroin. He slept in the corner while I listened and learned about pain, and how to kill, and why they believed such actions were necessary. Bobby didn't hear many of those conversations; he'd heard them all before and may have written some of them. Occasionally he would wake with a start, grab a pencil, and start writing. Then he would look over at us like we were strangers and go back to sleep.

He awoke one night and scribbled a poem about an Anglo named Toth who would go to prison because there was a doubt about his loyalty to the revolution, and because Fidel did not have time to sort through a person's politics.

The conversations went on, broken only by the time I spent on the ship. I'd return weekly. We would ride bicycles up the coast, sometimes sleeping on the beach. We'd go fishing. Occasionally we'd buy fruit from people who were on their way to the markets.

Once we were stopped by police. While Julio talked to them, Gaby stood close to me and began acting like she was turning a trick—smiling, teasing, being irritated with the delay, asking for money to buy beer for everyone (which I gave her, but which the police declined). It was a strange, yet arousing, incident. I was responding to her differently than I ever had. When the police finally left, Julio said, "More names for the list."

Gaby told me I was not a very good actor. I could have told her that. I certainly wasn't hiding how I felt about her.

Julio always referred to his "list" whenever he had a run-in with anyone who worked for the Batista regime. Whether he had an actual list I never knew. Years later, when the revolutionaries had successfully defeated the military dictatorship, it was said that Castro had a list of the names of people who had caused the people great suffering. It was said further that these people were arrested and executed—no questions, no trials. They were, it was said, given exactly what they had given to the Cuban people. Whether it's true or not I do not know. I do not approve of summary executions, but I can damn sure understand why it happens.

The Case of the Missing Springfield Rifles

Around this time, the navy replaced the old Springfield rifles—the bolt-action .30-06s if I remember correctly—with the new M1s. The Springfield was becoming obsolete, we were told—a good rifle, but the M1s were superior. With the help of a chief gunner's mate, who was gay and whose passion for a beautiful man with a golden tan was greater than his fear of losing his retirement, Julio ended up with the old Springfield rifles from our COM DES DIV 302 destroyer group, which was made up of the USS *Bronson* (DD668), USS *Smalley* (DD565), USS *Cotten* (DD669), and USS *Daly* (DD519). "Oh, yes," Julio would say, "I sure do love your old chief gunner's mate. Too bad he isn't in charge of the armory on the base."

During this particular period, Julio was always on the move. He had little to say, and when I visited he was often not there. But Gaby was always there, and having her to myself for a couple of days was perfect.

She once said to me, "I think you fall in love too easily, Jose."

"I've fallen in love hard. Falling easily is preferable."

Those were good times.

When Julio returned he would be relaxed, ready for bike rides, conversations, and cooking. One day, soon after returning from a trip to the Sierra Maestra Mountains, he was sitting with Gaby and me in the same park where we first had met. We were eating rice and beans and drinking Hatuey beer.

Julio asked me if I'd tell the chief gunner's mate that he wanted to see him early Sunday morning. "He knows where to meet me. Tell him it is important that he is there."

Before I could answer him, Gaby reached over and put one hand on her brother's arm and the other on mine. With a confidential tone to her voice and a smile on her face, she said, "Now I think Julio is a prostitute, just like our mother was a prostitute. I wonder if I will be next?"

Gaby laughed. Julio laughed. I laughed. I laughed out loud! My sudden laughter startled everyone in the meeting room and interrupted the *gusano* banker. The SERTOMA Club members turned and looked at me; they were shocked, and they whispered to each other and shook their heads in disapproval. There was nothing I could say except, "Excuse me."

(I should clarify our relationship with the old chief gunner's mate who was gay. He had almost thirty years in the navy. Had his homosexuality been discovered, he would have been kicked out of the military in an instant. He was easily persuaded. Would someone have "blown the whistle" on the chief if he had refused? Not a chance.)

Kicked out of SERTOMA

The speaker continued on and on about "Castro and his thugs" and how they had created a grim military dictatorship on his island paradise. When he finished, he asked if anyone had any questions.

I said I had a few. By then I had had a few too many Old Styles. First I asked him if he was opposed to Castro closing down the thousands of whorehouses that were run by U.S. organized crime, which split the profits with Batista's military police and probably the bankers.

The room became suddenly quiet.

While he was thinking about the first question, I asked him why he hadn't described how 90 percent of the Cuban people lived in abject poverty with no access to education or medical care until the Cuban people's revolution removed the U.S.-supported military dictator and the organized crime.

I asked him why he hadn't informed the SERTOMA Club of how the revolutionaries had received more help from navy personnel than from any Communist countries. And why he hadn't mentioned that U.S. corporations owned 75 percent of the farmland, and paid Cuban laborers pennies a day to ensure that stockholders got rich while babies died of malnutrition.

I asked him to please describe the slums, the sweatshops, and the exploitation of child labor that personified U.S. corporate involvement in Cuba—the gambling and whorehouses, the poverty, the lack of schools for the poor.

Looking around, I could see that everyone thought I was an outrage. I'd had too much to drink and I was angry. This Cuban banker's rap had brought back too many memories, too much rage. Anger and too much beer had brought me to my feet to spill my rage. I had a problem all right: I was unable to turn my anger into the kind of poetry my partner Tom Kuncl would spew forth when he was still sober enough to get to his feet in front of whoever was handy.

As a result of my outburst, I was kicked out of SERTOMA and labeled a crazy recalcitrant— which I probably was and am, but why scare people?

You can't be too careful. Not a good idea to mix politics and too much Old Style beer at the meeting of a social service group.

So the SERTOMA Club suffered an uncomfortable few minutes. They'll never know that they suffered far less listening to me than I did listening to the Cuban banker. I'm sure the banker had never been asked such questions—questions I'm sure they had all put out of their minds by the end of the day.

In looking back over my life, I believe that this outburst was one more element in the government figuring out that I was speaking about my own personal involvement with assisting Cuban revolutionaries. During the period I am talking about, the navy was lecturing personnel about the revolutionaries. They were quick to use the term "Commies." We were constantly being reminded that we had to be careful about who we associated with on the island. Bobby Vaughn's presence on the island, the fact that he had spent time with the revolutionaries in the Sierra Maestra Mountains, my association with him then and later in Iowa, the possibility of the government investigating and finding out that all of the Springfield rifles from our destroyer squadron were never turned in when they were exchanged for M1s—all of the above may have led investigators to identify me as a subversive who may have provided Castro with weapons from our squadron's arsenals.

Little did they know.

Looking back, the one thing that I found rather funny is that the chief corpsman who everyone thought was gay was gay, and no one gave a damn. A grizzled, tough old chief gunner's mate was a closeted gay and (almost) no one had a clue. The gunner's mate had fallen hard for Julio.

Bombed Out, Burned Down, and Charged with the Crime

In the summer of 1966, my vehemently pro-union weekly newspaper, the *Citizen-Times*, was deliberately burned down, and I lost what little perspective I had regarding justice or even the remote possibility that "right" could prevail—at least where either the newspaper or I was concerned.

It happened in Cedar Rapids, Iowa, during a period of intense union activity involving firefighters and wholesale grocery workers. The firefighters were being fought by the city and by every fire-department administrator on local and state levels. The other group was locking horns with a wealthy grocery-chain owner. Our newspaper, the largest weekly in the state, was with the workers 100 percent. My partner, Tom Kuncl, had a knack for describing the anti-union groups and individuals in a way that caused them to suffer serious attacks of apoplexy—particularly in city hall. For those and other reasons, we incurred the wrath of the city, the fire-department hierarchy, the state fire marshal's office, and a legion of others. We had friends among the rank and file in the cop shop and the fire department, but everyone above the rank and file treated us like pariahs, troublemakers who were giving the city a bad image.

Since working on the *Citizen-Times* paid nothing, we were lumped together with the unwashed, undesirable elements and shunned by 90 percent of society. We worked hard; and frequently, after a week of hard work—thanks to the generosity of workers—we found our table loaded with cold beer and schnapps. We were less gracious drunk than sober and consequently were only welcome in those taverns that catered to the workers.

Then the newspaper was torched and we were burned down.

It was bad losing the newspaper and equally heartbreaking losing the building, an old church where the Wright Brothers' father had been the preacher. The church had a history, a ton of stained glass, and a great location; the old fellow who owned it had bent over backwards to help me buy the building.

While the fire was raging, two firefighters smashed through a window to a second-floor room where they thought I was sleeping. Not finding me, they turned around and got out moments before the room exploded. At one point, over the intercoms that connected all the vehicles, a firefighter shouted, "We're trying to find the chief. Has anyone seen him?" There was a pause. Then someone who didn't identify himself responded with a note of humor: "The chief was last seen leaving the *Citizen-Times* newspaper building by the back door shortly before the first explosion was heard."

Broke everyone up. So here was this scene. Fire trucks, hoses, flames, smoke, people risking their lives, and the rank and file laughing and joking about the chief. Even though retrospectively, over forty years, I'm confident the chief wasn't the arsonist, it was no secret that he hated the *Citizen-Times*, the staff, the editorials, and particularly Tom Kuncl.

Following the fire and a lengthy investigation, I was charged with arson. The charges shocked many people, including me. We had recently spent $45,000 on a large Royal Zenith web-fed press; we were expanding, were making money for the first time in four years, had relocated downtown, and had the financial backing of a wealthy insurance-company owner. All of these positive developments carried no weight. Nor did the fact that over the objections of our backer I had dramatically cut back on our insurance policies because of the high premiums. After four years of working 16 to 20 hours a day without pay, sleeping in the office, using petty cash for cold cuts and white bread, pounding the pavement six days a week for nickel-and-dime ads, and pitching the churches on Sunday, I wasn't going to spend profits on insurance policies.

Because of prejudicial actions by the prosecutor, the charges were thrown out. I thought that was the end of it. However, the prosecution persisted, charges were again filed, and I was indicted for the second time. A year later, I finally appeared in court.

Over the course of that year, the harassment never ended. At times, the stress was so great that three or four days of work would just disappear from my mind. My inability to remember critically important parts of my day became a serious concern for my friends. When I was "with it" I was crazy angry. When I was "out of it" I was worse—according to my staff. My blackouts had friends concerned.

I was free on bond. I had managed the 10 percent necessary to get a bond.

One night about four months after the fire, while I was working late at our $30-a-month storefront, a deputy sheriff showed up with the woman who owned the local bonding company. She claimed I was preparing to leave the country; therefore, she said, she was arresting me and suspending my bond, as she had the power to do.

I was stunned and told her I didn't have enough money to use the john at the bus station, much less leave the country. Regardless, she said, she was pulling the bond. The deputy nodded when she repeated that I was under arrest. Further, as I knew, I'd be out the fee I had already paid her. With no money, I'd sit in the county jail until they got around to a trial. I thought about what was coming and couldn't deal with it.

As they escorted me to the car, I decided I couldn't live like these people were forcing me to live. I told them they could shove their arrest warrant. I jerked loose and started walking away from them. They told me to stop. I refused. The deputy pulled his gun and ordered me to stop, and I told them exactly what I thought about him and his gun, the county attorney, the state of Iowa, and their individual parentage, and I kept walking while screaming, "FUCK ALL OF YOU, YOUR BADGES, YOUR GUNS, YOUR EVERYTHING. YOU ARE SICK BASTARDS. IF YOU WANT TO SHOOT, GO AHEAD AND SHOOT!" The sound of the hammer on the deputy's pistol being pulled back sounded like a couple of Ginger Baker rim shots. I thought they were going to kill me, and at that point in my life I didn't give a damn. I kept walking, waiting for the punch of the bullet! If you have ever been shot, you know what I mean by "punch!" They waited and waited, and finally they ran to their car, grabbed the microphone, and called for help. He was yelling something about an escaped prisoner and asking for backup. What a circus.

I walked across a large vacant lot to the apartment of my friends Janie and Paul Kelso. The deputy had watched where I was going.

Janie and Paul asked what all the yelling was about. I told them what was happening. The cops were going to be all over the place in a few minutes, I said.

Paul had this thing about health foods. He didn't have anything to drink with alcohol in it, so I accepted one of his special high-energy milk shakes. I knew I'd need something to help me make it through that night. I hadn't gotten half of it down before the sirens started. Seven squad cars converged on the intersection, and a bunch of boys in blue pounded up the apartment stairs.

When the police knocked on the door, I went peacefully.

The health food must have adversely affected my mind.

At the station, I was informed that new charges had been filed: resisting arrest, possibly unlawful flight to avoid prosecution, escape, and a few others. Most of the rank-and-file cops were embarrassed. I was booked and spent the night in the can with prisoners I was beginning to know by their first names. The next morning, someone said the right words. I was out on my own recognizance, out the fee I paid that scum bondswoman, and back on the street. I walked to the office and took a bath. Marsha Kaiser (Mushy), my right hand at the newspaper, was there working.

My only clear memory of leaving the jail that morning was the feeling that I was starting a new life. The whole episode—the arrest, the second arrest—had an emotionally cleansing effect on me. There were times when the whole system had frightened me. Fear of prison; fear of having people around who you knew were trying to destroy you; not so much the fear of failure as the fear of not winning—of not being able to stand up against whomever and whatever it was you had to stand up against.

The trial began on April 18, 1966. For the first week of the trial, the prosecution paraded the state fire marshal's investigators and arson experts before the jury and the news media. First to the jury and then to the news media, the "overwhelming evidence" against me, which amounted to nothing more than determined speculation, was offered by a confident county attorney. After a week, the prosecutor rested his case with a round of adjectives, arm waving, and finger pointing.

Like it or not, despite the prosecutor's lack of hard evidence, I had to face the fact that it didn't look good for me. A guilty verdict would mean a 25-year sentence. With all the hell we had been raising with the city, the courts, the county attorney's office, and just about anyone who wasn't cheering for the working class, I looked for no breaks. None at all.

We asked for and received a ten-minute break to collect ourselves for the defense.

Just as we were entering the courtroom, Bob Nelson, one of my defense lawyers, was called to the phone by the bailiff. Suddenly our case became a classic Perry Mason adventure.

We had received an anonymous tip. A city detective had gotten a look into the county attorney's files and found reports that the county attorney had suppressed scientific reports that would clear me of the arson charge. One report, he confided, was from the FBI's criminal investigation laboratory in Washington, D.C.; another was from an independent lab; and the third was from a chemistry department at a local college. There was no evidence in any of those reports to indicate that the fire had been set, and much to indicate that it had not.

Someone had set me up, and it had almost worked. Whether the detective liked me or hated them I never found out. Chances are he was one of those cops who had bought into a personal honor system that couldn't be set aside. Not when the law-enforcement hierarchy wanted to close down a newspaper that had been born over on the West Side in Czech Town.

The paper that published "All the News That's Pit to Frint"—one of Kuncl's favorite digs at one of New York City's "waterpumps." We were grassroots journalism.

He never told us his name. He just gave us the facts.

The reports had been in the hands of the county attorney within ten days after the fire, and he had hidden them—suppressed them—for damn near two years. A classic cover-up. While I squirmed, it had been business as usual for the county attorney. I sat there with a whole new understanding of why some people kill.

With this new evidence in hand, the case for the defense was not that complex. We had brought in the top arson investigator in the country—the man who had trained the investigators the state was using in their attempt to convict me. He testified that he could not believe anyone who had attended his school could have investigated that fire and reached the conclusions they had reached. In his own opinion, he said, the fire had started probably as the result of a broken light bulb or incendiary device, in an area far from where the state fire marshal said it had been deliberately set.

After his testimony was finished, one of the state fire marshals was recalled, and he was asked by either Bob Fassler or Bob Nelson if any outside laboratories had conducted an independent investigation into whether or not flammable agents had been used. The marshal admitted there had been at least two such investigations. He was asked where those reports were from. He said one was done at the FBI laboratory in Washington, D.C., and the other was done in the chemistry department at nearby Coe College. Upon further questioning, he admitted that the reports showed that no such agents had been found where the two fires were alleged to have been set, and that those reports had been in the hands of the prosecutor within ten days after the fire broke out.

(If you, dear reader, ever end up in court, I sure hope your day will be as sweet as mine was that day.)

With the news about the suppressed evidence in front of the jury, the state's case disappeared. The jury came back with a "Not Guilty" verdict, and I was a new man. Unresolved, however, were two interesting bits of evidence: (1) a utility truck, the same as or very similar to trucks operated by the city, was seen at the rear of our building, and (2) shortly after it was seen leaving the back of the building, people living in the house next door heard a muffled explosion.

Despite our own star witness's testimony about the light bulb, I believed for my own reasons that the newspaper fire had been deliberately set by someone. Why did I think so? I had studied the site for months. I had taken photos of every inch of the burned areas. I studied the textbooks on arson investigation that our own expert had authored. My conclusion was the same as his. The fire had started inside the back door.

What the state investigators had failed to recognize was how the fire had spread from the first floor up to the second floor, to emerge under the altar/stage area. The flames had followed the path of an "I" beam for approximately 25 feet and had burned through the floor in two places. These two burn sites "convinced" the state that the fire had been set in two places under the altar/stage. The FBI laboratory was unable to find any traces of flammable substances at or around these burn sites, however. Rather than accepting the FBI findings and continuing the investigation, as a competent investigator would have done, the fire marshal's team chose to ignore the scientific reports—they actually suppressed them—and stick to their original theory. Had they acted properly, they might have discovered evidence that would have led to a successful conclusion. Since they refused to do so, I can only assume that they were more interested in putting me out of business than in solving a crime. If they had studied the site and traced the fire to the source, they would have been looking for the utility truck and the driver.

For me to point a finger at who might have had reason to destroy the newspaper was fruitless—not because I couldn't come up with anyone, but because there were so many. The only people who didn't hate us were working-class people—union members.

Additional evidence we never had to use came from statements that had been made by the state fire marshal's investigators at an out-of-state conference. Two of them had gotten drunk and said, "We're finally going to get rid of Kuncl, Grant, and the *Citizen-Times*."

Before the defense rested, I pointed these facts out to my attorneys and our investigators. I wanted the state witnesses recalled and questioned about the site, about their charges against me, and, more than anything, about why the reports were suppressed for over a year.

They shook their heads and said, "Forget it. You're innocent. We did what we came to do. We accepted this case to prove you innocent, not to go on a crusade." I could understand their reasoning. What had to be done had to be done by me. After all, the two Bobs were court-appointed, but they dug into the case as though I was paying them hundreds an hour.

Some of the jury members were crying when I went over and thanked them. I thanked my lawyers, then walked out of the courtroom with a smile on my face and hatred in my heart for the local upper-echelon law enforcement. The press was there, and someone asked me what my plans were. I told them I was going to start a daily newspaper.

The fact that the county attorney covered up evidence that would have cleared me immediately and not tied up a bunch of people for almost two years was criminal. I wanted to burn them. Unfortunately, when offered advertising that I desperately needed to survive, I discarded the suit and went to work. A few months later I was dumped. Lesson learned.

How to Pay for a Daily Newspaper

Daily newspapers, even small dailies, cost lots of money. But as our insurance executive investor would say, "Shoot for the stars and you might hit the moon."

Kuncl would answer, "Ya! And if a pig had wings it would fly."

As for the insurance coverage, I learned another important lesson that day: You hire an attorney as soon as you have a loss. We had held off hiring one. The thought of giving an attorney 30 percent of the money needed to replace the loss was more than we could deal with. After paying for the equipment and the building, we'd be lucky if we could buy a round of beer at our 16th Avenue SW hangouts. Plus the insurance agent kept telling us that we'd get paid as soon as I was exonerated.

Needless to say, as soon as I was exonerated I called the insurance company. A few days later their attorney informed me that since I had not filed suit within the period stipulated in the policy, they were not going to cover the loss. I learned that Daddy Warbucks, our wealthy backer, got his investment back years later. But as usual, the rank-and-file working class got the shaft.

Back to the beginning—again. Would my worries ever end?

They ended—or appeared to end.

Living on the bottom rungs of the socioeconomic ladder for the past few years and having covered the courts, the unions, fights, fires, and killings, the depths of my anger soon got to someone who saw the possibility of putting it to good use.

The right offer—rather, the wrong offer—came early in 1967.

It was no secret that I had skills as an artist: "Use your skills to print money, and we will see that you make enough to do exactly what you want to do." I thought about the offer for as long as it took to drink a cup of coffee.

I went to work for a group whose desire for easy money was almost as great as my desire to get even. My knack for making the perfect copy, and my knowledge about chemistry to develop a sizing agent that gave quality paper the look, feel, and flexibility of good old American currency kept me busy for a year. I desperately wanted a newspaper, but along the way, my desire for the newspaper took a backseat to developing the paper and the plates. Creating money was science fiction, an addiction. I couldn't stay away from the drawing table, the plates, the chemistry. I was hooked. Strange as it may seem, I never thought of spending it, never gave any thought to the illegality of what I was doing, and never rested. I published an issue of the newspaper once a week and spent the rest of the time in a small one-room hideaway that was a combination laboratory, art studio, and printing plant. I was in another world, one created by hate and some Chicago acquaintances.

The world was all new to me, and it was fascinating—for a while. I became so engrossed in the work that I could do little else. I was generating money to run the paper and meet a modest payroll. I didn't think to pay myself. So, when I was arrested and charged with counterfeiting, I thought about it and had to face the fact that I was cursed with bad karma. No sense in making excuses or copping a plea. Again I called Nelson and Fassler—my two Bobs.

Later that day, I was sitting with the Bobs trying to explain what I had done. After I had answered all their questions, Fassler said to Nelson, "We won't have any trouble winning this case."

Nelson looked at Fassler like he was nutso and asked him what he had in mind for a defense.

"Why, temporary insanity. What else is there?" Fassler laughed as only he could laugh—loud, louder, loudest, and right from the heart.

I could have walked away from most of the charges, but rejected adding any complications to my life that were not already there. As a result, life was considerably safer and mellower at Leavenworth—you never gain anything by dragging others to prison with you.

The trial itself was boring. I spent days answering the federal prosecutor's endless questions with a simple "I just don't know." Every time I said, "I just don't know," Nelson and Fassler would look at each other and shrug—the gesture saying, "We should have gone with the insanity plea."

The judge knew, though, and he didn't waste any time. He rewarded me with five or six 10-year sentences and tossed in an additional 5 for conspiracy. I entered Leavenworth in November 1967—a Pilgrim, so to speak, a couple of weeks in front of Thanksgiving.

When the two federal marshals dropped me off at Leavenworth, one of them took me aside and gave me some advice. "You have to be mighty careful in there, Joe—there's sex-crazed men on the other side of those walls who haven't been with a woman in a long, long time. Don't let them get to you."

Don't let them get to me? I thought. If there were men in there who were so hard up they saw me as a desirable love object, I wasn't heading into a prison; I was heading into a bloody insane asylum.

One last story about the money. Around the time I was finishing the money, a bright young high school student who had been hanging around the office getting occasional writing assignments had been given a key to the office. Being an inquisitive young man, he had discovered my hidden room and had borrowed some of the fruits of my nighttime labors. He had passed over the $10s, $20s, and $50s for the $100s with twenty-seven different serial numbers. He told me years later that he was working on a story of his own. After I had been cooling my heels in Leavenworth for three or four months, he and some friends got a little drunk after a football game and walked into the tavern a few steps from the old office. There, he laid a $100 bill on the bar and asked for a case of Old Style. As soon as the other patrons saw the bill, they went through the litany of jokes that my "temporary insanity" had generated.

"Check that C note!"

"Got a list of those serial numbers?"

"Let's look at that bill."

And they all did. They gathered around and studied the $100 bill that Bobby had laid down, and they all agreed that it was good old American currency—the real thing—not one of Joe's bills.

When the kids were picked up for public intoxication later that night, my young friend had a couple thousand in his backpack. One of the men who had been in the tavern the night before saw the front page of the morning paper and, in a letter, told me about what had happened there.

His letter arrived a couple of days after the story broke in the newspapers. The wire services had also picked it up. He was an old drinking buddy, who went into great detail describing how he and others had checked the $100 bill so carefully and decided it was real. The news of the story and the failure of the folks at the tavern to recognize a phony $100 bill spread through the prison population. Suddenly I was a bit of a celebrity. Those who heard the story learned I was the only first-time offender in the prison. This realization had my fellow prisoners convinced that the money was so exact and the paper so close to perfect that even though I had no previous record, the government was burning me with a 65-year sentence. I was aware enough to know I would never do all that time.

Behind the Walls

The community of the walled prison is much the same as life in the big city. It's a hot, explosive environment 24 hours a day. You have to be careful what you say and do. It's a little like living in a thimble that's being held over a Bunsen burner.

The prisoners run the walled prisons. They do everything, from the cooking of food to some of the counting of prisoners.

I'm not talking about the prisons where federal and state courts send the lawyers, doctors, preachers, financiers, and politicians—the scum who are able to buy time in the country-club prisons. I'm taking about the walled prisons, where the system puts the disenfranchised—the have-nots.

To sentencing judges, the "haves," with money for the connected attorneys, are prime candidates for rehabilitation. The "have-nots," the poor with no connections or resources, end up behind the walls, where they learn how to hate. Regardless of the fact that serious criminality crosses all economic levels, those with money end up in the country clubs, with unlimited visits from loved ones who can bring in lunch. The poor fill the end-of-the-line prisons, where the word "rehabilitation" has as much substance as cow shit in the springtime.

If the word "shit" continues to appear in this story about the PDI, it's because shit is the one substance that immediately comes to mind when I think back to life inside the walls. The custody, treatment, medical, religion, and recreation departments of every prison I have ever been in, visited, or written about have been for the most part supervised by guards who have failed at life in the free world, have earned GEDs, qualified with eighth-grade educations, and gone to work for the government. People I have shared this observation with tell me there are exceptions to this statement. A couple have told me about good guards. They could be right. Out of the many I have known, however, I only met one.

The preachers were the worst guards. Many a prisoner, weakened physically and emotionally by the stress, has learned the hard way that you don't talk to anyone with a guard's classification. Preachers of all denominations are classified as guards. They even get guards' pay. They'll betray you faster than a guard with ulcers.

Never tell the chaplain anything you wouldn't tell a guard.

This observation, I should add, has come to be accepted by a minimum of 90 percent of the prison population worldwide—that every prison preacher, be that preacher a representative of Baptist, Catholic, Lutheran, or any other of the Christian groups that make up world Christianity, is a guard first and a representative of all that Jesus of Nazareth held most dear second. Without exception they have obligated themselves to the state. They ALL report to "the man." They agree to do so when they take the job. Their livelihoods—not just the food on their family tables, but even their children's health insurance—depends upon the state. They follow the rules or they are out.

It was hard to imagine that a group claiming to be devoted Christians could condone these conditions, condone the brutality, condone the lack of official concern.

The more I distance myself from an otherwise painful period in my life, the less painful it becomes. Consciously or unconsciously I suppress the pain and misery, the sadness, the lonesome times, the fear. On the top of the memory heap are the successes, the victories, beating the chaplains, ripping off the test answers for the college entrance exams for the prisoners who needed that college acceptance to make parole and would never have been able to pass it on their own.

I still feel a rush when I think of how we broke into the chaplain's office to find that our suspicions were true—he had been intercepting mail from free world people at the Unitarian Universalist Church of the Larger Fellowship (CLF) in Boston. They were sending us books, and the chaplain was stashing them in a locked closet in his office. For all we knew, the Unitarians were ignoring our requests.

Unitarian Universalists Turn to Crime for CLF Books

Here's the whole story. It's an important one to me because it was one of two incidents that happened behind the walls at Leavenworth that helped me gain the reputation of being a person who could be trusted. The incident stretched over a year and involved the formation of a Unitarian Universalist fellowship in the federal prison system.

It was a community-organizing experience—organizing under the most difficult, repressive conditions. Just the kind of challenge that a rag-tag group of so-called religious malcontents needed to make their lives interesting. And what a year it was. We were surrounded by adversaries: the prisoners' "religious leader," the chaplain, who was a Baptist; the warden and the assistant wardens for custody and treatment; the ever-present guards; and a directive from the Federal Bureau of Prisons in Washington to deny the UUs everything. The highlight of the year was our publishing coup—a slick issue of an illegal underground magazine, published and distributed throughout the prison—and not a single UU group member or supporter busted.

The incident began in 1968 when a Chicano named Frank Sepulveda somehow found out I was for the most part a Unitarian Universalist. He had been trying to start a Unitarian Universalist discussion group for years, with no success. During his attempt to start a UU fellowship, he had read some articles about my activities as a Unitarian and was pleased to discover I was a prisoner.

Frank asked me if I would like to join his non-group. I was new and wary, but since Frank wasn't looking at me like I was a love object, I signed on.

The group now had two members.

Our request was a simple one. We wanted to get some free thinkers together to talk about religion. Among other topics we wanted to discuss were the conflicts between reason and creed. Frank had a way with words. Of course he had been working with words for nine years. He was serving a 15-year sentence for possession of an amount of pot that was so small it couldn't be measured—so small it couldn't even be smoked—in the bottom of a jacket pocket. Those were the days when they locked you up for not paying tax on your pot. Frank claimed that forcing a person to pay taxes on pot was unconstitutional. He had been trying to get the federal courts to stop and reread what the Constitution said about self-incrimination. He had filed actions on those grounds again and again.

This filing ritual usually took from twelve to eighteen months. Frank persisted. Year after year he fought the government, and he ultimately won his case; however, it was Tim Leary's lawyers who picked up Frank's work and got it before the Supreme Court for a win. Unfortunately, what should have been the Sepulveda Decision ended up in the law books as the Leary Decision. (Neither Sepulveda nor Leary should have been locked up.)

One day Frank's nine-year-old son, who had never seen his dad outside a prison visiting room, arrived with his mom for a visit. If I remember correctly, Paul Kelso and his son Devin were visiting me. (Paul had been an editorial writer at the *Citizen-Times* newspaper; however, his primary source of income was performing folk and union songs around the Midwest.) A guard reached out and grabbed the boy as the gate opened and he started to run into the visiting room. The kid, to the great delight of every prisoner in the room, jerked away and said, "Keep your hands off me, punk!"

Frank's whispered response was, "We are going to end up catching some heat for that remark." Everyone in the room had tears in their eyes from stifled laughter. There were things you did not want to get caught laughing at.

Frank not only had a way with words, he was patient.

Normally prisons love to see groups form. It looks good on paper. People with drinking problems had a group. Gamblers had a group. Drug, sex, and food addicts had groups. The Jaycees, Toastmasters, Catholics, Jews, and Black Muslims all had groups.

The request that we submitted and resubmitted was really quite simple. Yet the request continued to be denied.

When we pressed the chaplain for reasons, we were told: (1) We didn't have a sponsor (there were no UU fellowships or churches in the area, but in such cases the chaplain automatically sponsored any group with a religious affiliation); (2) there were already too many groups in the prison; and (3) we required guard supervision because we were a security problem and they couldn't spare a guard.

Something was wrong. We called a meeting. Arthur Rachel, from a few cells west of me, had signed on, so we had more members. The group wondered if we had missed something. There were many crazy organizations in that prison. How could the religion of Thomas Jefferson and Albert Schweitzer be considered crazy or dangerous? Certainly not the religion of Walter Kellison, a poet and the minister of the People's Unitarian Church, Cedar Rapids, Iowa—the only Unitarian I personally knew until I met Frank Sepulveda.

No crazies in that crowd.

In fact Frank was very much like Walter Kellison. Both were calm, quiet men who radiated a sense of strength. I'd had some serious conversations with Walter. He once asked me how it was that I ended up in the middle of so many losing situations. By "losing" he was referring to the involvement of our newspaper with so many seemingly hopeless crusades. We had been laughing over some of the situations my partner Tom Kuncl and I ended up in. At the time, I explained that the person to whom I attributed my proclivity to stick my nose into matters that many would consider none of my business was my mother. Mom's name was Magda Christine, but everyone called her Peggy. Mom, my four-year-old brother Duane Lee, my sixteen-year-old aunt Edna, and I lived in a small two-room apartment in Fargo, North Dakota, back in 1936. I was six years old and it was the height—perhaps I should say depth—of the Great Depression. We were poor.

Life became more interesting when a young sixteen-year-old runaway named Norma Deloris Egstrom rented a small room next door to us. She was pretty, quiet, and shy. Shortly after she moved in, some of the women in the apartment building decided that they wanted her to move out. Being too pretty, too young, and not in school, she was seen as a danger and a distraction to the men in the building.

I remember Norma coming to Mom in tears asking for help. She explained that she had had a tough life with a stepmother who was "cruel," and she had to strike out on her own. My mom had quit school when she was thirteen. Her dad had been killed in a hunting accident, and as the oldest of nine children, the job of running the farm had fallen on her. Mom listened and took Norma under her wing. She stopped the petition that was being circulated by going door to door and talking to the wives who saw Norma as a problem.

As the weeks passed, Mom, Norma, and Edna had many long discussions trying to figure out how best to use the meager resources Mom was so willing to share. Within two small rooms, I was witness to Mom's generosity and her concern for the welfare of others, a concern she passed on to me. (Ultimately I would carry my concerns to extremes and end up in prison. Guilty, unashamed, and in some circles understood.)

My brother and I shared a closet for a bedroom. Norma's room was on the other side of the closet wall. If Duane and I were noisy or misbehaving, Norma would knock on the wall and say, "Settle down, boys," and we would settle down. Frequently she would sit with us. Duane attracted women. He had large brown eyes and eyelashes that women always noticed and praised. She would sing for Duane and he loved it. Norma finally got a job singing at WDAY radio, which was only three blocks away from where we lived. In fact, Mom worked nightly as a cleaning woman in the Black Building, home to WDAY, a nine-story building that was Fargo's only "skyscraper."

One afternoon I was hanging around when Norma came walking down the street like she owned it.

"Is Peggy home," she asked? She wasn't.

"Would you tell her to check the marquee of the Powers Hotel when she gets home?"

I waited until Norma went inside, and quickly ran the two blocks to Broadway. The Powers Hotel was a block to the right. On the marquee in huge letters was:

THE POWERS HOTEL
PRESENTS
MISS PEGGY LEE

Norma Egstrom had changed her name to Peggy Lee: Mom's name and Duane's middle name. She had been advised to change her name and again turned to Mom. I recall Mom saying that no one deserved success more than Norma did. In those days nothing was more important than having a job. So many were unemployed and poor. So many were homeless.

Later that day, after everyone had seen the marquee, we had a little party with cake, coffee, and much hugging and tears. Many years later, I mentioned to Mom that I was surprised Peggy Lee never contacted her.

"She has called," Mom said. "More frequently many years earlier, but she never forgot those difficult days."

My Norwegian immigrant mom. Our 100-pound heavyweight.

Kellison pulled many stories about Mom's childhood out of me. It was hard to imagine a thirteen-year-old running a farm, but she did it. Then, when she was fifteen, she took a job working with a doctor in a small town twelve miles away. She would ride her horse to town, summer and winter; work for the doctor for two days; and return to the farm.

One day the doctor got a call from the former governor of North Dakota. He was looking for a couple of immigrant girls to work for him in his mansion in Fargo. Mom was only fifteen, but the doctor said that she and her younger sister could do the work. Mom was put in charge of seeing that meals were prepared, and she supervised the cleaning. They each earned $20 a month, and that $40 kept the family together.

A few weeks after they moved into the governor's mansion, the governor's wife accused Mom of stealing food. Mom went directly to the governor's office and informed him that she had never stolen anything and could not work for anyone who made such accusations.

"My sister Mabel and I are resigning and returning to the farm in Minnesota," she said to the governor.

The governor asked if there was anything he could do to convince them to stay. He explained that his wife suffered from an emotional problem and frequently made accusations that were groundless. But nothing would placate Mom. Finally the governor offered to double their wages. Eighty dollars a month in the early 1900s was a considerable sum and ensured that the family would survive until her siblings were old enough to contribute.

During one particular election, the governor gave Mom and Mabel each $10 and told them to vote a straight Republican ticket. He even had his driver take the girls to the polls. They were both kids, immigrants with only a seventh-grade education, not anywhere near old enough to vote, but Mom was a reader. When they got to the polling place, Mom instructed Mabel to vote a straight Non-Partisan League ticket. That was a historic election, when workers took over all elected state offices. All the bureaucrats were removed from office and there was much rejoicing. Years later, Mom would think back and talk about how troubled she was accepting money to vote Republican and voting the Non-Partisan League instead.

"It was dishonest and bothers me to this day," she reminisced. Then she would add, "But what would have caused me much greater emotional pain is if I had voted Republican."

What a gal.

When Frank and I asked the associate warden in charge of treatment for help, he told us to go to church on Sunday if we wanted religion.

We went back to the chaplain. He was pissed. In prison "No" means exactly that. "No!" When a prisoner doesn't accept the "No," he is considered either stupid or a troublemaker.

"What you two do with your lives is your business," the chaplain told us. "But as long as I'm in charge of religion around here, there will be no anti-Christian groups meeting in this prison."

Unitarians are many things, but they are not anti-Christian. Since we couldn't get a room for our UU meetings, we decided to meet out on the yard. We posted handwritten notices around the prison announcing the meeting.

The notices had been up about two hours when Frank and I were told to report to the captain, the man who handles discipline problems on a day-to-day basis. He told us that the notices were contraband, notices had to be approved by the chaplain, we had not been authorized to enter the areas where the notices were posted—and if it happened again, we would be sent to Building 63: "the hole."

We resubmitted requests and sent copies to George Marshall, minister for the Church of the Larger Fellowship at the UU headquarters in Boston. We also asked him for literature and books.

After about a month, we wrote to George Marshall again and asked why they hadn't sent the books. We got a fast reply. "First order was sent. Two more boxes of replacement books and literature sent today."

Another month passed. No books from UU headquarters.

By this time, six or seven months had passed. Seem strange? You have to remember that nothing happens fast in prison—except killings.

During this time, other prisoners were becoming interested. But since it was becoming known that being a Unitarian Universalist wasn't going to count for points at a parole hearing, most of the prisoners who came to listen and ask questions decided it wasn't worth being hassled about.

But some stayed.

We began proselytizing. The jailhouse lawyers were informed that every time they raised a constitutional issue on behalf of themselves or a fellow prisoner they could thank a Unitarian. Since many of the best jailhouse lawyers were doing heavy time, they were unconcerned that the administration was hassling us. To some, the hassling was what attracted them.

The Black Muslims asked, "If we can meet but the Unitarians can't, just exactly what is it the Unitarians advocate? Must have 'bad' politics if you can't meet without a guard."

As a diversion our group began attending regular church services, but we refused to allow the chaplain's clerk to add our names to the attendance list. We claimed that taking attendance was only crowd insurance and that it was discriminatory. The church attendance record was part of the information given to the parole board. It took a long time to get the practice stopped. When we did, the number of prisoners attending church services declined drastically.

Meanwhile, the chaplain would scream at us when we went to his office to ask about our books. Since George Marshall had told us he had sent the books, we knew the chaplain had them. Drastic action was needed.

One day, as soon as the chaplain and his clerk left for lunch, one of our new members, who was also a lock expert, walked four of us into the chaplain's office so fast I couldn't believe my eyes. Quickly, he locked the door behind us, then picked the locks on both desks, both filing cabinets, and the closet. In the closet were the four boxes of books and literature.

Our mission was half completed.

All books of a religious nature that came into the prison had to be stamped and signed by either the chaplain or the head of education. While the books were being spread out on the floor, the rubber stamp was located and the books were stamped while I signed the chaplain's name—I'd worked on duplicating his signature since we decided to take the "law" into our own hands. I signed fifty-seven books in five minutes. The pamphlets were all stamped, but I only had time to sign fifteen or twenty. Almost everything was carefully put back; desks, closet, and filing cabinets were relocked; and we were out of there with enough copies of some books to provide damned interesting reading for our few members.

We had made it in and out in 16 minutes and 28 seconds without anyone seeing us. My first B & E had been planned perfectly, but what fascinated me most was watching a man walk up to a locked door and, with what appeared to be three little steel "toothpicks," open it in seconds, with barely a pause in our forward motion. Twelve years later, James Caan starred in a movie called *The Thief*, a Michael Mann–directed movie that used this man as a model. The man was a professional. Contrary to what the movie portrayed, though, he did not use guns in his work.

That evening we had our regularly scheduled, unofficial non-meeting to determine a future course of action. Only four people knew about the break-in. Actually five. The chaplain knew. We decided he couldn't say anything without admitting that he had stolen our mail. He would have been in the clear if he had simply rejected the books and returned them. Keeping them was a "no-no," and that "no-no" determined our course of action.

First, we sent him a letter thanking him for approving the books and literature and being so supportive. We asked him which room he wanted us to use for our meetings.

Needless to say, he provided us with a meeting room, but only under certain conditions: We couldn't post notices in the prison that we were meeting, or that the fellowship even existed; only ten Unitarians could meet at one time; and a guard had to be present at all times to ensure that nothing threatening the security of the prison was planned.

Over a year had passed—but organizing and the risks involved had kept us busy and our emotional juices flowing.

Once a month, Emil Gudmundson, director of the Prairie Star District of the Unitarian Universalist Association, drove down from Minneapolis, 800 miles roundtrip, to lead a discussion group. Don Vaughn, minister of the First Unitarian Church of Wichita, drove over from Wichita once a month—a 400-mile roundtrip. Emil brought more than a lecture on Unitarian Universalism. He was a direct link to a way of life in the free world. Our discussions about Unitarians and Universalists during the religion's formative years were history as exciting as the history Howard Zinn was writing about. I had Zinn's book *Vietnam: The Logic of Withdrawal* and would later get a copy of *Disobedience and Democracy: Nine Fallacies on Law and Order.*

We named the group the Michael Servetus Fellowship, after the young Spanish writer who searched for, but could not find a mention of the Trinity in the Bible. Servetus not only wrote about his fruitless search, he traveled around Europe discussing it publicly. He made a serious mistake when he inadvertently wandered across the border into Switzerland, home to the infamous Calvin. Servetus, unaware that Calvin had a standing arrest warrant out for him, was arrested and brought before this God-fearing Protestant reformer. Calvin had no time for any "truths" other than his own. The kinds of truths Servetus was seeking and discussing were so abhorrent to Calvin that he promptly tied Servetus to a stake in the town square and burned him alive.

We felt a distant kinship with Servetus after being forced to interact with the chaplain for so many months. Servetus (as opposed to God) knows, our punk chaplain would have burned our books if he'd had the gonads for it.

Then, as if dealing with the chaplain wasn't enough, the Bureau of Prisons objected not only to our forming the group, but to our choice of the name. Rev. Don Vaughn called on the warden and informed him that the American Civil Liberties Union was stepping in and preparing to file a lawsuit. That bit of information helped the warden backpedal, and removed the final barrier to the Michael Servetus Fellowship, Leavenworth Federal Penitentiary—the first in the federal system.

Looking back and remembering that particular Protestant chaplain, with his degree from some academic Baptist factory, makes me want to step outside and scream. These guards with divinity degrees from half-assed little colleges associated with religious groups scattered around the country, cranking out preachers who jump at the chance of government or civil service jobs where they can preach greed and opportunism, make me sick. Prisoners waste away in solitary fighting for fair treatment for the sick and emotionally distressed, while the chaplains look the other way. Get used to it . . .

A Unitarian Universalist News Underground and Behind the Walls

With that fight over, we decided we owed an explanation to the entire prison population, in the form of an introduction to our Unitarian Universalist Fellowship. We gathered information from the books George Marshall had sent us—the books the chaplain had stashed in his locked office closet and was so reluctant to part with.

We sifted through the information, put together a booklet about the religion Thomas Jefferson favored, and went underground into the system that the prisoners control—the system that operates right under the noses of the guards. Books were given to typists, who passed pages on to prisoners in the print shop. There, type was set, or laid out, and the proofs were smuggled back into the cell blocks. Once we corrected the proofs, they were smuggled back into the print shop. In the print shop, pages were printed and folded. Then they were collated, covers were added, the binding crew took over, and the final step—distribution—was taken care of. I can't explain how it happened. The project involved many more people than I was comfortable with. But it was out of our hands—each UU member was covered. We had nothing, not even a penciled note, linking us to the publication.

We were pleased.

Five weeks after we decided to "go public," one thousand 20-page booklets suddenly appeared throughout the prison. It blew some minds. Imagine such a circulation when everyone's every move is scrutinized. No one was singled out. No one, with the exception of the chaplain calling Frank and me out, was accused of anything. To this day I believe the assistant warden decided to forget it ever happened, rather than give the situation the possibility of generating adverse publicity. Ignore it. It will go away. The chaplain was hotter than two rats making out in a wool sock.

"MAN'S OBLIGATIONS ARE TO MAN," the booklet's cover cautioned.

They were in the cell houses, on bulletin boards, in the factories, the tunnels, everywhere. Each booklet began: "Better to believe in no God than to believe in a cruel God, a tribal God, a sectarian God . . ."

The booklet contained answers to questions that had freaked out the Baptist chaplain: What is Unitarian Universalism? What do UUs think about prayer? About Jesus? God? Heaven? Questions about hell were unnecessary in Leavenworth, but they were included. Artie Rachel and Frank agreed, saying, "What the hell, why not?"

We believed in the inherent worth and dignity of every person. No need to dress it up with a bunch of ecclesiastical claptrap. We could make a case for everyone's right to justice, and for convincing our fellow prisoners that equity was one of the deterrents to deviant behavior. We were providing resources a person could use in the free world and in a cell. It's a big step up getting rid of the Biblical hocus-pocus the guards with collars were laying on their captive audience.

Our Michael Servetus Fellowship was credited (in the booklet) with publishing Leavenworth's first underground publication. We claimed innocence, contending that someone was trying to set us up. We maintained that what had happened wasn't possible. How could a 20-page booklet be typeset and printed when supervisors were around the printing presses at all times? It couldn't happen. How could it be collated and stapled? Not possible. How did it get distributed? Where did the paper and cover stock come from? How was it trimmed?

We had a message we felt was compelling and were eager to share the information, but all we had were a few books that arrived with no magic wands.

Only a few knew, but no one admitted to knowing, and there wasn't a snitch in the print shop underground. We had over fifteen members in the fellowship and no one admitted anything to the man; neither did the men from the print shop or the men who distributed the booklets throughout the prison. It was absolutely incredible. A real coup. I thought of the White Rose with great fondness and respect: The White Rose was a small group in wartime Germany that published an antiwar flier condemning Hitler. Weeks before the end of the war, a brother and sister, Sophie and Hans Scholl, were caught and beheaded.

Frank and I were called to the chaplain's office. We assumed he would have something to say about THE BOOKLET. He damn sure did. As soon as he saw us, his face turned as red as a stuffed beet, and he started screaming, "Just what the goddamn hell are you two sons of bitches trying to do?"

I'll never forget Frank's answer: "Hey, man, my boy is going to be nine in a few days. He wasn't born when I came here for less grass than a person could smoke. What am I doing? Well, today, just like yesterday, I'm trying to keep from going crazy in your fuckin' circus."

I just shrugged my shoulders and in what I thought was a righteous tone said, "The Lord moves in mysterious ways, HER wonders to perform."

On the way back to the cell block, I said to Frank, "For a minute I thought someone had gone to Baptist confession." Frank laughed. "It's a wonder someone didn't. Hell, Jesus only had thirteen members and one of them was a snitch. Our *followers* . . . ," and when he said *followers*, he did a little guitar-playing pantomime as we laughed our way back to the cell block. "We have a tight little group. Let's go to work."

Meanwhile, for his own efforts in hiding our mail and lying about it, along with making a minor name for himself fighting the Muslims and the Unitarians, the chaplain was later promoted by the Federal Bureau of Prisons to head the entire chaplaincy program in Washington, D.C. Interesting. Had we decided to file charges against him, we would have brought the entire system down on us. Our only consolation was knowing that he knew he was spending eight hours a day exactly where he belonged: in the prison we shared.

A couple of months after our meeting in the chaplain's office, Frank's conviction was overturned. Timothy Leary got credit for the Supreme Court decision, but Frank had done all the work. The government had been prosecuting people caught with any amount of marijuana with failure to pay income tax on the weed. Frank had been shooting off legal briefs for years pointing out that paying taxes on pot would have been self-incrimination. When Tim Leary's lawyers saw how sophisticated and well-researched Frank's briefs were, they jumped in and filed. Leary's name provided front-page fodder for the daily waterpumps. The Leary Decision should have been the Sepulveda Decision. Leary admitted it to me years later.

The second incident that helped give me a trustworthy reputation was funny, but it could have turned out badly.

After I had been there a few months, I was called into the office of the lieutenant who was in charge of Custody. Anxiety bells went off in my head as I tried to figure out what I had done to warrant a call from *Custody*. I was wracking my brain for a clue.

As soon as I told his clerk who I was and he nodded toward the closed office door, I saw his name and made the connection. He had called me into his office because he had remembered an incident we shared years before. Back then he had been the federal jail inspector. Tom Kuncl and I were publishing the *Citizen-Times.* His job was to inspect any jail that had been designated a place where the federal government could hold prisoners. He traveled to cities and towns all over the country, including Cedar Rapids, Iowa.

It was no secret that the Linn County jail was in poor condition. It was miserably cold in winter and stifling hot in the summer. The food was terrible. Security was so poor that prisoners were able to leave the jail for the night by crawling in and out through heating vents.

When we learned about this, I contacted one of the prisoners, who came out and brought me back in late one night. While I was inside, I interviewed a couple of prisoners, took their pictures, had my picture taken with them to prove I had been there, and then crawled back out. I had broken into and out of jail. I thought I had a great story. But I was advised to clear it with a friend who was a member of the National Lawyers Guild. He checked the law and told me I would probably be charged with a felony crime if the story and pictures were printed.

"They are not going to ignore this level of transgression, Joe," he explained. "Proceed at your own risk. Great story, but you'll be writing the next chapter from the Linn County jail."

We didn't use it. It would have been a wonderful story. It finally leaked by word of mouth, probably prisoners, but so many of the immediate circle of provocateurs might have been the culprits. We never considered those loose lips to be snitches—they were more like comedians.

Shortly after that jail "break," we learned that the federal jail inspector was arriving in town to inspect the Linn County jail. Tom Kuncl decided we had to interview him as soon as he completed his inspection. We knew the jail would be approved, but we also knew that the jail would not meet the basic requirements. Unfortunately, once he found out some newspaper reporters were trying to corner him, he enlisted the aid of the deputies to avoid us.

He avoided us going in and coming out of the jail.

We staked out his hotel room.

He changed hotels.

But a room clerk tipped us off and we were waiting for him when he drove up to a motel on the edge of town.

As soon as he saw us, he jumped back in his car and drove off. We were unable to find him after that. Later we learned he had driven 130 miles to Des Moines before he thought it was safe to stop and get some rest.

Finally he and I were face to face; unfortunately, the meeting was on his turf.

As soon as I recognized him sitting behind that big desk in Leavenworth's custody office, I knew I was in big trouble. If he was vindictive, he had the power to make my life a perfect hell in that prison.

I walked up to his desk, and instead of waiting for him to speak—which was the rule you did not break—I said, "I hope you understand the trouble I have gone through to finally catch up to you for this interview."

Thank God (or rather Servetus), the man had a sense of humor. He laughed long and hard and asked me to sit down and tell him how I happened to be bad enough to be where I was.

Every administrator has a prisoner clerk. These clerks keep track of everything that transpires between prisoners and administrators. If you step into the lieutenant's office, shut the door, sit down, and start talking, it looks bad—very bad. You'll end up an outcast—regardless of what you talk about.

I told him how pleased I was that he had a sense of humor, but that if he wanted information on why I was there he would have to get it from the official record. He didn't like my answer, but he smiled, glanced at his office door that I had left open, and understood. The smile never left his face.

By the next day, everyone knew the story. Grant, number 84219, had chased the custody lieutenant out of Cedar Rapids, Iowa, when he was the federal jail inspector. The population loved it. It is a rare happening that allows a prisoner to come out a winner in any conflict—minor or major—with a prison official on this level.

One lesson I have learned over the years is, when you are facing a situation where you cannot win, you have two choices: use humor, or get loud and make sure as many people as possible are paying attention, because you know you are going to get hurt.

Prison: A Mirror of the Free World

Walking those endless miles "on the yard" inside the Federal Penitentiary at Leavenworth over forty-two years ago, I came to the conclusion that the prison population, with only a few exceptions, reflected the free-world population.

Fourteen years later, in the mid-eighties, I was back in a state prison. PDI no longer existed. I was in the Anamosa Reformatory serving six months for manufacturing a controlled substance. That charge translated into my being held responsible for a few wild pot plants that a vindictive sheriff found growing on a farm I held the title to. The fact that I didn't live there didn't lessen my responsibility in the eyes of the court. The person who was found picking the pot took a walk by swearing he was picking it, rolling it into joints, selling them for ten cents each, and giving me the money. It was absurd and everyone knew it. I had rented the land to an Iowa County deputy sheriff and wasn't farming anything. Friends were living there and had a huge garden to supply the Catholic Worker houses in Iowa with fresh produce. At the time, Iowa had more CW houses of hospitality than any state in the U.S.

I laughed all the way to an Iowa reformatory.

However, it turned out to be an interesting six months. I was older than most of the prisoners, and my reputation had preceded me—particularly with the guards and administrators.

My first prison job, this time around, was in the laundry. Prisoners put their socks, T-shirts, shorts, and other whites into mesh bags that were washed in huge machines. When each prisoner came back to the sorting room to pick up his clean clothes, we checked his number and put the bag in a cubicle with a corresponding number. Occasionally the guards would order us to check all the bags to make sure no prisoner had items of clothing without a number (possession of unnumbered items—contraband—was illegal). We were ordered to turn any bags with illegal clothes over to the guards.

Most of the population was age twenty-five or under. Many prided themselves on how tough they were and on how much time they had done. It was a typical prison with this exception: In Leavenworth, serious arguments were rare. If there was a serious conflict developing between two men, it was either resolved calmly or there was a killing. In Anamosa there was endless yelling and screaming and threatening behavior, but there were no killings.

The first time, after I started working there, that we were ordered to check laundry bags for contraband, one of the prison toughs found a bag with unnumbered socks and started walking over to the guard with the bag. "Wait a minute," I said. "Let's talk about this." He came back and rejoined the circle of ten or fifteen prisoners who were inspecting the bags.

"If you give that bag to the guard, someone is going to end up in trouble. We can't be causing that kind of trouble. If you find any illegal items, take them out of the bag and throw them in the lost-and-found bin."

He thought about what I said. He had to make sure he wasn't being made to look bad. "What if I get snitched off for not turning the bag in?" The thought of getting in trouble for helping another prisoner he didn't even know was unthinkable.

"What if you get snitched off for turning the bag in?" I answered. Now he had to think about dealing with whoever might get written up.

Damned if you do, damned if you don't.

"Look at it this way," I explained. "The guard is making us do his job for him. It is not our job to act as cops. We only have to sort the clothes. If we turn someone in for having unmarked socks, we are participating in that person's getting busted. I don't know about you, but I'm not getting paid to be a cop." Then, to make sure he didn't feel threatened by me, I added, "And I know you aren't working for the man."

Before anyone could say anything else, I asked him to give me the bag. He did. I took the items out of the bag, threw them in the lost-and-found bin, tied the bag shut, and went back to work.

Conversations stopped while the men thought about what had been said. Some seemed perplexed. They didn't understand their role in the peaceful order of things.

"It's interesting to watch how the prison operates," I said to the group. Then I asked them, "Who does all the work?"

"We do all the goddamned work. The prisoners do all the work and take all the crap," a number of them said all at once.

"That's why it's important that we make sure life goes as smoothly as possible for everyone. If we turn in every bag with clothes that are not numbered, ten or fifteen or more prisoners are going to get written up. A man could lose good time. Someone may get knocked off the list for a one-man cell. They may be looking for a way to stop someone from making a move to minimum security. All because the man has successfully turned prisoners into snitches."

"What you are saying could get you in trouble, Grant," one of the men said. "What if someone here goes to the man and snitches you off for not turning in those unmarked items of clothes? What would you do?"

"Well, I wouldn't deny it, because the man always takes the word of a snitch over the word of the person who is being snitched on. I'd just tell them that I thought they were causing themselves more trouble than a pair of socks was worth. I didn't turn the guy in, because to do so would cause me trouble (I'd be a snitch) and the guy trouble (he'd be violating rules). If I ended up in "court" for not turning him in, I was only causing myself trouble. I'd rather be in trouble with the man for not being a snitch than in trouble with the prisoners for being a snitch. I had cut the trouble in half. I might give me a free bag of popcorn at the next movie."

The men liked my story. Lots of laughs. But I made my point.

One of the other prisoners smiled and said, "If I get caught not turning a prisoner in, I'm gonna say, 'I'm just trying to save you a bunch of paperwork, Boss!'"

Everyone laughed again, and for the rest of the afternoon we kept coming up with excuses to tell the man. Responsibility rehearsals. Memorizing your lines for the next performance. Peacekeeping practice. Helping your brothers. And that is exactly what happened. I was snitched off to the guard, he called me out, I told him exactly what I had told the prisoners, and he agreed. He tore up the report. He surprised me.

The Prisoners Can Vote . . . But!

The following week I was elected to the inmate council. Since I hadn't been a prisoner for the required amount of time, the custody officer removed my name and they had another election. The inmate population reelected me. The administration took me off and filled the vacancy with an appointee.

A vote is a terrible thing to waste. "Teach your children well . . . ," I told the warden.

It was the third inmate council I'd been denied a seat on. But I knew that a time would come when all the good, common-sense rules that have developed over the past three hundred years in the prisons of the world would someday come together someplace. I had hoped it would be the PDI, where we could refine them, get rid of the crap and the egos, and end up with a slim little volume of customary law that prisoners could use as a guide to what is right and wrong from the prisoner's perspective. Not something to make war with, but something to make peace with.

"Your vote is precious—use it," I'd tell my fellow prisoners.

This incident, as much as any, convinced me that these young prisoners could and would act responsibly if they were given reasons to do so. My talk with these guys about our obligation to look out for our brother prisoners and try to avoid creating problems had an impact. No one was ever turned in for having an unnumbered sock or T-shirt while I was still there—not because anyone feared me, but because the decision was one they could make on their own.

One other incident took place that changed the general appearance of the population. When we sorted the shirts and pants, the clothes were jammed into the cubicles assigned to each prisoner. Each of us was assigned a block of cubicles. I decided to fold all of the clothes before I placed them in the cubicles. I'll put the responsibility for having that little hang-up, folding my clothes, on my mother. It was such a simple, easy act. The clothes were all hot and fresh from the huge driers. It didn't take me any longer to shake and fold a shirt or a pair of pants than most of the workers took to separate clothes and stuff them into a cubicle.

When we finished the sort that day, my section of cubicles stood out from the rest. It screamed "NEATNESS," and there was no way anyone could avoid seeing it. When the prisoners came for their clothes after work that day, those whose numbers were in my block made a big deal out of the fact that their clothes seemed to have been pressed. They seemed pressed because we sorted when they were still warm from the driers.

Pressed clothes are available to anyone who wants to pay for them. Walking around with pressed clothes made a prisoner stand out from the masses.

Prisoners asked, "Why go to the extra trouble?"

"Because the man wants us to look like a bunch of trashy losers," I answered.

Within a week, everyone was folding the pants and shirts. The laundry-room workers began taking pride in how neatly clothes were stacked in their block of cubicles.

A Proliferation of Child Abusers

One major population difference I could see between this prison and my first, fourteen years earlier, was the presence of an extraordinary number of prisoners who were child molesters. There had always been child molesters in the can, but in the past they were few and far between. They were considered the dregs of the population and were the recipients of every prisoner's anger or frustration. They were raped by the aggressive, beaten up by whoever took a notion, and verbally abused by everyone. Yet in the brief span of fourteen years, their numbers had increased so drastically that they were a significant percentage of the prison population. A group to contend with. A voting bloc. Old men, young men, married men, fathers, you name it—they were a group. And they were out there walking the yard like respectable prisoners. They even had their own block of cells separate from the regular prison population.

So, does the prison population reflect the free-world population before or after the proliferation of convicted child abusers? I've come to the conclusion that fourteen years earlier, when I was in Leavenworth, it didn't. The prison population has been playing "catch-up." Today's prison population is a more accurate reflection of society. Be that as it may.

Prisoners. A cross section of society. Living with them, constantly interacting, studying, observing, learning. It was a Philip K. Dick novel. Real. Unreal. Never have I lived in such an oppressive environment. Never have I seen "justice" meted out so swiftly. At times I felt so vulnerable it made me sick. At other times I felt invulnerable—unbeatable. For the most part, however, I was a constant witness to hopelessness, futility, and waste. At times it exhausted me. Occasionally it energized me. There were times when it inspired.

It was interesting, for instance, to watch how the conscientious objectors during the Vietnam War affected their fellow prisoners as more and more of them began showing up in the walled prisons. Suddenly the prison population had to contend with prisoners who did not lie, cheat, or steal. When a CO was asked about the conduct of another prisoner, he didn't lie to disassociate himself from what he had observed. It didn't take long for them to learn to stand on their Fifth Amendment rights. They simply refused to answer.

There have always been prisoners who feel an obligation to help their fellow prisoners, but the COs went public with it—taking it from the unusual to NOP: normal operating procedure. They were, with rare exception, pacifists. There were times when convict thugs—the prisoner equivalent to the guard's goon squads, who took orders from the man—would play rough with COs; but for the most part the COs earned the respect of even the toughest, most cynical cons. The fact that these gentle people were even in prison was one more example of a judicial system that had become as evil as some of the defendants who ended up before the bench, and as evil as some of the judges behind the bench.

In the Sandstone (Minnesota) Federal Prison, where I was sent from Leavenworth, I met a number of COs. One evening I came up with an idea that I believed would get their endorsement. My plan was to contact the president and inform him that a group of COs were willing to change their politics and join the military. They would be taken to Minneapolis for a press conference and dinner, and then to the recruiting station to be sworn in. At that point they could change their minds, or disappear in the crowd and head for Canada. Most thought it was a great idea that would get great press when the COs arrived at the recruiting station and changed their minds. As the plan progressed, one of the COs, a young, slight fellow, said he wouldn't participate because it called on him to lie. There was no convincing him. In the end, all of the COs told me they admired the idea but would not be able to live with the lying.

Another Grant failure, but what great in-the-can-doing-time fun.

As long as nonviolent people are imprisoned for their antiwar convictions, a critically important element of civilization has been ignored or rejected by our society. We all suffer for it. Prison was a difficult adjustment for most of the COs. They were unprepared for the irrational violence that surrounded them. Unprepared for the rapes that took place during group showers, with all but the participants going about their business as though nothing was happening. The insane, irrational criminality—the violence, different than any I had ever known.

I knew that rage could provoke a person to kill, but I had never, before Leavenworth, seen a killing that wasn't preceded by some show of emotion—a display of anger or rage. Not so while I was at Leavenworth. Words. Calmly spoken. And suddenly there was violence. A seemingly normal conversation ended with a person dead. And as quickly as it had happened it was over. Men walking around a body as though it wasn't there. The crowd smoothly drifting away in an ever-widening circle, with no one facing in. Nothing seen. Nothing heard. It was tough on COs.

I observed their lives and the lives of others in prison. Through it all, observations provoked perplexing questions.

For example, why is it that as soon as a person is convicted of a crime, he or she is abandoned by the law? Why do prisoners, be they convicted of pandering, prostitution, perjury, or murder, suddenly become nonhumans, not worthy of an iota of attention when they are raped, assaulted, denied medical attention, starved, held in solitary confinement without trial for years, and generally treated in a manner that will guarantee that the petty offender will become tomorrow's armed robber, and those carrying today's anger will walk out tomorrow harboring a potentially deadly rage?

Only a few weeks into my new life, shortly before Thanksgiving, I was deep into Henri Troyat's biography of Tolstoy. Couldn't put it down. I took it with me to the dining hall. I was eating and reading one evening. Suddenly blood splashed across the pages of the book. I quickly looked up to my left and watched a prisoner with a slashed throat at the next table fall forward into his food. Blood was spurting wildly. A man passed behind me and a discarded shiv came to rest under our table.

"Don't look!" a friend muttered as he calmly stood and walked. I wiped the blood off the open pages with my shirtsleeve, slammed the book shut, and placed it in my lap. Before I could figure out what to do next, my friends were heading for the exit. I thought all hell would break loose, but nothing was happening. No alarm. No yelling. Just a man, face down on his food tray as his life pulsed away.

I had dropped off my tray and was almost at the exit before a couple of guards, eyes focused, pointing, and attracting other guards, walked rapidly toward the lifeless body.

Perhaps the most perplexing question I asked myself while on the inside looking in was this: For all the brutality (by prisoners and guards); for all the lying, cheating, and stealing (by prisoners and guards); for all the shakedowns (by prisoners and guards), how is it that so many prisoners survived the insanity and, facing the same situations that originally, for whatever reasons, combined to place them in prison, successfully put their lives together, made it out, and manage to stay there—against all odds.

Rule by Tradition

The rule of law, which we hoped to establish in the prisons back in the seventies, does not exist in any prison in the United States. There is state law, legislated law, and the law of force, threats, and arbitrary punishment, but the "rule of law" as we think of it in the free world does not exist in prison. Prisoners, therefore, survive through guile, muscle, gangs, as informants, or by cutting deals. Nevertheless, one doesn't have to spend much time in prison to discover that an elaborate system of customs, "informal" rules, does exist. These unwritten laws, accepted simply on the strength of tradition, probably began to take shape when the Quakers released prisoners from their single, solitary cells, where isolation with only the Bible for a companion was doing then what the same treatment does to prisoners today—it drove men nuts. Once the prisoners were out of their solitary cells in Philadelphia (where prisons as we know them today were invented) and began mixing and interacting, social "agreements" began to form. A code of behavior developed.

During these hundreds of years, prisoners have managed to survive the barbarity of prison with the help of these unwritten "rules." The society of prisoners, no differently than the free-world society, needed a code that they could live by—could survive by.

In the dining hall at Leavenworth, for instance, if you were sitting at one of the four-person tables by yourself or with a friend and another prisoner needed a seat, he would ask if it was okay to join you. Then, he would sit quietly and not join in the conversation until he was spoken to. You could eat an entire meal with a person at your table who seemingly didn't hear a word that was said, didn't look at you, didn't seem to be there.

Whether it was a cell, a bed in a dorm, or a table in the dining hall, your personal space was something that no one entered unless he was invited. The great majority of the prisoners had a tremendous respect for another prisoner's space. You could die for not respecting it.

Usually, the longer a person had been inside, the gentler and the deadlier he became. He could respond with thoughtfulness, a totally unexpected birthday gift, or deadly force if someone broke a "law" that he lived by. "If I don't enforce my law, who will?" I was told by an old-timer a few cells down the line in B Block. A new fellow had moved in and had brought a guitar with him. He was strumming the guitar. I was aware of it, but was painting and paying no attention. Suddenly a quiet voice said, "Stay out of my house with your music." And the music stopped. There were places to play your guitar. The cell block, where your music entered another person's "house," was not one of them. In Anamosa, few prisoners had respect for their fellow inmates.

Another rule: "Do your own time." This is one of the most basic rules. You hear it many ways. "If you can't do the time, don't do the crime." Defining "Do your own time" is not as simple as it first appears. One prisoner will say, "Don't let your problems spill over and affect the man in the cell next to you." Another will say, "Look out for number one, ignore what's going on around you, and keep your mouth shut." Another will state, "It means that no one wants to listen to an endless litany of blaming others for the reason you're in prison. Shut up and 'do your own time.'" It's a rule that goes both ways. It benefits the administrators and the guards when prisoners "do their own time" and refuse to go to the aid of a fellow prisoner who is being treated unjustly by guard or prisoner. On the other hand, it's a very positive rule when prisoners understand that they must respect other prisoners' space, privacy, and rights.

In 1988, Professor Richard Oakes, founding dean of the Hamline University (St. Paul, Minnesota) School of Law, initiated the first systematic examination of that system when he began contacting—and being contacted by—prisoners from around the world. These prisoners were in turn carefully researching those customs in their own prisons that had literally become law. He concluded that customary law, although it existed and functioned for many, never made it to a form where it could be studied and adopted as a means to bring the rule of law into the prisons.

Like Professor Richard Oakes, I believe that these unwritten rules must be collected, studied, and published, then made available to all prisoners to use in their relations with prison guards, administrators, and other prisoners. "Law and order" continues to be a major concern of people in the free world. Believe me, for much longer than anyone in the free world can imagine, it has been of paramount concern inside the walls of prisons as well.

Dick Oakes, unfortunately, died young. His heart gave out. He had graduated from the University of Minnesota Law College and quickly determined that his law education was lacking. He founded Midwestern College of Law and designed the curriculum. Unbelievably his law college was granted accreditation during its third year. As soon as that happened, Hamline University, St. Paul, asked if he would move to Hamline. He agreed, with a few conditions, and today his legacy lives on.

As a union activist who had walked picket lines with the Laborers, the Packing House Workers, the International Brotherhood of Electrical Workers (IBEW), and the Teamsters, I understood how management attempts to fragment groups of organizing workers. In the same way, the prison population was also being fragmented by the authorities. Turn the blacks against the whites, the old against the young. Keep the populations fighting amongst themselves. Keep the population from organizing. Keep the population from bringing anything that resembled the rule of law into the prison.

The "man" had been carefully coached by the psychologists and psychiatrists. The old stimulus/response games were being played to the hilt. Rewards and punishments. Outrageous rewards, inhuman punishments. Transfers, segregation, every tool of the trade used and learned in hundreds of years of suppressing individuality, of punishing, of breaking people's spirits were available and in use. Many of them were common knowledge; most were not.

There was a time when a snitch was despised. Someone who could not be trusted was an outcast. However, with more and more perks being introduced into the system—good time, parole, more liberal visits, mail, minimum and medium security prisons—the temptation for a prisoner to ingratiate himself or herself with guards became greater and greater. When a prisoner who is facing the loss of a couple of years' good time can avoid the punishment by informing on an acquaintance who is running numbers, he or she frequently does so.

My first serious mistake inside the walls was as memorable for what didn't happen as for what did. Contrary to popular thinking, and regardless of *Miranda et al.*, even the courts cannot help the prisoner who threatens the stability of the system. I threatened the stability of the system.

I had kicked around in a number of prison jobs in Leavenworth until one day in 1968 when the chief surgeon discovered that I had had a modest exposure to science and anatomy (Boston University) that had provided me with a fair degree of familiarity with medical terminology. He had been without a clerk for a couple of weeks, and the paperwork on new prisoners was a mess. The job of the chief surgeon's clerk was to type medical summaries from the chief surgeon's scribbled notes that were made during the superficial physical exams that each new prisoner received. My ability to decipher his medical hieroglyphics thrust me into a job that provided me with the one possession no other prisoner in the joint had—an office of my own. My office was small, but it afforded me more privacy and freedom than I ever believed would be possible in that prison. No guards, no prisoners, no one.

Directly across the hall from my office was another small office where the psychiatrist worked. The psychiatrist was a Berkeley grad whose mannerisms were extremely effeminate. Most prisoners thought he was gay, and since most of the old-line prisoners were right-wing flag wavers who hated "draft dodgers, faggots, and longhairs," he was seen as out of place behind the walls. For the year or so that I worked across the hall from him, I watched him gain the respect of most of the prisoners. It was not unusual for prisoners counseling with him to allow their pent-up anger and frustration at the prison and the system to explode. They would curse him, scream, jump up and down, and pound the table. One day I asked him why he put up with such abuse. "That talk means nothing. Better they get rid of the anger yelling at me than going out and killing someone."

The chief surgeon was not so sensitive. In my opinion, he was one of the coldest, most sadistic men I have ever known. He treated me like a human being simply because there was no one else available who could do the job as well as I could. The job was such a cakewalk that no pay came with it. I took care of that problem within the month. I worked slowly, with a fixed, pained expression on my face, until the chief surgeon asked me if $20 a month would speed me up. I said I thought it would be worth a try. He did and it was. Soon I was typing the medical histories and interviewing all new prisoners regarding their medical histories.

Since I was questioning every prisoner, and the prisoner didn't know where the official questions ended, I began asking my own. I was interested in substance abuse—alcohol, drugs, and others. Had they been drinking when they committed their crimes? Had they used drugs? Did other members of the family? Parents divorced? How many times? Siblings? et cetera, et cetera, et cetera. I even initiated visits to Building 63—the hole—to get medical histories on prisoners who were never allowed to join the general prison population.

Some of the residents of Building 63 were an elite group who had committed the only unacceptable offense: they had attacked a prison guard or administrator. The ultimate crime. They got special treatment. They were endlessly transferred around the federal prison system and never saw a cell block, the mess hall, the yard, or the commissary, and rarely received mail. They lived in the hole. Prison to prison to prison. I managed to spend time with prisoners in solitary. One prisoner, Red Hayes, had been in solitary for thirteen years. I began asking him questions about his medical condition and he looked at me like I was crazy. He stood in front of his cell, eyes registering disbelief. His face twisted and he started shaking his head back and forth, faster and faster. I stepped back. He began blubbering. A guard walked over and slammed the outer door closed. Later I learned that occasionally, to show their total disregard for the welfare of a prisoner in solitary, they would bring in a torch and weld the outer door shut. The only opening was the slot where they passed the prisoner his food.

When the chief surgeon learned I had been questioning prisoners who were placed in solitary immediately upon arrival, he freaked. He read me the riot act, but he kept me in my job. I never returned to Building 63.

As the supervisor in education was fond of reminding us, "A little education is good job insurance." His clerk also had a cushy job. He was writing the supervisor's thesis for his master's degree. Job insurance.

I carefully coded all of the information I gathered, using a master form that enabled me to put small pencil dots and pin pricks on hundreds of pages of my journal. Unless you looked closely, the dots were lost on the page of handwritten material. In the course of a couple of years I gathered extensive histories on over one thousand prisoners, who had served an average of four prison sentences before getting to the Big Top.

Even though I went to great lengths to keep the journals bland and free of any controversy, they were snatched when I was being transferred, and I didn't realize it until I was 1,000 miles up the road in the Sandstone, Minnesota, prison. A guard later told me that much of my accumulated belongings were trashed. When the guards who search prisoners' belongings (before the boxes leave the prison) watched me show up with five regulation-sized boxes of books, journals, and fifteen-plus paintings, when the rules clearly stated that each prisoner was only allowed one box, they were pissed. I ended up getting read the riot act by the guards. One said, "I haven't seen this much shit come out of a cell since the Birdman was here stinking up the prison."

He was referring, of course, to Robert Stroud, the prisoner who did extensive research on canaries while at Leavenworth. A movie, typically Hollywood as far as the facts were concerned, was made of Stroud's years in prison. Burt Lancaster starred. Stroud's hobby had started at Alcatraz. Old-timers at Leavenworth described him as "strange . . . very bright . . . crazy . . . reclusive . . . dangerous . . . non-dangerous . . . good guy . . . weird." The only thing everyone agreed on was, "His birds created a smell that permeated the cell block." He also collected more "stuff" than regulations allowed.

I had gotten by with breaking the rule. Could have been because I was the chief surgeon's clerk. Could be I was just overlooked. The transfer relegated me to the position of just another prisoner.

The marshals chained me and led me off. Three weeks later, my paintings and art supplies showed up, but the journals were gone. The day-to-day scribblings of nothing substantial were looked at and trashed, just to piss off a prisoner. *My* notes, *my* paper, bought with *my* money. Years of research gone. Thankfully, they never knew how important the material was to me. So it goes . . .

But let's get back to my friend, the chief surgeon. Since I was able to put together a pretty good medical history, he and the director of the hospital called me in one day and told me they wanted me to document fire and emergency drills that never took place—drills that had to be held for the hospital to maintain its accreditation. They explained what they needed, showed me the forms, and sent me over to the dentist's clerk who had been doing them.

"This is easy, fun, gives you a chance to express yourself creatively, and, if breaking the law is your idea of fun, this is the job for you," Jim explained.

So I began creating these complex drills. I'd decide on a scenario. For example: A fire breaks out in a closet, on the second floor, across the hall from where oxygen is stored. I would describe in great detail how the prisoners were evacuated, where the most serious custody cases were taken, how the ambulatory cases were moved, and on and on. For the disaster drills, I even designed menus and had the cooks preparing food in the yard after a Kansas tornado had destroyed two cell blocks, the kitchen, and the mess hall. I would get so into these fictionalized happenings that the reports would sometimes be 8, 10, 15 typewritten pages. Designing the scenarios was fun, and the surgeon, the director, and I would sometimes laugh about the complex situations the "well-trained staff of the hospital was able to deal with in such a professional manner."

It was funny all right—really funny. It was part of my job. But the thought that if a real emergency ever happened the staff would not know how to evacuate that hospital began to bother me. A fire, any kind of serious emergency, could end up costing people their lives. In the midst of abject boredom, a conscience reared its self-righteous head. Strange how it so frequently contributes to a person's self-destruction.

I mentioned to the director and the chief surgeon that it might be a good idea to actually hold the drills. We could really train for an emergency, I suggested. Training would not disrupt our work day, our scenarios would be documented with pictures, and the two of them would be held up as examples of how top-notch hospital administrators ran a prison hospital. They looked at each other with smiles that bordered on laughter and told me to forget it.

Their refusal to hold actual drills, a prerequisite for a hospital to be accredited, kept digging at me until I finally decided to do something about it. A friend had documented all of the federal rules that were being broken. All the past falsified drills were in the files. I had also researched the law. Falsifying official government documents. The signing of official forms that contained false information. These were felony crimes. How quick I was to point a finger at officials involved in criminal activity. I sincerely believed that I had only to send the documentation to the attorney general's office to end the abuse. I was going to personally charge them with the crimes and substantiate the criminal activity by submitting the proof. It was risky. It was perfect. I was looking for action.

I didn't realize how thin the ice was where I walked.

The only difficulty would be smuggling the information out of the prison. Prisoners are allowed to send sealed mail to the attorney general. By law, prison administrators are not allowed to open mail that prisoners send to lawyers, federal officials, or members of the Senate or the House of Representatives. But they did. Fortunately, I had a friend, a fellow prisoner, whose job took him in and out of the prison a couple of times a week. He was an old guy from Iowa, doing his time on the farm nearby. Frequently he would smuggle letters in and out for me. I gave him the letter with postage on it. (That was another method I used to generate extra income. I'd clean up cancelled stamps so they could be used again.) A business envelope thick with documented evidence with the appropriate amount of postage. He slipped it under his shirt without looking at it.

With that out of the way, I felt better.

About an hour later, a runner came to my office and told me to report to Custody. When

I got there, I was met by my friend and a guard. The guard took the two of us into a room, closed the door, and pulled out the letter. I had been caught, and my friend had been nailed with me. Very serious. This was not just any letter.

The guard was the only guard I had developed any respect for. I had never seen him harass a prisoner or play any of the typical games guards play.

The letter was opened, and all the copies of the last four or five fire drills and emergency drills, signed, with cover letter, were laid on the table. He folded everything up, put the material back in the envelope, and handed it to me.

The guard was being very calm about this. "I opened it because of how it was being sent. Had to be sure you guys were not planning something serious. Since this letter is addressed to the attorney general, I'm not going to tell you what to do with it and I'm not going to give it to Custody. But I will tell you that if this letter gets to the attorney general's office, you are going to be the most miserable prisoner in the federal system. You will do every day of your sentence. You will never see good time. You will have your cell torn apart at least once a month, if you ever have a cell for a full month. You will spend hard time on the road again and again and again. You will become familiar with the hole in every maximum-security joint in the system. You will not have visitors. You will get crap for food, and you will have the most shit detail jobs available in this entire system. You can appeal your case to court, but you know that access to the courts takes so long you will have already lost by the time your case gets there, regardless of the final legal outcome. Now, if you think that kind of misery will be worth blowing the whistle on the hospital director and the chief surgeon, go for it. Because nothing will change, Joe. Absolutely nothing. I'm not going to mess with any mail to the attorney general, so you decide what you want to do with this letter."

With that, he waved us out.

We left. Once outside, my friend turned to me, and he was as white as the (old) Johannesburg, South Africa, City Hall, with a tinge of green around the edge of his jaw.

"Jesus Christ, Joe, you shudda' tol' me what you was doin'. If'n anybody else had caught me with a letter like this we'd never see daylight again! I'm too old for this kinda shit."

We were on the yard at the time. When I got back to the hospital, I tore the contents of the envelope into very small pieces. Then I filled the sink with water, mashed the pieces into a mush, and flushed them down the toilet.

Lesson learned.

The more I thought about what had happened, though, the more I realized that there was no one I could have sent that information to. No one in the Federal Bureau of Prisons or its parent operation, the Justice Department, would protect the person blowing the whistle on their own system. Absolutely no one. But, I reasoned, if prisoners had their own newspaper, run by ex-prisoners who understood how vulnerable a prisoner was, that letter, that story, would have been published, and I would have had the protection that comes with being able to reach the public with the story. At that point in history, 1968, there were some liberal newspapers, but their liberalism normally had a life of two days, if you really had a story that was dynamite.

Fortunately I had smuggled a duplicate set of records out with another friend, who saw that it was sent home. Three years later, I made a copy and hand-delivered it to Norman Carlson, director of the Federal Bureau of Prisons. He was hot about some stories I had written in the PDI concerning conditions in the federal system. To show him I wasn't trying to make him look bad, I gave him copies of the material, explained what it was about, explained what criminal acts were involved, the danger to the prisoners in the hospital, and other related pieces of information, and asked him to talk to the hospital director and the chief surgeon. I threw away a great story, but I felt it was worth it to convince him that my attacks were not personal.

After I gave him the material proving that top hospital administrators were committing a crime that carried three to five years plus fines, I sent word to a friend who worked in the hospital inside Leavenworth. I told him what I had done and asked him to keep me informed of any changes. He sent word out to me every few months for a few years. Nothing changed. The disaster and fire drills were still works of fiction, still signed by the hospital administrators and submitted as true.

No question about it. The prisoners needed a newspaper, a voice, with a second-class postal permit—the same second-class permit the *New York Times* and the *Washington Post* and the other daily and weekly newspapers received from the U.S. Postal Department. Only with that permit could our voice—our newspaper—get inside the walls to the prisoners. We had to have a newspaper that would allow us to spill our guts. To scream poetry and prose. To cut through the endless reams of reportorial gobbledygook. To write letters to the editor that you knew would get published. To sit down with cheap pens and tablets of lined paper and write exposés that you knew would be published a few weeks down the line. A newspaper to wipe our emotional asses with. Such a newspaper would be hated by all except a handful of wardens, guards, and prison administrators. Most would try to keep prisoners from subscribing. But as a newspaper with a second-class permit, every establishment newspaper in the country could be coerced into asking, "If this one newspaper, a newspaper with a second-class permit, can be banned, who might be next?"

The second-class permit took me out of the true "underground" category of newspapers. We were not the establishment. We were an "underground" newspaper in the truest sense of the word. But that permit gave us clout that we would use.

A prisoner could count on no help from the courts. The free world had no way to see inside the prisons. Prisoners then and now are shut out, shut off, shut up. Everyone took the abuse. The rotten food, the sexual abuse, the psychological abuse, the beatings, the isolation in the population, and the solitary confinement were the rewards you received when you screamed for justice. The strong fought back, took their lumps, and went on. The weak folded, were crushed, ended up whipped punks or broken men and women who would never recover or regain a sense of self-worth.

The kind of suffering that is the most intolerable is the kind that holds no relief in sight. You take your lumps knowing that the longer you stand it, the more it's going to hurt. Giving up sometimes helps, but you always pay. And through it all, you know that there is nothing you can do. If you had any resources, you wouldn't be there. If you had money for an attorney good enough to take on the system, your problem would already have been taken care of.

The prisoners in the end-of-the-line prisons needed a voice. Hell, all the prisoners needed a voice.

If we were going to suffer, knowing that we would never have a day in court, we could at least suffer knowing that we had had our day in print.

Having a "day in print" is the major dream of many prisoners. That and getting out. There are many minor dreams. An unlimited supply of books to keep the sexual juices flowing. A decent meal. Some spice. A jar of hot sauce. Someone to write to. Letters. Quiet. Equity. But mostly, wanting to spill your guts about your life. Why you did or didn't do it. The arrests. The sleazy lawyers. The lying cops. The judges who neither hear nor see. The hopelessness. "If only I could tell my story!" prisoners lament. "If only someone would listen! I wish . . ."

But wishing isn't enough. One morning some years later, after I had been released and after PDI had come into existence, I was eating pancakes over by the Bronx courthouse with attorney Bill Kunstler, who was now on our advisory board. I wished for something. Bill looked up from his pancakes and said, "Tell you what, Joe, you pray in one hand and wish in the other and let me know which one fills up the fastest."

Having a day in print. Telling the prisoner's side of the story. In my cell, into my journals, I spilled my guts every day. I would rage with a pencil and my pads of lined paper. I would scream. Accuse. Threaten to file the class-action suit that would end the abuse. But you file a suit and it takes sixteen months getting to the judge, who dismisses it quietly and sends it back and you start all over. Or else you win, which is just as bad. The judge sends the cease-and-desist order to the prison. The prison ignores it. You file again asking for the prison to be cited for contempt. Sixteen months later the judge sees it, reads it, and sends it back for a correction or clarification.

With a newspaper it would be different. BAM. INTO PRINT. There it would be in black and white. PRINT. People believe print. There is a magic in print. Particularly NEWSPRINT.

How often could such a newspaper be published? It would have to be a monthly. Even that might be too costly. Maybe a quarterly.

Who would buy it? Some prisoners could afford it, but for the most part the prisoners who needed it couldn't afford it.

And so, while I was still in prison, that great builder and destroyer of dreams moved in and began to take over. I said to myself, "The law schools would subscribe. Yeah! And the libraries. Yeah! And free-world organizations that were concerned with the welfare of their fellow human beings. Men, women, and children who were being treated like animals. YEAH! Damn right! I knew about printing costs. I knew about deadlines and layout and setting type. Boy, did I know! And I knew that in these United States I could sell three or four thousand subscriptions at, say, $6 a year. No, $9 a year. $6 for prisoners. NO! $6 for prisoners who could afford it. $1 for prisoners who couldn't. And free to those with absolutely no resources at all.

With pencil and lined tablet, I pored over the numbers. Over a million and a half people passing in and out of the city, county, state, and federal systems each year. A multibillion-dollar industry. A work force of hundreds of thousands.

I worked on it and convinced myself that the publication would be successful. NO. Not just successful. The publication would be a steppingstone to focus the attention of the free world on the plight of the prisoner. As a result, thanks to the illuminating effect of an internationally circulated newspaper, change would come to the prison systems of the United States and the world.

If you're going to dream, dream big.

The first step was getting out. Then I had to raise money to get a publicity piece to colleges and libraries. Then, with all that money, I would have to wheel and deal for the equipment

I would need to put together the camera-ready copy. I would need enough left over to pay the printer. I would need a vehicle reliable enough to get us to and from the printer, and big enough to haul all the newspapers back to the office for addressing and mailing.

No sweat.

"Laying Out My Winter Clothes"

I began seriously planning for PDI soon after my fellow Unitarian Universalist Frank Sepulveda was transferred. I spent more time now observing the goings-on inside the prison. I paid more attention to the unwritten rules that many of the prisoners lived by. I talked with the old-timers.

What I found was, as I have said, a slice of the free world. We had it all and more. Long-smoldering feuds. A legal profession. The peacekeepers. The assassins. The poets. Capitalists, socialists, anarchists. The weak and the strong. A class of poor, a broad middle class, the wheeler-dealers hustling through their financial ups and downs. At the top, a handful of power brokers. Just as in the free world, that reliable old rain barrel theory applied inside the prison—the scum rising to the top. Many had even linked up with community organizations like the Jaycees.

One day I was sitting out in the yard watching the endless stream of prisoners walk by. One young fellow came over and sat down near me. He hadn't been there long. I remembered interviewing him when he came through the hospital. All the required questions. Have you had such and such? All the prison hospital medical stuff. Then my own questions. His was a particularly sad case. He had a serious learning disability. He had stolen a car and taken it across state lines. He had done it again and again. He was, in the eyes of the law, "incorrigible." Tell him anything and he believed you. Ask him to do anything for you and he would.

I had come across him one day a few weeks earlier. He was sitting in the middle of a driveway between two buildings. I asked him what he was doing.

"The next truck to come driving by is gonna kill me," he said.

"Why do you want to die?"

"The Bible said that if you give it'll come back to you three-fold. I've been giving away everything I get from the commissary. Nothing has ever come back to me."

"Who told you to do that?"

"The chaplain's clerk."

I explained to him that the verse didn't mean he would be rewarded here on earth. Rather, I said, "The rewards will come to you in heaven." Since he had placed so much faith in the Bible, I explained that Jesus didn't want him to give to people who already had more than he did. Instead, Jesus wanted him to share with people who were suffering. I didn't have much faith in the brand of Christianity that was being peddled in that joint, but with some people you have to be very gentle. He decided to go to his house instead of waiting for a truck.

The chaplain's clerk was an officer in the Jaycees. This time the fellow looked like the problem was more than waiting for a return on donated candy bars.

"How you doin'?" I asked.

"I been makin' friends in the Jaycees. Good friends."

"Great."

"I made thirteen new friends at the meeting."

"Exactly thirteen?"

"Yeah. Exactly. Thirteen."

"Who were they?"

"I don't remember names, but I counted them."

"Do you try to remember their names?"

"No. I just count. There was thirteen Jaycees that fucked me. They told me that every time I let a Jaycee fuck me he would be my friend."

He was starting to cry. He was twenty-four. Maybe twenty-five. Young for his age. He looked nineteen. The Jaycees loved him.

"I think you should tell them that you hurt real bad. Tell them that you may have to go to the doctor if anyone fucks you again. Tell them you think you have some kind of infection."

I knew how much the thought of infection would affect them. They'd all start using rubbers.

Sitting there talking and watching him suffering. Thinking that the great majority of the Jaycees were closely associated with the church. Most were members of the choir. You see them with their Bibles. Their little New Testaments. The only emergency that had me turning to one of the little New Testaments was when I ran out of cigarette papers. It worked, but a steady use would put more ink in my lungs than was healthy.

Like the free world. The women bleed. Without women, they manufacture substitutes and the subs bleed.

When I first arrived, I was invited to a meeting of Trailblazer Jaycees, so named because they were the first Jaycees chapter in the federal prison system. After my introduction, I was asked what I'd like to accomplish while I was in prison. I told them I'd like to convince the prison Jaycees group to drop out of the national organization because it is a sexist group that is primarily interested in the business interests and advancement of men. The president took me to the side and, while tapping me on the chest with his index finger, told me he would kill me if I ever talked like that again. I slapped his hand away. Other prisoner Jaycees jumped up. I turned and walked out of the rec center. The original Trailblazer charter incentive plan: Do as you are told or die.

When I got back to the hospital, my friend Jim K —— asked how the meeting had gone. I told him what happened and he looked at me like my days were numbered.

"Christ-all-mighty, Joe, don't you know anything about the crazy who heads the Jaycees?"

I shrugged and asked, "A crazy? Right here in the can?" I was laughing.

"Well, Beryl McDonald, to make a name for himself, scrambled over a 15′ wall protecting men in protective custody. The snitch Mickey Cohen was on the other side, and Beryl beat him so viciously with his bare hands that he thought he had killed him and bragged about it when the guards took him to Building 63.

As it turned out, Cohen lived, but he was a vegetable and never recovered. I avoided the rec center from that time on. I did help some prisoners who were Jaycees with plans for a project they were unable to put in the proper format to submit for approval. Strange as it seems, there were many prisoners who were unable to read or write. They could manage a signature, but little else.

I took a second job in the education department, helping prisoners pass their GED tests. I needed access to all those locked areas, and my lock-expert friend joined me.

We had run into a situation concerning the college entrance exams. Prisoners with parole dates coming up were allowed to take the college entrance exams to show the parole board they were good risks to make it in the free world if their parole plans were approved.

We were able to coach those taking the tests, and it was rare that a prisoner didn't score high enough to impress the board. Suddenly the test threw in a new section on grammar. Picking the "correct" sentence was never that difficult. I did not know English grammar, but I had read enough to know when a sentence was correctly written—or so I thought. The new tests devoted a section to sentence structure, but with a hitch. In the new section, two sentences were offered with instruction to pick the sentence that was the MOST correct. They all sounded perfect, and to an untrained grammarian, both were perfect.

My friend came through with the new tests so we could study them in our cells at night. Again, he saved the day.

My Dilemma: Hobby Craft or Jesus

As my plans for the newspaper took shape, I began discussing the idea with friends I could confide in. Very few of my friends encouraged the idea. Most of them had much more experience with prison populations than I did. Maybe it was my naiveté that made it happen. Whatever. After some interesting escapades and scares over the next ten- or twelve-month period and a transfer to a medium-security joint in Sandstone, Minnesota, I was released on parole.

Before you can "walk," you have to check out of each department in the prison. That means you have to personally go to each department head and have him sign a release form stating that you have nothing of value that belongs to that department. When I got to the chaplain's office, I put on my very serious mask and asked him if I could talk to him for a moment.

He was wary, but he invited me into his office. I sat down and explained that I was leaving, and that I was faced with a seemingly impossible problem. I had to make a decision that I had been struggling with for days. He was all ears. He couldn't believe he was listening to this kind of talk from the fellow who had helped shove a Unitarian Universalist fellowship—the first inside the federal prison system—down the throat of the Federal Bureau of Prisons in Leavenworth years earlier. I explained that I had wrestled with the problem for days. Now I had to choose. I couldn't work it out by myself and needed his help.

He came out from behind his desk and sat down beside me. The chaplain had this look of disbelief on his face. He put his hand on my shoulder and reassured me that he would help in any way he could.

"Do I have your absolute confidence?" I asked.

"My office is like the confessional, Joe. You know that," he answered.

That remark almost broke me up, but I held the serious look. My eyes were kind of watery as a result of holding back the laughter. He was in heaven. I looked him in the eye and explained, "You know I'm being released." He nodded. "You know I have to check out with all the departments." He nodded and said, "Yes, Joe. How can I help?" I explained that since yesterday, I had two departments remaining to sign my release forms. My problem was that I had been going to the departments in their order of importance. With the religion and hobby craft departments the only two remaining, I couldn't decide where to go first. "Would you help me, Father?" I asked. "Should I have you sign or should I go to the hobby craft shop first?"

He froze. He took his hand away from my shoulder and stood up, walked to the chair behind his desk, turned to me, and called me a son of a bitch. As I stood up to leave I added, "That's right, priest, but a son of a bitch who thinks the philosophy of the good carpenter is a gas as opposed to your adulterations of Christian brotherhood and sisterhood."

He had answered my question. I headed for hobby craft. Sometimes I didn't like the way I responded to clergy, but damn, they were impossible. You couldn't reason with them. The damn fools had the perfect leader. A carpenter clean. Why peddle all the hocus-pocus pie-in-the-sky crap when the man they had was as easy to sell with the truth as with the bullshit.

The next day, the chaplain had the final word in the matter. Before he would sign my checkout form, he made me wait three hours.

No, I take that back: Even with the wait, it was a pleasure watching him sign his name right below the director of Hobby Craft's signature.

Buck Naked at the Liquor Store, Minneapolis, Minnesota

I stepped out of that northern Minnesota federal prison ten days in front of Christmas. John Eastman was there to greet me. I had just made a terrible mistake and was in a vile mood. The associate warden had seized one of my paintings—a combination sculpture/painting that I knew was going to make me enough money to start the newspaper. I didn't find out what they had done until I picked up my parole papers and was stepping out of the prison. I had fifteen or twenty paintings to load into John's station wagon. Right away, I saw that they had removed the sculpture part and given me only the painting part. I returned to the window and asked the guard on the other side about my missing art. He said I used federal property to make it. He was talking about scrap metal that had been discarded. From my papers, I took out the document giving me permission to use the scrap. The guard said, "We'll let the warden decide. He'll be back in a week."

It's at times like this that the boys are separated from the men. I should have torn up my parole papers and refused to leave. Hindsight has convinced me that if I had shoved my papers back through the slot and refused to leave, I would have been given the sculpture. If I had been thinking clearly, I would have realized that they would have had to give me the sculpture—because I had already been officially paroled, the papers had been signed, and if I had refused to leave, they would have had to charge me with trespassing and call the local sheriff. If they had done that, the news media would have heard about it, and the story would have made the local news. Subsequently, the story would have hit the wire services and gone national: "Prisoner artist arrested for refusing to leave slam without his art."

That particular sculpture, made up of scrap metal, was a powerful piece—the best piece I had ever done. I might have turned to art full-time if I had stayed for a showdown that evening. Who knows? Who cares? Art is the grass that is always greener . . . Maybe it's what I'll do when I grow up.

But I was infected with "getting-out fever." I wanted out, and I was one door away from freedom. I was ready to walk. John was standing there. My paintings were loaded. I turned to the guard. "Will the sculpture be safe until I call the bureau in the morning?"

"Absolutely!" he answered.

I believed him. Can you imagine my stupidity? I believed him.

Believing a guard! Allowing your wants to override experience. I'd simply call the director of the Federal Bureau of Prisons in the morning and scream. There was no way they could take my property away—not just my property, MY ART.

As Greg Brown sang in one of his originals, "Dream on, Little Dreamer, Dream On," I was dreaming. Head in the clouds, free clouds, and on the road again, and didn't that cold air feel and taste just great?

Heading south toward Minneapolis on I-35, John asked me about my plans.

I did a quick sketch of my prisoners' newspaper, sang the "Money wouldn't be a problem for long" song as John raised a skeptical eyebrow and gave me the look we had both seen hundreds of times as we articulated past dreams.

"No problem," I insisted, gesturing toward the paintings stacked neatly in the back. "I'll sell my paintings and use the money to get started."

"What were you smoking before I arrived?" John asked, reminding me of the many times the wave of a distorted view of reality washed away dreams we figured were carved in stone.

"Nothing that comes close to this," I said, and we cruised.

I felt so good wheeling down the highway with a cold beer and a little smoke that the three-hour drive to Minneapolis seemed especially short. John had a never-ending supply of inspiring stories. He had written scripts that were produced, had been in movies, and was as gifted a writer as I have ever known. Invariably the good guys always lost, but the ride was worth it and the stories memorable.

I have a John Eastman story that never gets told. Dropped here in the middle of an ex-con coming-home story, it might fit.

We had both worked in radio, but radio to John was an extension of a magnificent imagination. He started in radio in Miami at the same time Larry King started his radio career in the same town. One night John had a singer from Count Basie's orchestra on the air, discussing jazz and life. When his shift ended, he took her down and hailed a cab for her. All the blacks stayed in a hotel a long way from the strip where they performed. A cab pulled over and John opened the back door.

As the woman was getting in, the guy yelled, "I don't take niggers. Get the fuck out of my cab!" She shrugged it off and got out. John freaked and went after the cabby. The resulting fight cost John his job. A columnist for the *Miami Herald* devoted a column to the incident, praised John, and remarked that he was disappointed the radio community didn't support Eastman.

As a result of the publicity generated by the newspaper, Larry King invited John to sit in on his radio show, which was broadcast from a houseboat in Miami Bay. Larry was the other popular radio personality in town at the time, and tickets to his broadcast were limited. Larry was married to a bunny from the Miami Playboy mansion. During the three hours or so that John was on the air with Larry, something happened between John and Larry's wife. They didn't speak, were never introduced, and did not know each other in some past existence.

But when John finished the show and left, she stood up and left with him. They left Miami for Iowa, married, opened an advertising agency, promised each other "No more show business," and settled down in Marian, Iowa. It was an ideal existence until John wrote a show for *The Fugitive*. They asked him to come to L.A. for rewrites and offered him a couple hundred thou to stay on and join the writers. He wired the "good" news home and grabbed the first flight out. When he arrived he found a note. "NO MORE SHOW BUSINESS!" in bold block letters. She had returned to Miami, filed for divorce, and a short time later she and Larry remarried. It didn't last.

We were rebounders. Frequently hopeless rebounders.

John and I had shared hopeless situations many times prior to my going to prison. He once said he wanted to write my biography—adding: because I had been involved in so many great failures. That possible claim to future fame would lend nothing to a resume.

Approaching the Washington Avenue exit on I-35 in Minneapolis, I asked John to turn off and drive west on Washington Avenue. Along the way, clusters of street people were gathered around an occasional barrel, nursing fires with scrap wood and rolled up copies of free weekly tabloids to keep warm. We pulled into Discount Liquors' parking lot, and I ran in for a case of Leinenkugel's. As I returned to the car carrying two cases, one old man asked, "Want to share a couple of those holiday beers, mister?"

"Hell, yes." I put the case down, grabbed four longnecks, and motioned for John to come join us. John isn't a beer drinker, but he got into the spirit of the moment. We opened the back of the wagon, set the cases inside, popped four "Linees," and raised our beers to peace. "Merry Christmas all around," I said.

Christmas was only a few days away. These two men were cadging drinks in a liquor-store parking lot and freezing their asses off. I knew these guys, good old guys, and they were in a worse prison than the one I had just left. Like Jerry Samuels wrote in his song, "Prisons and Prisons, My Daughters and Sons / The very worst ones have no bars and no guns."

"This ain't exactly beer-drinking weather," John said.

"Bullshit," the older of the two men said. "It's always beer-drinking weather, partner."

I asked them what they would be drinking if they had a choice.

"They got some Four Roses on sale that would damn sure warm us up."

I handed John my beer and came back with a couple of quarts of Jack Daniels.

I handed each of them a bottle. "Merry Christmas! A Jack Daniels Merry Christmas, fellows."

The old fellow in the ratty jacket was damn near jumping up and down. I couldn't make out what he was saying until he put his teeth in his mouth. "This'll warm things up—really warm things up tonight."

John was stamping his feet, and I was wondering what it would be like living in a prison where your heat source was a 30-gallon barrel. It must have been 10, maybe 15 degrees at the most.

Since I had planned on changing into some old clothes that John had brought up from Iowa, I handed the old guy my overcoat.

"This and the bourbon will keep you warmer."

Suddenly the old guy was giving me the once over. "What ya got on your mind? What are you after?"

His partner became indignant in an almost aristocratic manner. "Shut up, fool. Ya got a new overcoat and the best bottle of booze I've ever seen you sucking on. This dude's comin' on like Santa Claus and not asking for Jack shit."

John was laughing so hard he was crying.

I handed the other guy the sport coat I had on.

"What size shoes you wear?" I asked him.

He didn't even look down. "Any size ya got."

I took my shoes off and handed them to him. He glanced at them, sized them up, and put them in his coat pockets. I started unbuttoning my shirt.

The old man looked at John. "What's your friend been smoking?" he asked, laughing. The old guys were becoming animated, kind of dancing around.

I handed him the shirt, which he held up and admired while I took my pants off. "Thirty-two waist?"

"Hot damn! Me exactly, but what are you gonna wear?" he asked, glancing around to see if anyone was watching us.

I took my shorts off. John handed me one of the bottles and I took a drink.

"Goddamn! I do not believe this is happening," laughed the old guy, with tears freezing in his whiskers. His partner glanced down and said, "If it gets any colder and you don't get some clothes, you may have trouble finding your dick to take a piss."

Both of them were laughing as hard as John. It was a bizarre scene. I was down to my socks and couldn't feel the cold. Like swimming in Lake Superior, it's so cold you don't feel it when you jump in; however, in two or three minutes your joints start aching.

I flashed on my old Navy buddy Don Pelvit running six blocks through the snow one January night in Minneapolis, naked and barefoot. It was 33 degrees below zero.

I took my socks off, held them up. "Want 'em?" The two guys were looking at my feet like they expected my toenails to have fingernail polish on them. "Give 'em to me," said the fellow with my shoes, and I tossed them over.

A woman came out of the liquor store laughing and yelled, "Curtain time! You guys are freaking out the store manager. He's calling the cops."

We all piled into John's wagon. He was laughing so hard he could barely drive. I dug a pair of old Levis and a sweatshirt out of a brown paper bag. A few minutes later we were eating burgers from White Castle and washing them down with Jack Daniels.

We dropped the old guys off some place on Lake Street and continued south on I-35.

John's observation as we cruised was typical: "I never expected a scene like that when we stopped for beer."

When I reminded him of a time he freaked in Miami and climbed a tree naked and was half covered with Band-Aids for a week after, that triggered another round of stories and laughing.

It was so good being out.

Throughout the remainder of the trip, John talked about making films. He had sent me one film to show our fellowship, but Custody had taken it away and returned it to the film company. I had asked a guard who was one of a team who screen films what it was about. "Some nuns walking around down in Mexico. Strange shit," is the answer I got. That film,

The Day Love Died, was later used in a successful United Way fundraising effort and was one of the most successful, award-winning films the United Way ever used.

"Who's going to buy your newspaper?"

"Libraries."

"Why?"

"Because I'll give them material that will blow their minds."

"No one cares."

"Only because the material hasn't been presented to them in an acceptable format!"

I had convinced myself! No one could reason with me. No one could change my mind. John had known me long enough to know that the stories were true. He had freaked often enough, been fired from enough jobs, stared at enough rejection slips, been married and divorced and remarried enough times that he knew how important it was to be able to tell your story.

We drove all night. It was like old times, being with a friend I could dream with.

When we reached Cedar Rapids, John asked me how I felt.

"I feel pure. Nothing to hide. No place to go but up." What I lacked in discipline I figured I could make up for with enthusiastic bullshit.

It had been a great drive. I think I'll always feel a chill across my buns whenever I think of standing naked in that parking lot by the Discount Liquors in Minneapolis. But that kind of cold I could deal with; watching the sun come up as we drove south through the rolling, snow-covered Iowa farmland, with the air so clear and sharp that it brought tears to my eyes, was equally memorable.

This was an off period in John's life. Nothing permanent. John dropped me off at his small apartment, gave me the keys, and said he'd see me in a couple of days. I went in. John's place was always as good as home, and it was good being home. I needed rest and time to organize my thoughts.

The next morning I called the Federal Bureau of Prisons and explained about the painting and the sculpture.

Two hours later, a fellow from the bureau called me back and said that the sculpture had been destroyed. "They figured it was prison property, so it was taken to the welding shop and cut up with a cutting torch. It was junk."

I made few non-prisoner friends while I was locked up.

I'd make fewer in the next three years.

Prison Art Attracts Collector

A phone call to Eli Abodeely got me space to paint for a month in one of his downtown hideaways. Another call to the People's Unitarian Universalist Church got me space for an art show.

I had left prison with enough art supplies to last me ten years. When you paint in prison an interesting thing happens. Prisoners come by and watch. They see you doing it and it looks easy. They send home for money for supplies and tell the family to send photos. "I'll have oil portraits for you in a month," they reassure the folks at home. The money arrives; they buy the oils, brushes, and a couple of "how-to" books; and everything they touch turns to mud.

They finally end up making a deal with one of the prison artists. You get the supplies and you paint them a picture or two they can send home.

I slapped more oil on canvas in the next thirty days than I had in my entire life. No style, no nothing. Just a hodge-podge of emotion. Pictures that I hoped would sell—if not for the art, at least for the curiosity.

My show was memorable for two reasons. The first reason was that I met a person who was interested in two of my paintings but wanted to see them hanging before making a choice. I agreed to bring them to the person's home that night.

I found the place on the east side of Cedar Rapids in a neighborhood of luxury homes. A long, curved drive led to a huge entrance. Just inside the entrance was a Marvin Cone painting. Pretty heady company. On the tour of the home, I saw originals by Grant Wood, Picasso, and Matisse, and what seemed to be more early American traditional paintings by artists I didn't recognize. I was overwhelmed—not just seeing the art, but because this person was interested in my two paintings, one for $400 and a small one for $120. In my wildest prison dream of getting out and having a show, I never imagined that I would ever interest anyone with this kind of an art collection.

A huge staircase led up from the front entryway. On the first landing was a prime spot for a large painting. Upon entering the house, it was the first spot you saw.

"I think the large one might look good there," she suggested.

I agreed with her.

"The warm colors will be complemented by the woodwork."

I had never seen that much woodwork in a home in my life. Plus it was a painting I had done in a day. "Angular Compromise." Two figures. Hard to tell if a man or a woman was compromising. John had named it. It was a steal at $400.

We went upstairs to look at it from above.

It was beautiful.

At the top of the stairs was a large area with more stairs leading off in three directions. The area was lined with bookcases and built-in seats.

"Would you care for a drink?"

"You bet!"

As the drinks were being poured, I looked at the books. They were all matched sets. Some of the sets had twenty-five or more books in them. All appeared to be bound in leather, or at least material that looked like leather.

I didn't recognize the titles or the authors, but it didn't take me long to realize that I was not looking at the classics. *She Was Daddy's Little Girl* and *Cheerleaders Romp*. Many years would go by before we'd see a marquee with *Lawyers in Lace* on it, but I'll bet the book was there if it was in print. As I gave the books a closer examination, I was aware that I was being watched. I took a book off the shelf and opened it. Clit lit. Hundreds of books. Expensive matched sets of cheap trash. I'm not talking erotica. No Henry Miller or Anaïs Nin in this collection.

I couldn't believe it. The collector from hell. Grant Wood and Marvin Cone behind the Green Door.

"You like to read books like those?" I was asked.

It was clear where this evening was headed. No sense in playing games. "Which do you prefer, the large painting or the small one?" I asked.

"I can't make up my mind. I like them both," was the response, spoken slowly while my glass was being filled with the first Calvados I'd ever tasted. I've wondered about Calvados for years. It was what Ravic always ordered in Remarque's *Arch of Triumph*. I could smell the book, see the Minneapolis Public Library. I don't think he ordered Calvados in the movie.

"I'll buy the small one because it's the better of the two paintings. I'll also buy the large one if you will spend the night."

I sat there with my Calvados. What would Ravic say? I couldn't believe this. Was it the fascination of being with a newly released prisoner? I thought about the $400. Ravic had Ingrid Bergman. Maybe it would have been possible if she hadn't looked so much like Charles Bukowski.

"We could read to each other."

"I'm really sorry. I'm driving a borrowed car and have to return it in half an hour."

"Could I have them until tomorrow night?"

"Sorry. I have obligations." Obligations? I sounded like a fool.

I was grateful to pick up $120.

The second memorable happening was that I made $2,500 from the art show. If the sculpture that had been ripped off by the guards at Sandstone had been in the show, I would have made $7,500.

Chapel Builder Busy Building Wardens

A week earlier, I had moved to Iowa City and enrolled at the University of Iowa. An interesting incident happened to me when I arrived. While in prison, I had taken some correspondence courses, mostly in criminology, from the University of Iowa. The professor who I sent my lessons to, Professor Caldwell, was the author of a widely used criminology text. I had poured my heart into those lessons, submitted typewritten papers that would run 30 and 40 pages, always returned with an "A" boldly marked across the first page, usually followed by "Remarkable" or "Good work." Years later I'd sit around with teaching assistants from that same department. The long papers only elicited groans, they told me. The papers would be passed around. Care would be taken to not spill any beer on them. The best ones were the shortest. No BS. Just the facts.

As a prisoner, I had been impressed by Dr. Caldwell. He had headed the department and authored an important text. He had praised my work. On my first trip to Iowa City to find a place to live, I stopped at his office to meet him. It was a typical office, narrow and long. Books lined the shelves from floor to high ceiling. Sitting behind a large desk that was stacked with books and papers, he looked smaller than he probably was.

He recognized my name immediately and welcomed me to Iowa City. We talked about the various topics I had written about and my interests: prison, his department, what I would probably find at the University of Iowa. I never mentioned the PDI.

At this point I revered the old professor. Finally I asked him the question I had come there to ask. Thinking that he would be the centerpiece of a lengthy article in the PDI someday, I asked him, "Dr. Caldwell, you have been involved not only with the subject of criminology but with the prisons and prisoners of Iowa for many, many years. What do you believe is the most important contribution you have made that has been a benefit to Iowa prisoners?"

He leaned back in his chair, shut his eyes, and was deep in thought. Finally he leaned forward and looked at me. There was a dramatic pause. Was it practiced? I'd never seen him lecture. "My most important contribution? That's easy. I'm responsible for the chapel at the Anamosa Reformatory. I'm prouder of that than anything."

It figured. He was nothing but a guard. The guard from the department head's office. It seemed like every time I turned around, some script for a grade B movie was happening before my very eyes.

I sat there looking at him. He seemed to expect a response. I didn't say anything. I just stood up, thanked him, and left. I couldn't believe it.

That department at the University of Iowa, I later found out, led by the likes of Caldwell, turned out more federal prison wardens than any other single institution of learning in the country. And the federal prison system, then and now, contrary to the public relations drivel that is ejaculated from Washington, is one of the most repressive systems in the world. It was bad then. It is worse now. Behind the repression, brutality, and behavior modification units are a bunch of wardens from this department—from the University of Iowa.

Getting Organized on the Cheap

The new year found me in a small, cheap furnished room three blocks from the University of Iowa on the southwest corner of Jefferson and Van Buren. I wasn't carrying much with me: an easel and some art supplies, a few books, and odds and ends of new used clothes. My personal needs were few.

The PDI, on the other hand, needed a nonprofit, tax-exempt corporation, a board of directors, and money. What that added up to was a serious need for contacts and advice. I'd also need space for an office, at least one extraordinary staff member, and ultimately a home large enough for a staff that I figured would grow to fifteen when we were publishing. All I had were a few ideas and the money from the sale of paintings.

That money was earmarked for emergencies. Staffing of the PDI was not going to be easy. I wanted ex-prisoners in key positions. I knew prisoners who had developed those necessary skills while serving long prison sentences. Unfortunately, they were still inside, with little chance of getting out.

To save money, I applied for and received tuition assistance. When I learned that I could use it to help pay my rent, and that I could qualify for grants to cover the rest of my rent and my living expenses, I enrolled full-time.

Culturally, economically, and politically, Iowa City was the place to be. It had an excellent university symphony, and complete symphony orchestras in the two senior high schools; the best rock concerts, opera, and a remarkable university drama department; the Bijou, where two art movies played nightly, year round, for 50 cents; and reasonable rent. You could walk anywhere in town. Politically the university campus was boiling over with antiwar activity. Opposition to the Vietnam War was drawing the kinds of crowds Vivian Stringer would draw years later with the Iowa women's basketball team. Sit-ins at Old Capitol. Gentle people making a nonviolent statement while the jocks ran across their bodies.

At my first sit-in, I needed every bit of restraint I could muster to keep from reaching up and smashing one of the sadists in the groin as he ran across the group. Long conversations with conscientious objectors while I was a prisoner had partially prepared me for these confrontations, but I still had problems. At times, I still felt that the solution was to "take arms against a sea of troubles."

Every night, crowds would gather. Occasionally they would spill over into the streets. Banners would be unrolled, poster board would appear, and just as quickly paint and brushes. An American flag would appear, upside down, draped across the front of a house. The Iowa City police would come pounding on the door. Jackie Blank would come out and refuse to take it down. "It's a legitimate distress signal. A nation distressed. I'm signaling for help!"

The police wanted no part of that scene. Every day it became increasingly more difficult to break away from the discussions, the planning sessions, and the teach-ins to attend classes. That problem was soon solved when the action of the streets moved into the classrooms. With increasing frequency, students were challenging instructors about the significance of what they were teaching. "If universities are teaching people to think, why are we in Vietnam? Why are there people without food, housing, jobs . . . ?"

Some students who objected to the interruptions would counter with, "We're trying to get an education! Why don't you take your rhetoric someplace else?" To them, activists responded, "What the hell do you think I'm here for? I'm paying tuition just like you are—but I want more for my money!"

Endless questions, accusations, and confrontations.

One day a group of students challenged an instructor about a comment he had made in an offhand manner. After some give and take, the instructor finally got angry and told the students, "If you don't like what I'm teaching or how I teach it, you can get out."

One of them jumped up and said, "Wrong! Either you begin to deal seriously and responsibly with these issues or you can get out."

Thinking he was involved with just three loudmouthed radicals, the instructor called the university police. When they arrived, the three students were addressing the entire lecture hall about the use of police to back up instructors who "were out of touch with reality." As the police advanced on the three, 95 percent of the rest—over three hundred students in all—got up and began to leave the hall. The three disappeared in the crowd. When calm returned, only twenty or so students remained. The great majority agreed that changes were needed.

I had been away from school for a long time. What I saw now was more than students demanding an end to a war they believed was unjust and illegal. They were demanding the right to participate in the decision-making process. They wanted some say in what they were being taught. The most vocal students were being singled out as troublemakers, and no doubt they were. But the trouble they were causing had been a long time coming.

In many ways the university's attempt to stifle dissent reminded me of my recent life in prison. Prisons have always been intractable as far as rules are concerned. You do as the state tells you, or else. In prison, you refuse an order and you land in solitary confinement.

You don't get kicked out—you get kicked farther in. When prison personnel find themselves in a situation where they are wrong and a prisoner is right, they simply change the rules. No discussion permitted.

Traditionally, neither prisoners nor students had any say in how their institutions were run. But now, as I became acclimated to my new environment, I saw that educational institutions were changing. The PDI would act as a catalyst to open prisons to greater public scrutiny, I vowed. As a result, change in the prisons would be possible also. Making prisons more democratic would not be easy. Once people realized that only a small percentage of the prisoners were a serious danger to society, change would come.

Punishment for radical activity was a reality on the campus. Some of the more conservative students, especially from the fraternities and the athletic department, would catch antiwar activists alone and rough them up a bit. During sit-in demonstrations, the leaders invariably ended up getting kicked around, stepped on, and punched when they were being carried or dragged away. Vietnam veterans who were opposed to the war were often attacked. A young bearded veteran with a flag sewn on his sleeve upside down was set upon one night by a group of ROTC students, who ripped his dog tags off and whipped them across his face again and again. He was cut rather badly, but he refused to press charges against them or tell anyone their names, even though he knew the students who had attacked him. He had seen and participated in all the violence he could endure in Vietnam, he told me. "There is nothing anyone can do that will cause me to fight—ever again."

Sobering. Your anger would boil. Understanding would be almost impossible. But finally, painfully, you realized that he and others like him were right. The resolution of disputes through the use of force and violence accomplished nothing positive and led only to more violence.

And just as it was tough for the most active protesters, it was also tough for many of the instructors. I was awed by the sophisticated methods young students used to pin instructors down on issues pertaining to the war. There were groups that seemed to be devoting all of their time to the war. They were constantly producing and distributing fliers, and making amazing demands on instructors.

In my previous life as a full-time student many years before, I had always viewed professors as intelligent, dedicated, educated people. Frequently we students didn't like their regimen or their methods, but we never thought to challenge them, to treat them like equals. Now I was watching professors being dragged out of their ivory towers and knocked off their pedestals.

For example, at the beginning of one semester, a professor who had been head of the department the previous year was putting everyone to sleep. Finally a young man stood up and started making his way to the aisle. "Pardon me. Excuse me. Pardon," etc. etc., he was saying in a conversational voice as he squeezed by the students seated in the cramped lecture-hall seats. The professor stopped speaking and was watching him work his way past students.

"May I ask where you are going?" he said to the young man.

The student stopped, looked at the professor, and said, "Yes." And stood there.

"Well?" the professor asked.

"No, I'm not well," he answered. "I signed up for this course thinking I'd get my mind fucked. I'm certainly not going to listen to this drivel for the rest of the term." And out he went.

I had never heard the word used in reference to mind stimulation and gratification, but I understood.

A number of other students must have understood as well. About 20 percent got up and left.

Interesting.

Hot, Dusty Roads between Prisons

During the summer of 1970, I made a month-long swing through Nebraska, Colorado, Texas, Oklahoma, and Kansas. Unfortunately, because I didn't have a car, I had to travel by bus. I had picked up an assistantship from the University of Iowa Communications Department to produce a series of half-hour radio shows. I was tape-recording editorials written and read by editors of prison newspapers. The tape recorder weighed 45 pounds.

With no money for cabs or rent-a-cars, I walked miles from the bus station to the walls at Huntsville, Texas; got in; recorded a couple of editorials; talked, planned, listened; and left to walk more miles up and down those hot Texas roads, swearing that a time would come when there would be money for a taxi, a van, or a rented car.

Back on the bus. Over to Dallas and a visit with Judge Sarah T. Hughes, the federal judge who made the news when she administered the oath of office to Lyndon Johnson after Jack Kennedy was assassinated. Jackie, stunned and bloodied, looked on. Judge Hughes would provide us with a feature article for the front page of the first issue: "LAW AND SOCIETY: Where Do We Go from Here?" It was a thoughtful article by a person who was looked upon by the public as a venerable member of the judiciary, and by those who had been tried in her court as either a blessing or a curse. Most important, every warden in the country knew Judge Sarah T. Hughes. If any wardens decided to ban the PDI or to seize issues from prisoner subscribers, as I anticipated could easily happen in Texas, I wanted the National Lawyers Guild to wave that front-page story at some federal judge when we demanded that the First Amendment rights of prisoners were as sacred as those of a judge.

On my trip through Texas, I rested a few days with my friends Paul and Janie Kelso in Dallas, caught my breath, cursed the 45 pounds of tape-recording equipment, took in a Janis Joplin concert, and continued crisscrossing the country visiting prisons.

My last stop before returning to Iowa City was Leavenworth, Kansas. The walk from the bus station to the "Big Top" was a long one. I always seemed to be arriving around noon. The sun was as unmerciful as it had been when I walked the yard behind the walls. Now I had no more luck getting in than I had once had getting out. I waited a long time. When I was given the final no, I left. Out on the front walk I stopped and looked back. Through the windows, five stories high, I could see my old tier. I heard a "Yo, Joe," and it sounded like my friend the Green Lizard, a most remarkable, gentle, thoughtful artist who had lived a few cells down from me. From a nearby speaker came the admonishing "Move it, Grant."

A woman with two young boys was leaving and asked where I was going. I kicked in $5 for gas, and they dropped me at the bus station in Kansas City.

By the time I arrived back in Iowa City, an extraordinary amount of mail had accumulated, mostly from prison editors who had interviewed me, and prisoners who had read about me in their newspapers. All of their letters encouraged us to publish—to get that first issue out.

The response from prison editors was more than I had hoped for. Some who sent me editorial contributions were Mary Vangi, editor, *The Clarion*, California Women's Institution, Fontera, California; Henry Moore and raulrsalinas, *The New Era*, U.S.P., Leavenworth, Kansas; Jerry Nemnich, *The Interpreter*, Colorado State Pen, Cañon City, Colorado; Erik Norgaard, Danish Prison System, Denmark; Arnett Sprouse, *Georgia State Prison News*, Reidsville, Georgia; Verna Wyer and Mark Suchy, Sandstone Coffeehouse Organizing Committee, Minnesota Federal Prison, Sandstone, Minnesota; Cathy Kornblith, *Connections*, San Francisco, California; James Farnham, *The Presidio*, Iowa State Pen, Fort Madison, Iowa; James R. Caffey, editor, and Jim Bishop, the *Jefftown Journal*, Missouri State Pen, Jefferson City, Missouri; James Williams, *The Voice*, Southampton Prison Farm, Virginia; Lee Harg (aka Wesley N. Graham, who would make it out in time to share the editor's job with Rex Fletcher, who, as you'll read, we were able to get out), *The Signet*, U.S.P. Leavenworth, Kansas; and Harley Sorenson, *Prison Mirror*, Minnesota State Pen, Stillwater, Minnesota. (Harley went on to become a top-notch journalist working for major dailies. Years later he would meet up with Becky, the PDI's first full-time employee, who was on her way to support the Indians at Wounded Knee. Harley was covering the story for the *Minneapolis Tribune*.)

Poetry came from Celeste Clark, Jerry Nemnich, Linda (a resident of Hillcrest School for Girls), Johannes von Gregg, Bones Kennedy, Gary Ayers, Freda Pointer, S. L. Poulter, E. M. Matzko, and a fellow named Benavidez.

Other contributions came from Oregon, Rhode Island, Israel, Michigan, Maryland, Illinois, Ohio, and Indiana. Not all were from prisoners. Walter E. Kellison, the Unitarian Universalist minister at Peoples Church in Cedar Rapids, sent us an inspirational Easter sermon to share with the many readers we hoped to have in prisons.

One of our big surprises was an article from United States Senator Hubert H. Humphrey, who wrote, "Let's listen to ex-cons for a change." (An interesting note to share about Hubert Humphrey: I met him briefly once in 1970. I told him about my plans for the PDI, and he shared some of his thoughts with me. I never saw him again until 1976, when we passed each other at Washington National Airport. I knew he had been ill, so I walked over and said, "It's good to see that you are feeling well, Senator." "Thanks, Joe," he answered. "I wish I had some time to talk. I'd like to hear more of your ideas about changing the prisons." And he was gone. I couldn't believe that he really knew who I was. I later learned that he never forgot a face or a name. He was also a close friend of my mother, who worked in the bakery where he and his wife Muriel shopped.)

For the next few weeks, I spent more time than usual in my room, recuperating from my exhausting trip. The window by my work table gave me the opportunity to observe a young woman who lived next door. When the weather was mild, she would sit out on the back porch of her second-floor apartment and study. Observing led to sketching, and soon I had the oils out and was running down one of my favorite escape routes—painting.

When it was finished, I looked at the painting for a few weeks, then finally walked over and introduced myself. We became close friends despite our more obvious differences—Shar-lane was attractive, intelligent, and quiet, and she paid her bills. Just what I needed: a role model to fall in love with. In the following months, our relationship grew into a commitment to each other that continues to this day—without benefit of clergy, I should add.

Also during this period, I was leaving for a 7:00 class one morning when I saw a wild rabbit get hit by a car. I brought the rabbit into my room, sterilized the cuts, and closed them. The rabbit was a quick learner. Within two weeks it was depositing its pellets on newspaper in the corner of the bathroom.

One morning I woke up to find that the book I had laid on the floor the night before was covered with pellets. The book was *The Arms of Krupp*, about the German military industrialist Alfred Krupp. This was certainly a special rabbit, I thought. I named it Israel.

Israel did one other thing that I will never forget: The rabbit discovered a small stash of hashish behind a chest of drawers next to my front door. I had moved the drawers in myself, so I knew a previous resident hadn't left it. I hadn't left it. But if I were caught with any drugs, I would get a minimum of five years with no chance to defend myself in court. Within ten minutes, I wrapped the package securely, walked to the post office, and mailed it to my parole officer in Des Moines. I then wrote a brief note, stuffed it in an envelope, and tacked the envelope to the front door. On the envelope I wrote: "ATTENTION INVESTIGATORS WITH SEARCH WARRANT. PLEASE READ BEFORE ENTERING." The note explained that the stash had been found and had been mailed to a federal law-enforcement agency in Des Moines. They came that day, saw the note, didn't search the place, but did contact my parole officer.

From that point on, my parole officer called me every couple of months. Best parole officer I ever had was an Iowa farmer. Come to think about it, he was my only parole officer.

Community Support Grows for PDI

Given the political environment at the university during this period, I had thought that most of my support for the PDI would come from there. I was wrong. The departments where I thought I'd find interest and support turned a deaf ear: criminology and sociology had many interests, but communicating with prisoners was not one of them. The most interest came from folks in the psychology department, the Writer's Workshop, and the Poetry Workshop. Vance Bourjaily, from the Writer's Workshop, was genuinely interested, both in opening lines of communication and in the space I'd be devoting to poetry and art in the publication. Not only did he put me in touch with ex-prisoners in the workshop, he also agreed to take a seat on my board of directors.

Despite the lack of further interest on campus, my own increasing commitment to antiwar activism, and the increasing commitment of so many others, were leading me effortlessly to resource people throughout the city, including a group of business people who appeared willing to front some money for a newspaper. Or, as I had come to refer to it, a monthly journal.

In my daily contacts with them, I'd describe the desperate need for a newspaper that would open lines of communication between prisoners and people in the free world. It was the right time to be talking about prisons. Liberals were everywhere. Normal, law-abiding people were spending nights in the can for demonstrating, smoking pot, acting up in magistrate's court. Young innocents were going to the can, and a straight, free-world society didn't like what they were hearing about prisons, or the city and county jails.

It was, to be perfectly honest, the ideal place to be, and the perfect environment for the PDI.

Through it all, I indicated, but didn't specifically say, that such a newspaper would make money. At the thought of a return, chipping in $500 to a $5,000 nut looked okay. It all depended on how much money you had and whether you had a social conscience.

Within a few months, I was living a couple of blocks south of Burlington on Van Buren, the one block in Iowa City that was as close to a slum as any street in Iowa City could get. (Now it's all apartment buildings—no character at all.) On both sides of me were welfare families and a corps of kids ranging in age from five to sixteen. Most of the families were in trouble with the police. Some of the teens had spent time in Iowa's juvenile prison.

In the winter of 1970–71, Joe Johnston, a young attorney, agreed to help me form a nonprofit, tax-exempt corporation. I decided to call it PHASE IV. In a feature article that appeared Saturday, January 2, 1971, in the *Des Moines Register*, Larry Eckholt explained:

> The purpose of the *Penal Digest International* is reflected in the meaning of . . . the corporation's name—PHASE IV.
>
> "First, a man commits a crime and is arrested; that's phase one," said Grant. "Phase two is incarceration, at which time, hopefully, you decide you don't want to continue phase two.
>
> "Phase three is education. And the fourth phase is assuming an obligation to your fellow offenders—helping to find solutions to the problems."

The four phases: violation, incarceration, education, and obligation. In that first article Eckholt wrote, "Libraries are enthused, Grant said, because 'there's nothing else like [the PDI] in the country.'" I would get the surprise of my life when we made our first promotional mailing to libraries, universities, selected individuals, and wardens around the country.

Around this time, two new friends who had a small public-relations firm—Jerry Mansheim and Loren Bivens—met with me and listened to my ideas. We spent the evening talking. A couple days later, I met again with Loren to see the plan he and Jerry had laid out for presenting those ideas to a carefully chosen group of business people, educators, elected officials, and possible investors. Their roughed-out presentation would use slides and possibly film. He asked me for a theme, I gave him one—the plight of the prisoner with no way to communicate grievances—and we went to work.

They became my advertising agency, public-relations agency, idea board, and source of unlimited help. All the good ideas in the world are worthless if you lack organization and the necessary experience to present them to the people who can help turn them into working projects.

Loren and Jerry designed an attractive packet containing news articles, carefully written press releases, professional photographs by Jerry, information about the nonprofit corporation that was forming, and a description of the PDI and its goals. When I presented my plans for an international journal that would open lines of communication with prisoners, the news media moved right in for a story.

The importance of the press releases cannot be overstated. They are the difference between a reporter getting all the carefully thought-out statements—the phrases and buzzwords that stick in his or her mind and sell your idea—and the reporter missing important points altogether. Reporters use releases as backup. Often a complete article is no more than an edited version of a press release that you yourself write.

Not that writers are lazy or incompetent—on the contrary, they are always incredibly busy and writing against deadlines. They'll spend enough time with you to be sure they are not being led down some "primrose path." Once they're satisfied they have a good story, they will get the information they feel is important to the story. Later, when they are writing the story, the press release provides them with answers to all the unasked questions. The more information you provide, the better your chances are that the story will touch on the subjects you believe are most important.

While the formal presentation was being planned, I was busy contacting the local and regional representatives of companies that manufactured typesetting equipment. When approaching a manufacturer about possibly purchasing very expensive equipment, you have to achieve one of two goals to get that equipment on a trial basis: convince them that you are absolutely trustworthy and will not cheat them—or convince them that you are absolutely trustworthy and will not cheat them.

When the packets were ready, I personally delivered them to all the representatives I had contacted.

Jerry also designed our stationery. Pure art. It screamed "stability."

Knowing we were going to need top-flight legal advice, I contacted nationally respected lawyers, authors, and activists to make up our advisory board. Some I called; some I wrote. All accepted. Our advisors were front-line activists: William "Bill" Kunstler, Stan Bass, Julian Tepper, Diane Schulder, Jessica Mitford, and Kitsi Burkhart. As the commercials would claim years later, "It doesn't get any better than that."

Meanwhile, news articles, feature pieces, poetry, fiction, and other items of interest continued to come in from prisoners.

Some of these prisoners were standouts. One, Rex Fletcher, had been in prison for nineteen years. He was editor of the newspaper at the Oklahoma State Pen. His column was humorous and filled with insights. Often, Oklahoma dailies reprinted his columns. By the end of the year, I had decided I wanted him for an editor. He informed me that his chance of making parole was zero.

Another person I wanted was Charles DuRain, a cartoonist who had become a fixture in the Kentucky State Pen. The parole board had been laughing at him for over twenty years.

This wasn't going to be easy.

Hawkeye Foods owned a large building at 405 South Gilbert, a few blocks from the university (in Iowa City, everything is a few blocks from the university). There, I set up the PDI's first office. The space was split down the middle. We were on the left. On the right was the Crisis Center that Howard Weinberg had started. A few years down the line, Howard would head the Iowa Civil Liberties Union.

Howard was sitting around the office one day and saw a poem by Jerry Nemnich, editor of the Colorado State Penitentiary *Interpreter*, that was scheduled to go into the first issue. He read it and wanted a copy:

WORTH
avocado seeds turn
black
for the chisel.
&

> someday
> I'll carve a rose
> a black rose
> the mythical kind
> you always hear about
> but never see.
> I'm no carver of ironwood or teak.
> I'd be of no use at the monument works
> &
> I'd be hopeless & even frightened
> at the thought of shaping jade,
> but
> an avocado seed . . .

Before long, I was getting calls about Jerry. Local poets and bookstore owners wanted to hear him read. He would have loved it, but the warden at the Colorado State Penitentiary had other ideas.

Soon, wardens throughout the state heard about my plans and began inviting me to visit their prisons. My initial relationship with the wardens was fairly good—not until the PDI's second year did some of them begin to actively oppose our existence.

Laurel Rans was the warden of the Women's Penitentiary at Rockwell City. The first time I heard from her was in a letter asking if we could help a young woman, an ex-prisoner, relocate in Iowa City. I drove to Rockwell City to meet her and talk to her about the PDI and about using our headquarters as a halfway house for prisoners—men, women, and children—who were returning to the community.

Laurel was the ideal warden. Open and direct, she was a no-nonsense administrator. The prisoners respected her, and I believed her to be trustworthy and a person whose counsel would be valuable. I was right. Again and again she proved that she was as willing to trust a group of ex-prisoners to help other prisoners as she was to trust the established state agencies.

During that first visit, sometime in mid-1970, I told her also of my plans to participate in a workshop on corrections at the university, and asked if some of the women from the prison could participate with me. I'd asked that same question of the wardens at the men's reformatory in Anamosa and the penitentiary in Fort Madison, but they couldn't, or wouldn't, cut through all the red tape to give me any men.

Laurel, however, thought the idea was excellent. When I asked her if I would have a problem keeping them for a weekend, she said, "Just stay out of trouble. I'm releasing them to your custody."

Pretty heavy. I'm living under the supervision of a federal parole officer with the admonition to not associate with other ex-prisoners, and suddenly I'm given custody of four women from the women's penitentiary for a long weekend. I checked my parole papers and found no mention of having prisoners in my care, so I figured, "Why not?"

As it turned out, we spent our days on campus participating in panel discussions, our evenings listening to good music and making the rounds of the clubs, and our nights in the home of the woman who had been arrested for hanging the flag upside down to signal that the ship of state was in a state of distress. Jackie Blank became an important part of my life during this period. Until I bought the home at 505 South Lucas, she opened her home (and a very nice home it was) to me and a number of prisoners who ended up in my care on weekends. There wasn't enough floor space in my small room for a chair, much less overnight guests.

In the end, we had a terrific and productive weekend, the first of many that would follow. Panel participants impressed the audience, we partied afterward in a secure section of town, the fireplace roared, and the food was exceptional. But most important, a warden had decided to take a chance with a group of society's losers. A circle of friends formed that weekend that continued long into the future. And the trust that Warden Rans placed in those women and in me did as much to help get the PDI going as did the investment in time and money by our board of directors, advisors, and friends.

The news coverage from that weekend was a great help, too. I wish we could have held a press conference and told them the whole story, how we sat on the panels and spilled our guts, emotionally naked, and then escaped to some quiet club where we could talk and relax. Those were important times for the women. They were busy. They were *free* for a few days. They were supporting each other when the questions started coming at them from skeptical audience members. Reaching inside themselves, they answered questions normally left unasked. Nothing to hide. At home for the first time in a long time. Relaxed. Responsibility's rewards.

Had the truth been known, if everything we did had been public, Laurel Rans would have had more trouble from Iowa Corrections than she deserved. As a warden and a woman, she was as considerate and trusting as any warden I ever knew.

Yet, even in Iowa City, racism was present. A young parolee arrived in town, and I met her at the bus station to help her get settled. We were walking around downtown Iowa City. When we came to Donnely's, a well-known "watering hole" in town, I asked if she'd like a beer and we went in. I ordered two beers but didn't have cash, so I wrote a check—just as I had done many times before. It was refused. Then it struck me. I was with a black woman, and I had never seen a black person in Donnely's.

Then it got painful. I had friends in the place. I looked around. "Does anyone have a couple of bucks until I can cash a check?"

Nothing. Not a word. I regretted not grabbing a bar stool and sending it through the front window. We left. It was the first time she had ever been refused service. I took her to Jackie Blank's for the night and went home. Jackie was a gem.

Following that weekend, John Clark, a computer consultant at Westinghouse Learning Corporation, introduced me to the right man at the right time, and Westinghouse Learning Corporation gave us the desks and chairs we needed. It was remodeling time. They even loaned us a truck.

Permanent transportation, however, was becoming a problem. With our nonprofit status secured and our federal tax-exemption status working its way through the IRS, I started looking around for a van. Once again we benefited from favorable media coverage. I found what I was looking for, a large Chevy van, and the dealer was enthusiastic about leasing it to the corporation. Unfortunately all of our money was earmarked. The van had to wait.

One day, shortly after the Eckholt article came out, I received a call from a William McDonald. Bill had read about my plans and wanted to sit down with me to see how he could help. The next day he drove to Iowa City, and we spent a few hours talking about prisons, prisoners, rehabilitation, jobs, and my plans for the PDI. Bill was a typical Iowa farmer, plainspoken and sincere. He had helped a number of people who had had problems with the criminal justice system and was especially interested in helping children. He was, without question, a good man.

Around that time, I had just received a folder of poetry and short stories from some of the youngsters doing time at the Hillcrest School for Girls in Salem, Oregon. Bill was looking at the poetry and came across a poem I had decided to use in the first issue of the PDI. It was a poem by a young girl named Ellen:

> PEOPLE, so busy bein' black, that they never be people;
> PEOPLE, gettin' their kicks, kickin' others while down;
> PEOPLE, getting their kicks, kickin' man in thorn crown.
> PEOPLE, wonderin' what to do with, rather than for, kids;
> PEOPLE, coverin' superficial topics deeply and deep topics superficially
> PEOPLE, coverin' superficial topics deeply and deep topics artificially
> PEOPLE, drawin' immoral morals from lives best left unled;
> PEOPLE, drawin' immoral morals from books best left unread.
> PEOPLE, sayin' "how is he?" meanin' "can I get his bread yet?"
> PEOPLE, sayin' "how is he?" meanin' "is he dead yet?"
> PEOPLE, lovin' people whose love is all a lie;
> PEOPLE, lovin' people whose love will never die.

The entire folder of material, but especially that poem, struck a responsive chord with Bill. He knew that he would not be able to initiate any kind of a rehabilitation program on his own, but he wanted to help. His concern was genuine enough that I asked him if he would like to take a seat on the board of directors.

By that time, my board consisted of the following individuals: attorney Joe Johnston; author Vance Bourjaily; John Clark; Sharm Scheuerman, former Iowa basketball star and coach for a year, and now a realtor; Richard E. (Dick) Myers Jr., a one-time Republican legislative candidate and the owner of Hawk I Truck Stop on I-80; Miles (Mace) Braverman, vice president of Hawkeye Wholesale Foods; Myra Mezvinsky, wife of our district congressman Eddie Mezvinsky; Dr. Magorah Maruyama of the Social Science Research Institute, University of Hawaii; and prison poet/editor Jerry Nemnich. Bill's response was positive and enthusiastic.

While he was there, I received a call from the manager of the Davenport office of a major manufacturer of typesetting equipment. The manager offered to loan me all the equipment we needed to get the publication ready to go to press. The problem was, we had to pick up the equipment ourselves.

When I hung up the phone, Bill said, "You need some wheels . . ."

Two hours later, a Chevrolet van that could seat eight adults was ours. Bill had given us money for the first and last lease payments, and enough extra for the next two payments. It was so easy I thought Bill had some in with the dealership. Two years later I was to learn an interesting lesson about leased vehicles.

One of the staff had been driving the van, and wires shorted out under the dash and caused a fire. The van was still drivable, but it needed work. In all this time, I had only made two payments on the lease. The dealer had never contacted me about being overdue, so I just kept driving. Finally I drove it into the dealer and made him an offer. If he would repair the damage under the dash and replace a cracked window and a couple of tires, I'd start making payments. Sharlane was with me and very pregnant. The dealer was apoplectic. He stood and pointed a finger at me and seemed prepared to give me hell. But he glanced at the door of the general manager's office and saw that it was open. He walked over, closed the door, and asked me what the hell I thought I was doing.

"Just trying to get a good deal so we have wheels," I said.

After an hour of talking back and forth, it became clear to me that something was not right. This fellow was not saying what I expected. Instead of cussing and threatening, he was just saying I had to do something about all the money I owed. He was being much nicer than any car dealer I'd ever met. So I said, "Fix it or keep it." I had nothing to worry about. They were leasing vehicles off the books and pocketing the payment—when there were payments. Interesting. Someone was stealing from the company, and they had involved a man without the means to make those payments.

I drove to Davenport, picked up the equipment—with enough supplies for the first three issues thrown in for good luck—and that evening I was setting type. By the next morning, I knew I had to have someone working with me who could type.

Since I was in the business of opening lines of communication between the free world and prisoners, I figured I might as well employ as many ex-prisoners as could fill jobs. I called a parole officer I knew. She was working with a huge caseload. I asked her if she knew of any typists looking for work. She didn't.

The next day, Becky Evans (see figure 1) knocked on the door to my room. She was looking for a job and had heard I needed a typist. When I asked her where she lived, she said she lived two houses up from me. We were neighbors. She was a little on the shy side, quiet, didn't have much to say, but she could type like a whiz. The problem was, she was only fifteen—too young for me to hire full-time. On the plus side, she confessed that she was on probation because she skipped school so frequently. Perfect. The only problem was, I needed a full-time employee, and this kid was only fifteen years old.

I told her I seriously wished there was a way, but I didn't think there was. She left, but said she would be back in the morning.

The next morning there was a knock on the door, and there stood Becky with her juvenile probation officer.

An hour later, I had a typist, Becky agreed to attend classes, I shook hands with her probation officer, and we headed for the office. On the way to the office—we were three short blocks away—I asked if she should go to school and join me after classes.

"It's almost noon. I'll go tomorrow," she replied.

To make a long story short, Becky loved the work, loved the people, and loved the idea of the PDI. Her probation officer monitored her work and stopped by the office frequently. After a few weeks, I was called into the office and the authorities made me an offer. Would I agree to be Becky's foster parent?

FIGURE 1. Becky Evans, the first PDI employee, hard at work as usual. So young she initially needed permission from the state of Iowa to work, she was there at the beginning and remained to the end.

I couldn't believe what I was hearing. They explained that they had been discussing it and had decided that Becky was doing so well, and such a dramatic change had happened, that they wanted to see how the arrangement would work out for Becky.

The next thing I knew, I was an official foster parent and Becky was the PDI's first paid employee. Becky was a rare self-starter. From the time she started, she worked two hours for every hour I paid her for. I had never met a kid who was such a pro at the typewriter. She set the type for the first issue—a 72-page tabloid. But I'm getting ahead of myself.

Becky was never an employee in the traditional sense. Her age was the problem. Becky was family. She lived close by and spent most of her time in my room or in the office. I'd never had anyone work for me who never had to be told what to do. Becky could do it all and was comfortable with the hours and the conditions, and to have her legally placed in my custody by the State of Iowa was blowing my mind.

Over the next few months, Becky and I learned the business. Between school and the PDI, neither Becky nor I had time for recreation. As for Becky and school, I soon learned what the problem was. She simply had no time for school, whether she was working or not. Money was scarce, and for many months the only person to get any pay was Becky, and she was giving her mom the majority of what she earned.

Loren and Jerry helped design a mailer to send to prospective subscribers. The first issue was shaping up. The presses we were using could print a 24-page tabloid. We had material for three 24-page signatures—a total of 72 pages for that first issue. The front page was reduced and used on the first page of the flier. Seven pages in total were on card stock. The last three pages were postage-paid return mailers: "Check the box and we'll send you the first issue free. If you like it, subscribe; if you don't, write cancel on the invoice and return it." The potential subscriber had nothing to lose. The mailer was beautiful. I was convinced that it would sell and we'd be in business.

In March 1971, with a little fanfare and a small addressing party, we sent out 7,000 mailers. Cost us an arm and a leg, but it was an important step. After dropping the bundles of sorted mail at the post office, Becky and I had a celebratory spaghetti dinner at The Mill. Owner and good friend Keith Dempster heard about the mailing, and he gave us dinner on the house. The only thing that would have made that dinner better was if Paul Kelso had been on stage with his great folk and union songs. Paul was always around in spirit.

The First Issue

After mailing out the flier, I sat back and waited for the postage-paid return mail cards to flood in. In a few weeks we would have a return of at least 50 percent. Why not? It was free—gratis. If you don't like it, just write cancel on the invoice and forget it. No obligation to inspect a 72-page tabloid—written, designed, edited, and marketed by prisoners and ex-prisoners. Curiosity alone would have people returning the postage-paid card. We couldn't miss.

When a direct-mail campaign brings in a 3 percent return, it is considered successful. I believed that the PDI's uniqueness alone would bring us a return of 50 percent or more. Not all of them would subscribe, but I knew that most intelligent respondents would at least consider $6 a fair investment for twelve issues. Prisoners could subscribe for $1, although we were encouraging them to spend $6 if they could afford to do so.

The response during the first five weeks was less than exciting. Three weeks after the mailing, two cards came in. A few days later we received three more. Another week passed and two more came in. Seven in five weeks, out of 7,000.

Hello, I thought. Is anyone out there?

With the response to the mailing in my hand, I understood clearly that the only people I could count on to support the PDI were the people who were unable to do so—the prisoners.

The lack of response from the libraries I could understand. In their eyes, our content was so specialized that no one besides prisoners and correctional employees would be interested. I had failed to convince them that 20 to 25 percent of the general population was interested in the problems facing prisoners and their families. Damn near that many had some kind of criminal record.

My greatest disappointment was the lack of response from the colleges, particularly those with criminology departments. I had fine-tuned my list so that the mailer was sent directly to the department heads, as well as to those professors who were well known because of books they had written.

What also mystified me was that no one called or wrote to ask questions about what I was doing. The PDI was the only newspaper dealing directly with incredibly serious problems—problems that concerned the public as well as prisoners. Our initial presentation to prospective subscribers had been professionally done. Yet it generated no response.

Equally distressing was my not being able to discuss the problem with anyone. Becky and I were the only people who knew. If I mentioned what was happening to anyone else, I would never be able to undo the damage. For those few weeks while I waited for postage-paid cards to arrive, I had imagined a flood of so many cards that I would have to borrow money to pay the postage. During that time, I would occasionally find myself sitting in the office late at night. Becky would be typing articles. I'd reach to the rear of the bottom drawer and take out the seven return mailers that we had received. Becky would glance over, see what I was looking at, and shake her head.

"I simply cannot believe that there are not more people who are curious enough to drop a postage-paid card in the mail to get a free copy of a publication of any kind," I would say for the fiftieth, sixtieth, or hundredth time.

Becky would shrug her shoulders and respond, over and over, "No one gives a damn about prisoners, or about you or about me."

One night, just as she was saying that to me for the umpteenth time, an Iowa City police car slowly drove by the office. Becky smiled and added, "At least not anyone willing to spend $6 on a year's subscription."

She was absolutely right. It took over a month for the facts to sink in—for me to under-stand and admit to myself that my dream of a widely circulated and subscribed-to monthly journal that would provide a power base to bring change to one of the most repressive prison systems in the world was not happening. There would be no wages for staff and travel and lobbying. There would be no research department, nothing for correspondents behind the walls. If the PDI was going to happen, it would have to be done on sheer determination, bluff, and a willingness to work without pay. The question was, how much determination could a person generate when the bank account had only enough money to cover a couple of months' expenses?

We were in trouble.

"Let's get a pizza."

Over pizza, Becky and I discussed options.

"If the PDI is going to press, it will happen because we make it happen, Becky."

"If we print the issue, who will we send it to? Surely you'll print more than seven copies."

"Somehow we have to generate some excitement."

Becky had been to all the board meetings. She had heard the details of my dream. More than anyone besides me, she was a believer. Becky I could confide in. I explained what I was going to do and asked her if she wanted to help. Since it was a week night and she wasn't allowed to party, she said, "Let's go do it."

We returned to the office—our sanctuary—and started filling out postage-paid return mailers. By morning, we had filled out about 3,000.

We were tired—but we felt satisfied. Every person, every department, every college and university that I had believed would request the first issue was going to get that first issue. So were the television networks, the top newspapers and magazines, some carefully selected wardens of federal and state prisons, chiefs of police, congressional representatives, a few authors, and some prisoners.

Believe me, I had my lists.

We locked up, had breakfast, and walked over to Van Buren for a quick rest. Becky still lived two doors up the street. A couple of hours later, we walked to the office, filled some brown bags with the postage-paid cards, and then went to the board meeting.

Everyone was eager to hear about the mailing. Becky and I walked in as if we'd just hit the lottery. All smiles. Shaking with what everyone thought was excitement—instead of exhaustion. Not being one to waste words, I just emptied the bags on the table and announced that we had a 43 percent return. These were business people, and they were stunned by the return. It was a higher return than any direct-mail solicitation they had ever heard of.

After a general discussion about what was next, I said that I felt safe in projecting a paid subscription base of around 20,000 by the end of the first year.

Then I explained that I needed $1,500 to pay for the return mailers, and $2,500 to print and mail the first edition of the PDI. The vote was unanimous. Combined loans from Dick Myers, Mace Braverman, Sharm Scheuerman, and John Clark totaled $4,000. Becky and I walked to the bank, then to the office, and went to work.

We had the money now for the first issue. We even had enough money to pay Becky. But we were only three months into the lease on the van, and I knew I'd be unable to generate the $225 needed to keep it. Not with the office rent, utilities, and printing costs—plus two separate places of residence.

The problem of housing was solved with the help of Sharm Scheuerman and his partner Steve Richardson. Using my GI loan that I picked up from my time in the navy, I bought a large three-story house at 505 South Lucas Street. The combined rent that we were already paying on separate places almost covered the monthly payment. I still had money stashed from the sale of my paintings. We were going to have financial problems, but we were going to get out at least two issues.

The house at 505 became synonymous with PDI, and we said goodbye to our sanctuary over on Gilbert Street. It became a pizza place called The Sanctuary. Bo Ramsey was the man behind the bar, and his days as a bartender would come to an end when he turned to music full-time and teamed up with Greg Brown. The Sanctuary had the best pizza in town.

With more room, a large house, a yard, and a great kitchen, more people began spending time at the PDI. Included, in particular, were some of the kids from welfare families I had been helping out.

Oatmeal and Love: Bringing Kids to the Table

The number of people who were living and working at 505 previous to our printing the first issue fluctuated between five and eight. That number, plus the constant flow of visitors, forced us to locate sources for large quantities of food. I think we were one of the first groups to check out the commercial food wholesalers around closing time each day. Staff members would show up to pick over the fruits and vegetables that were too ripe to be sold to the stores the next day.

Hawkeye Wholesale Foods provided us with quite a bit of food, thanks largely to David Braverman, patriarch of the Braverman clan, the founder of Hawkeye Foods, and a genuine friend. David's generosity was legendary. During the holidays, he would load up our van with turkeys and hams. Our staff, the welfare families, and the homeless, helpless drifters always knew where the groceries were. Maybe the old man liked us so much because he knew two things: that we could have all been working 9 to 5 making good livings for ourselves, but chose instead to devote our lives to the only prisoner-owned-and-operated halfway house in the country; and that we shared everything we had, no matter how much or how little. David recognized that we didn't share a religion, but we damn sure shared a philosophy.

As a result, we set a dinner table that was second to none and always had food to share with a dozen or so other poor families. We were the largest welfare family in Iowa City. We housed runaways, escapees, wanteds, people who were walking to the beat of a different emotional drummer, and children from preschool on up.

Although we applied for and used food stamps regularly, many of them went to families who came to us for emergency help. Families also came to us when they felt they were not being treated fairly by Human Services. When that happened, I was the one who usually accompanied them back to the office to lodge a complaint. I would listen to the long list of regulations concerning food-stamp eligibility, then argue my response. I'd listen and argue, listen and demand, listen and threaten, but I would never leave. Finally I'd walk over and start pounding on director Cleo Marsolais's door.

"Come," Cleo would call.

The aide would open the door. Cleo would be sitting at her desk, buried behind stacks of paperwork; all you could see was the top of her head.

I'd start right off: "Cleo, these people are desperate. I've never lied to you and I'm not lying now . . ."

Cleo would just raise a hand and wave for us to go away, yelling, "Just give Grant the goddamn food stamps."

If we could have cloned a Human Services army of Cleo Marsolaises, we would be living in a more equitable world today.

We became expert on living well with an incredibly small amount of money, thanks to the PDI's first vegetarians, Warren and Cathy Dearden. Warren and Cathy came to us in 1971 after Warren won a scholarship to the Writer's Workshop at the University of Iowa. Grove Press had just published *A Free Country*, a book by Warren that was not only entertaining, it resounded with the ring of personal experience. They were in Iowa City only a few hours before hearing about the activities at 505 from a woman at the Iowa Writers Workshop. That afternoon, they wandered in and introduced themselves (see sidebar 1).

SIDEBAR 1

A VERY ZEN GARRET (by Warren Dearden)

There's no way to talk about the *Penal Digest International* without talking about Joe Grant. For Joe wasn't simply the paper's founder and publisher, or simply the fundraiser and organizer who made the paper possible. Joe was literally the sine qua non of PDI—the only person on the planet, probably, who could have gotten such an unlikely enterprise off the ground, and the exemplar of the wholeheartedly altruistic dedication that characterized its staff. In a profound way, PDI was Joe Grant—a newspaper that reflected his radical analysis of American society and its justice system, dedicated to improving the lot of its most abused, most oppressed bottom rung.

"Oh, you've got to meet Joe Grant!" the receptionist in the Writer's Workshop office told me the day after my wife and I arrived in Iowa City, when she learned that I was an ex-convict. Joe was also an ex-con, she told me—a dynamic, fascinating character who'd started an underground newspaper for prisoners. "You'll really like Joe," she said, and offered to put me in touch with him. I think it was that very night when we met. I remember that he telephoned late one steamy August afternoon, introduced himself, and invited us for dinner at his friend Elinor's house; I know it was impromptu because I remember Elinor remarking that she'd given us her kids' dinners. After dinner, we sat on the porch and smoked, watched a lightning storm explode the torrid day, and laughed our asses off.

Joe and I were nonviolent, amateur criminals who'd both struck out at the outset of our criminal careers—me before I could get my thirty kilos of marijuana into the United States, Joe before the currency he had created got into the hands of its wrongful owners. We'd have probably been cohorts if we'd done our time in the same joint. But Joe came into my life at just the time I was reading Ferdinand Lundberg's *The Rich and the Super-Rich*, grasping for the first time the full implications of an oligarchic society, grasping that the law and the government were *always* tools of the ruling class, always used to oppress the common folk. Joe was a patented hero for my money in the struggle for the rights of the most oppressed, incarcerated victims of that system, playing for all he was worth a game that could end only in defeat, playing it for the sake of the difference it might someday make.

I pegged Joe for a con man the minute I met him: handsome, amiable, and amusing, with a head full of ambitious, improbable schemes and an absolutely mesmerizing voice, a syrupy radio baritone that dripped sincerity, that could charm the birds out of the trees. Yet I liked him enormously, somehow sensing that he was at heart the altruist he pretended to be, and that his concern for prisoners was genuine. Joe was a working-class, intellectual anarchist, like me—a freethinking, iconoclastic, idealistic revolutionary, full of goodwill and good humor, charity and fun. He was kind and tolerant of practically anybody he met, yet ready to ridicule any institution, especially those he believed in. I laughed at all of Joe's jokes and he laughed at all of mine, and on that very sound basis our friendship was founded. If my memory serves me right, it was that first night that Joe invited Cathy and me to move into the attic of his new PDI headquarters at 505 South Lucas Street.

My part of the bargain was to insulate and drywall the ceiling and so convert the bare attic into a living space. I'd never applied insulation or hung drywall before, but I was handyman enough to do a decent job—though hanging drywall on a sloping ceiling, professional drywall hangers have since told me, is one of the trickiest jobs they have to do. I boxed in the eaves at chest height, building chests of drawers so they were flush with the walls, storage compartments and shelves into the wall, and a desk where I could write under the front windows. The result was a big, bare space, 12′ × 30′ maybe, with sunny yellow ceiling and walls, no furniture but the desk and chair at one end, a mattress on the floor at the other end, and a rocking chair beyond it near the back windows. A very Zen garret.

One entered by a narrow, dangerously steep, head-bumping, railingless stairway from the second floor of the house. The electricity came up the stairs via a heavy-duty extension cord, from an outlet on the second floor, to power an electric heater at my feet in the daytime or by our bed at night; our light was kerosene lamps. But Cathy and I were hippies in 1971 who'd spent the past summer in a dirt-poor, beans-and-tortillas commune a mile and a half high in the Jemez Mountains of New Mexico, sleeping under a roof that didn't even keep the rain off. A warm, dry place was heaven to us. We actually called it our "log cabin home in the sky," after an Incredible String Band song Cathy liked me to sing to her. I wrote a couple hundred pages of *Children of All Ages* at that desk, including "The Little Boy Who Never Got Anything for Christmas Except Underwear" and "Little Lost Creek." Two or three times a day, a crew of PDI staffers would assemble there to smoke a joint. Shortly after dawn on March 11, 1972, my daughter Nimblewill was born in PDI's attic.

Joe probably counted on my getting caught up in PDI and joining the production staff, although we agreed specifically before I moved in that I would be busy writing fiction for the workshop and working on my novel. If he did, he was disappointed. But Joe got something from Cathy and me that he wanted in the Lucas Street residence: an example that made the house a home. We'd been living in communes for a couple of years between us, so we were practiced at communal spirit and were able to draw together an extended family out of a bunch of strangers. That was, to a large extent, what transpired among a core group—Joe, Merilea, Dick Tanner, Becky Evans, and Bob Copeland—who worked selflessly in that basement like slaves for PDI all through that winter of 1971–72. And Cathy and I (not to mention Nimble) were the instigators of it.

Buying and preparing the food was a big part of our contribution. We spent our food stamps and my tiny fellowship stipend on beans and tortillas, rice and vegetables, spinach lasagna, and other bulk foods and grains.

Cathy baked fresh bread every other day. Other people would rebel against the vegetarian fare occasionally and cook a meat dish for us all, but Cathy and I did probably 90 percent of the food preparation between us, and she did two-thirds of that, as well as probably two-thirds of the housecleaning.

All of this only reinforced the mother role her swollen stomach cast her in. A sweet, pretty mother-to-be in the prime of her twenty-three years, she was the spiritual center of the commune. Happy as she was to be in love and pregnant, she drew that PDI core into a tight, cozy family.

Joe was blessed in the people he attracted to PDI; although there were a few who couldn't fit in, the best were absolute bricks. Bob Copeland was a relentlessly genial Lake Forest graduate who'd somehow convinced his draft board to let him do his alternative service working for PDI. Dick Tanner was a Leavenworth graduate, a mercurial madman/genius from Oklahoma who'd been in jail the last ten years.

Dick Tanner rode his temper like a tiger, high on brotherhood and selflessness. Merilea was an artist and a junior-high school English teacher whose marriage had recently gone on the rocks—a woman looking for a place to live, an important job to do, and someone to love, who found 505, PDI, and Joe Grant. These talented people worked long hours for nothing under the worst conditions, in a windowless basement—much harder and longer, I daresay, than they've ever worked at paying jobs. Thanks largely to their unpaid labor, Joe was able to publish PDI nearly every month for the two years or so if its life.

Joe, as I've said, was the sine qua non of PDI: the provider of the means for housing and feeding the staff—of the paper, printing, and postage necessary to produce and deliver a newspaper without a line of advertising in it. Joe himself had not a pot to piss in, so he did it all on credit: on his own credit, as far as that would take him (not far); on the credit of his benefactors, mostly some Iowa City businessmen whom Joe had persuaded to join the PDI board of directors. Entirely on credit, he leased the typewriters, composing machines, and photocopiers, plus the van he drove around in; he'd purchased the Lucas Street headquarters with a no-down-payment VA loan. He of course charged the rolls of insulation and the drywall I hung in the attic. He bought his gasoline and tires on a credit card, naturally, and maybe the heating oil as well. "Charge it," he said airily, for as long as he could get away with it. What else do you say when you can't pay?

Subscription revenues at PDI were seldom more than $10 to $20 per day, money diverted by whoever got to the post office first, so very few of these bills were being paid. Overdue bills mounted around him the winter long; the clamor of unsatisfied creditors steadily swelled. Joe charmed them, cajoled them, made rosy, empty promises, and fended them off as well as he could. But the concerned inquiries of his board members began to swell also, and sometime around February or March 1972 the board assembled to question Joe about his finances and to take PDI away from him.

I knew nothing of PDI's finances. Joe kept them to himself, if he kept them at all. I never used credit; at thirty years of age, I'd paid cash for everything I ever bought. But for some reason—call it Joe's instinct for survival—he asked me to come along to the board meeting with him, and hence gave me an opportunity to repay him some of the debt I owed him.

It was clear from the moment we walked in that tossing Joe out on his ear was the basic conspiracy: a disaffected ex-PDI staffer, Wesley Nobel Graham, was there, ready and eager to succeed him. I don't recall the details of its unfolding over the next couple of hours, and I don't remember why they had to do it just this way, but eventually the basic shape of their plot became clear. They wanted Joe to produce a financial statement that would detail accounts payable; with that in hand, they were going to assume responsibility for PDI's debts and replace Joe as publisher. Up against the wall, Joe agreed to produce a financial statement after a two-hour lunch break.

I don't recall the total debt, but I remember that it wasn't that great a sum; the board had a fairly accurate idea of its size and was prepared to swallow it. By dinnertime, Joe was going to be out on his ass, and with him gone, the PDI family would disintegrate. Dick and Merilea and Bob were devoted to the cause, but they weren't going to work for nothing if their room and board weren't provided. Without them, PDI was doomed.

Maybe it was that realization that fired off my brainstorm: inflating PDI into a spiky, unappetizing blowfish in the very jaws of its predator. By accounting for the labor costs that had gone into PDI, I realized, we could effectively triple the debt. And because labor liabilities take precedence over other liabilities, Merilea, Dick, Bob, and Joe himself would each be entitled to between $5,000 and $10,000 in payoffs before any of the other bills could be paid.

You would've loved to see their faces after lunch when they got a look at that financial statement. Everybody knew that none of the labor that went into PDI had ever been paid. No one had ever thought of it till I did. But it was a legitimate debt just because Joe had put it down there, and each of the board members knew it as soon as he saw it. Watching them pass it around, seeing them change color as they read it, Joe and I had all we could do to keep from laughing. We heard nothing about assuming PDI's debts the rest of that afternoon, nothing more about replacing Joe as publisher. Firmly in command of his sinking ship, but with enough energy to bail water frantically for another eight months, he sailed bravely on toward oblivion, cranking out issues until it finally submerged.

Warren had taken an early pot bust and done some federal time. He was quiet, had a great sense of humor, and seemed to know what he was doing. For a person so small and slight, he moved around with deliberation and authority. That first night, we didn't even have floor space, so they ended up on the living room floor at the home of Elinor Cottrell, who was one of the most interesting and remarkable women I met in Iowa City, and whose friendship, still to this day, remains one of the highlights of my life.

Early the next morning, when Elinor came downstairs, Warren had just awakened and was standing in the middle of the living room, naked, facing away from her. Just as she was about to say good morning, he bent over, and it appeared that he was mooning her. Had she spoken, she recalled to me later, she would have been talking to Warren's butt. She turned and walked back upstairs, then came down a few minutes later when he was dressed.

Some time later, she asked me if I thought he had done that deliberately. I wasn't sure. He and Cathy hadn't been long off a desert commune in New Mexico where food and water had to be carefully conserved. Elinor was living in what appeared to be rather affluent surroundings. He might have decided to let her take a good look at the skinny ass of a man who wasn't impressed with the surroundings, or he may have been bending over to see what Elinor looked like coming down the stairs upside down. Maybe he was picking up his socks. I never asked him.

The next day they were back at 505. Cathy checked the kitchen, the stove, and the refrigerator, and walked through the house. After about a half hour she indicated that she wanted to talk.

"We'll prepare two meals a day, breakfast and dinner; make out the grocery lists; and see that someone does the shopping or do it ourselves," she offered. "We all clean up for ourselves, and Warren and I will live in the attic."

There was no question in my mind that Cathy was exactly what 505 needed. I was right. Soon Cathy was cooking two meals a day. Cathy was also working part-time at a pseudo-Mexican restaurant, the Taco Vendor, across from Keith Dempster's Mill Restaurant, and playing out a whole host of roles at the house: to Warren she was a wife and lover, to the women in the house she was a sister, to the kids she was a mother, to the men she was damned attractive, quick with a smile, always a pleasure to be around, and absolute boss in the kitchen and dining room.

At Taco Vendor, she scrubbed pots and pans during the lunch rush. Her boss was a man who seemed to have trouble with women who thought for themselves and expected answers to questions.

Women like Cathy.

Cathy would do her job, but when her Taco Vendor boss started laying "trips" on her, she would just look at him and smile. Finally he decided that she had to wear a bra when she washed the dishes—in effect, "Wear one or lose your job." I recall her getting that slight, lopsided grin on her face, slowly shaking her head from side to side, raising one eyebrow quizzically, and saying, "He is really fucked up." We assumed that her boss was having hormonal problems—among other things. He must have mellowed out, because Cathy continued working for him.

Meanwhile, the meals at 505 became legendary. The evening meal soon developed into the most important meal socially. Often, twenty or more people would sit together around our long dining room table. There, over casserole and salad, we caught up on incidents of interest that had been happening around Iowa City and the state and federal prison systems, via news reports from our correspondents in prisons around the world. Conversations touched on deaths, births, and suicides. One of the main thoroughfares from the east coast to the west was I-80; it was a rare evening meal that didn't find a traveler or two sharing dinner with us and bringing us news from the road.

Breakfast was always my most important meal. I had been raised on substantial breakfasts. My mother was a tyrant when it came to breakfast. As soon as you were old enough to work, play, or go to school, you left the breakfast table with the nourishment to carry your share of the load for the day. Fortunately for me, Cathy had graduated from that same nutritional school. Breakfast consisted of cooked cereal made up of a variety of grains, raisins, and nuts, with gallons of raw whole milk from Moss's Dairy. It always appeared that Cathy had made more than the regulars and visitors could eat. Yet invariably the last person to eat would be cleaning out the second of the two huge cast-iron kettles that were seasoned to perfection.

Breakfast was spread out over a three-hour period, beginning about 6 A.M., as people wandered in from the six upstairs bedrooms and the two basement bedrooms. It wasn't unusual in the morning to find people sleeping on the porch or in the backyard, or neighborhood kids walking in for breakfast on their way to the elementary school a few blocks away. With Cathy's touch, the house at 505 became a home. Of course she had a pretty responsive crew gathering for those meals. Many had spent long years lining up for food in prison mess halls; they knew what it was like living on a diet of the proverbial "cake and wine" while in solitary confinement.

The kids who came for breakfast not only were welcomed, but they became close enough to us that we started filling in for parents. Often teachers contacted us if there was a problem. We'd stop in and discuss grades, behavior, all of the issues that parents normally discussed.

One observation I made was that when the kids spent time at 505, their behavior, and also their grades, seemed to improve. I could easily understand why: They had people around them who were genuinely concerned about their welfare. They were getting good breakfasts and attention in a friendly, laid-back environment. Being with the kids, I learned this important lesson: The best way to rehabilitate screw-up A was to give screw-up A the job of helping screw-up B. I had the kids looking out for the grownups and the grownups looking out for the kids. I impressed upon the kids how important it was that they set a good example for the men and women who arrived at 505 fresh out of prison—and incidentally, I also carefully impressed upon these same men and women how important it was that they set a good example for the kids. The result was that the cons looked out for the kids, and the kids looked out for the cons.

During this time, I was frequently driving between Iowa City and Chicago because we had contacts there for bulk food—mostly 25- and 50-pound bags of rice, beans, and flour, and cases of canned peanut butter. On one of my trips, we struck it rich and were given much more than we would be able to use before the next shipment was ready. I asked around and ended up dropping some beans and rice off with the Black Panthers for their breakfast program.

I observed their program in operation and found that where we were feeding eight to ten kids, they were feeding hundreds, and the results were the same. The kids were healthier, their behavior in the classroom was more laid-back, and consequently they were learning more and they were learning faster.

The Free Breakfast for School Children Program was initiated by the Black Panther Party in January 1969 in Oakland, California. Members of the Panthers and community volunteers would cook and serve food to the poor inner-city youth of the area. Initially run out of Oakland's St. Augustine's Church, the program became so popular that by the end of the year, the Panthers set up kitchens in cities across the nation, feeding over 10,000 children every day before they went to school. Fred Hampton joined the Chicago chapter of the Black Panther Party in 1968; the breakfast program and the Chicago branch of the Black Panther party thrived as a result of Hampton's energy and organizing skills.

But in December 1969, Hampton was murdered when a task force of Chicago cops raided his apartment and shot him numerous times. When it was over and he wasn't dead, a cop walked over and shot him in the head—execution style.

There was no sign of this past trauma, which had stunned the Chicago chapter, by the time I visited them with food in 1971. Visiting the Panthers' breakfast program was as inspiring as watching our kids take the hand of a college student, go through that university cafeteria, and help themselves to the "magic" of endless varieties of healthy food.

Watching the children eating, in Chicago and at the University of Iowa, was a joy—an absolute joy.

I was impressed.

And I was depressed—because I knew that we could not mount that kind of offensive against hunger in Iowa City. To begin with, as far as 99 percent of the population was concerned, there was no hunger in Iowa City.

I was determined to get a breakfast program going in Iowa City, but couldn't figure out how to do so while keeping the PDI going and making sure enough money was raised each month to make the house payment, keep the folks who had no resources in shoes and clothing, and care for the kids who came by for breakfast.

One night I was making notes in my journal about some incidents that had happened to me and a few other Korean War veterans while studying at Boston University. The money we got from the GI Bill barely covered tuition. We had to earn what we needed for food, but on top of our academic loads, we had little time to work. As a result, we each made do with coffee for breakfast, a peanut-butter and jelly sandwich and a half-pint carton of milk for lunch, and whatever we could hustle at jobs for dinner.

One morning, my friend Eddie Doyle and I were having our coffee at the school cafeteria when a couple of young women from our college sat down next to us. On each woman's tray was a cup of coffee and a gigantic cinnamon roll with raisins. As we talked, one of them decided she couldn't eat her cinnamon roll.

"Will you eat that roll, Joe?" she asked. "I hate to see it go to waste."

Eddie and I looked at each other and smiled. Then, like John Belushi with his samurai sword, we split it—and it was gone.

"We should pay you for it," I offered.

"Why bother? Daddy has already paid for it."

With that, we headed for class. But the fact that "Daddy has already paid for it" kept echoing through my hunger-crazed brain. If Daddy had paid for it, why didn't I ask her to go through and get a tray full of food? Why didn't I ask four or five of those diet-conscious young women to do the same for vets who simply had no money for meals?

During lunch I brought the subject up, and they thought it was a great idea.

"No reason to let that money go to waste" was the unanimous decision. From that point on, breakfast was eggs, ham, bacon, potatoes, toast, fruit juice, coffee, and cinnamon rolls, all of which we enjoyed in the company of lovely coeds who enjoyed the company of the handful of Korean War vets who were trying to get an education.

School became a joyous experience. As a result of enabling those fine young women to become nurturing caretakers to a pack of insane veterans, and helped along by my own weird sense of humor, I was elected president of the Humanities Workshop at the College of General Education. CGE was referred to as the Tire Factory. With me, and with most of my friends, CGE was an affair filled with as much hate as love. I had been given a choice of either accepting CGE or taking a walk. My poor high school grades gave me no rebuttal.

As if the academic load wasn't enough to drive me nuts, the VA messed up some paperwork. Every day I would race home to the abandoned closet I rented at 529 Beacon and ask my landlady if my checks had arrived. Each day for four months, Mrs. Lusier would shake her head "no" and look at me with the ever-present question in her eye: "Is this guy for real?" Rent was accumulating at the rate of $7 a week (for a small room with a broken window); a piece of ¼" plywood separated my small room from my neighbor Jim, and only breakfast and lunch kept me sane.

I vowed daily that when my checks came, I would go out for a steak dinner and follow that up with a bottle of wine. When my checks finally came, two days before Christmas, I paid my tuition and rent, then called all my friends for a party at a corner tavern. I was there having a beer when they arrived, ready to party. Before they could yell for the bartender to send over a round of beer, I stood up and told them that I was here to spend every damn cent I had left after paying my tuition and back rent. I laid down two dollars.

"Have you had your steak?" Eddie asked.

"No money for food," I answered.

"You don't think that $2 is gonna fund a party, do ya, Joe?"

"Look at it this way," I said. "There's five of us. Two pitchers of beer will cost $1.50. That leaves each of us with a dime to make a phone call. If I can come up with the idea that is keeping us in food for the next four years, it seems to me that collectively we can come up with enough money for a few beers and, if not steak, at least pizza."

But that's another story, and the Boston scene was what reminded me that there were full-time students at Iowa whose parents paid for meals that were not being eaten. That being the case, why not give the meals to kids who needed the nutrition, the friendship, and a little adventure?

I contacted a few friends at Iowa, and we met to figure out how we could make it work. To begin with, someone pointed out that the laws of the University of Iowa made it illegal to transfer a meal.

"It would upset the computerized figures that have been worked out over many, many years," Al Frost said. "If people who didn't eat their breakfasts suddenly showed up and gave them to hungry kids, the balance would be upset and the system would go a little haywire."

"That means we can only allow people who always eat breakfast to participate in the program!" I offered.

Correct.

Everyone at the meeting always ate breakfast. All agreed to give them up anytime a kid showed up for breakfast. Together they were confident they could get as many other students as we needed, so that a college student would be available for every kid we brought to the school.

I had put out the word that I would pick up, feed, and deliver to school any kids who wanted to challenge the system. Specifically I asked for kids who were hungry, who wanted nutritional breakfasts so their grades would improve, or who wanted excitement.

Little did we know how much excitement we would generate.

We started out one Monday morning with about twenty kids, about half boys and half girls. We all met at the Burge Hall cafeteria, and there each student was teamed with a child. After introductions and an explanation of the game plan, the teams headed for the cafeteria.

Now you have to understand that these kids lived in a small, Midwestern college town. The university was the town's number-one employer. It was where all the action was: the best concerts, the best movies, the best of everything. Yet these kids were strangers to the school. Certainly they had never been in one of the cafeterias. Some of them would sneak around stealing whatever wasn't nailed down, or checking coin-return slots on phones and pop machines (they'd come away with a couple of dollars for an hour's work). With rare exception, they were not welcome on campus.

And now we told them that they could have anything they wanted and as much as they wanted—just like the students who were there for the full ride.

The first ones through the line were taking a sweet roll and a couple of cartons of chocolate milk apiece. I sat down with Lester Holderness and asked him why he didn't fill up with food as he did at 505.

"I dunno."

The idea of having that much food, or that kind of a variety of food, was beyond their understanding.

"Have some fun," I said. "Try a little of everything. Let's see who can sample a little bit of everything being served."

Suddenly it became a game. They headed back to the food line. Lester jumped in with a friend who was just starting, and soon everyone was trying everything.

After breakfast, I loaded them into the PDI van and got them to school on time. About mid-afternoon, some of the teachers called to find out what we were doing. I told them. They liked the idea and asked if they could recommend additional kids. I said, "There's always room for one more."

We had already decided to feed the kids every Monday, Wednesday, and Friday: Monday to get their week off to a good start, Wednesday for a mid-week boost, and Friday to give them a good start for the weekend. On Wednesday, the news media was there to greet the kids. I think it was Al Frost who told the press that every care had been taken to ensure that the computerized balance wouldn't be affected. He and the other students, he said, were only giving away the breakfasts they had been eating regularly since coming to the University of Iowa. The kids talked about their new friends at the university and admitted that they enjoyed trying the different kinds of food.

When the news media asked me if the kids were participating because they were not being fed at home, I told them it wasn't so much a matter of getting them food as it was helping them increase their commitment to education. I couldn't say that they were not eating nutritiously at home because I knew their mothers were doing the best they knew how. "This breakfast program is our way of making them feel that they are part of the system, and not outsiders," I said. "I want them to feel that the university is as much theirs as it is the students' who are enrolled."

The press liked my answer and gave us good publicity. No parents were made to look bad, and the kids were excited about the publicity. Normally the only time they paid attention to newspapers was when a relative had been busted.

The second week went by without incident, but during the third week we were tipped off that university security was going to be at Burge cafeteria to stop the students from giving the kids their breakfasts.

To avoid security, we went across campus to another cafeteria. By the time they arrived, the kids had eaten and were on their way to school.

Still, we knew the university wanted to stop the program, so we arranged to meet with a high-level university administrator. At that meeting, the students explained again that they had designed the program carefully, that only those students who had always eaten breakfast were involved, that they had the computerized lists to substantiate this assertion, and that they were going to be at Burge the following morning with the kids.

They were, and so were all four network TV affiliates, plus photographers and reporters from all the newspapers. When the students arrived, hand in hand with the kids, the police just stepped aside. The next morning, the university informed all the participating students that their final grades would be withheld and they would not graduate unless they stopped giving their breakfasts away.

The students called a meeting. About half were seniors and two were in grad school. Some of their parents had been notified by the school. The thought of a year's tuition being wasted and their children's degrees being held up caused them concern. Even some of the kids heard about the meeting and showed up.

I remember one of the kids saying, "I don't want any more of their goddamn food." It was probably Lester. There was no question about how the kids felt. They were turning their hurt into anger. The teams had developed a tremendous affection for each other, more than we had ever anticipated, but it was the kids who would end up being harmed if the program stopped—not because they would be losing those three breakfasts every week, but because they were once again ending up on the outside. The university was rejecting them. We talked about the rules and how rules for the most part should be obeyed. But this time the students decided that the university was being too inflexible. After weighing the worst that could happen—no grades and a year down the drain—the students asked the kids to stick with them for the rest of the semester.

When the university students announced that they were not backing down, the kids cheered them. It was an incredibly courageous act, but as Al Frost said to one of the university administrators, "Look into the future. Do you want these kids to feel that they are a part of the educational system of this state, or do you want them to feel like rejects—feel like outsiders?"

As usual the answer was, "I understand how you feel, but we have rules that must be followed." But although they occasionally called me in to discuss the situation, the university looked the other way.

It was an amazing semester. No more hassles from the university. Occasionally a television camera would show up, or a reporter from somewhere who wanted to do a human interest story, but for the most part the kids simply became part of the normal Monday, Wednesday, and Friday morning breakfast routine.

During that semester, we began to take kids with us when we traveled around the country fulfilling speaking engagements. They went for the ride and the sights. I recall one trip to Miami with Lester, Jeanie, Patrick, and Brenda Holderness; Chris and Diane Steckman; and Becky. Just before going to press with the first issue of the PDI, the American Correctional Association had called me and ordered a copy for everyone who was signed up to attend that year's convention in Miami Beach—well over 1,000 extra copies. I was to deliver them to Miami for distribution at the convention. I told the kids to inform their teachers and parents that they were going to Miami for a few days.

The preparation was hectic. Normally Becky and I packed enough food for two and hit the road. It was simple. With six children and Becky, it was more complicated. We packed the newspapers, then laid the sleeping bags over the newspapers. Each person was allowed one backpack, and we had eight sleeping bags. It was great just being with the kids and feeling their excitement.

We kept stops to a minimum. No soft drinks were allowed in the van while we were driving, and if anyone got road-sick they were to let me know immediately.

At a stop in North Carolina, the tourist places were selling beautiful multicolored rocks. I told everyone they could each buy one stone from the 50¢ bins. They looked at every stone in every 50¢ bin, and finally each had a souvenir. Two hundred miles down the road, it was so quiet in the van that I stopped to see what was going on. They were comparing stones—but not seven stones; they had twenty-five or thirty. I freaked and read them the riot act.

"What if you had been caught? We might have been hung up for hours getting it straightened out. And the humiliation would have been more than I could have dealt with," I said.

We were too far down the road to return the rocks and force the kids to go through that ordeal. They swore they would behave.

John Eastman learned that we were in town. He called a friend, Jim Montgomery, who had a public-relations firm, and suddenly these kids were looking out the top-floor window of the best beachfront hotel on Miami Beach. The phone lines to room service were hot. I didn't sleep for three days and nights; one night, Becky and Diane were missing until dawn and then had the nerve to walk into the hotel as though nothing had happened.

Drive a pseudo-father nuts.

We had three sensational days of swimming, sightseeing, visiting fine eating establishments, and counting cash that was being donated to help the kids have a good time. The money saved the day. As a result of interviews on radio and TV, people were coming to our hotel with contributions and invitations. Since the American Correctional Association said it would take a week or so to get the newspaper purchase processed, this gift money was all we had, and it got us back to 505. In the end, the ACA stiffed us on the price of the papers. No one was surprised.

I came to the conclusion that I could not travel with more than two kids at a time in the future.

Not long after our return, the university semester ended, and the university told the students they could have their grades if they agreed not to continue the program in the fall. The students met, discussed the offer, and rejected it. Talk about hard-assed, never-give-an-inch students.

In the end, the university relented. The students got their grades. Those who were seniors got their diplomas. Their looks of satisfaction at having successfully confronted the university were unforgettable.

Although it was a major victory, I had the feeling that one or more of the administrators had secretly supported the program, but had been entangled in the rules and regulations that had been in place for decades. Although they now were backing down, they didn't want students to view this breakfast program—this Oatmeal and Love—as a student victory. They also didn't want the television cameras and the newspaper reporters making heroes out of students who had sacrificed grades and graduation to feed some hungry young kids. So when they learned that we might hold a press conference, I was asked to try and discourage any news that would make the university look as though they had been "beaten." For the sake of those university administrators who were trying to help—and I later learned that Phil Hubbard had been the force that tilted the decision in favor of the students—the press conference was called off. I didn't have to mention anything to anyone, because the students did it all on their own—for which I was grateful.

The university was relieved when the term ended and the students left. They were doubly relieved that no one called a press conference to boast about the victory. After the confrontations that had taken place on campus after the Kent State murders the year before, the administration feared the PDI would attempt to use the breakfast program to our own advantage. In fact, we used the van to pick up and deliver students to breakfast and then to school, but early on I had stepped aside and let the students deal with the media. We were always there, but students like Al Cloud, who would move on from Iowa to work for Liberation News Service, the AP/UPI of the Vietnam era underground press, provided leadership that was so calm and laid-back we never had to step in throughout the crisis.

Law Section Attracts Jailhouse Lawyers; First PDI Generates First Subscribers

Meanwhile, the staff continued to expand. For six months, beginning in the middle of 1970, I worked hard with correctional officials and the legislators from Oklahoma to get Rex Fletcher paroled from prison. He had been in longer than was necessary. He didn't deny that prison was a just reward for armed robbery, or that his escape warranted an extension on his sentence. However, thirty-three years in the can was a bit much for a man in his fifties. He was writing and loving it. He had a job waiting for him in Iowa City, and enough politicians urging a positive response to our petition that the parole board had to give serious thought to releasing him. The State of Iowa had already agreed to accept him as a parole transfer.

Finally I was notified that Rex would be released on March 24, 1971. He came straight to Iowa City and the PDI.

A few weeks later, Wes Graham arrived from Leavenworth.

A couple of months after our two ex-prisoner editors were in place, we added our first "non-offender" to the staff—a junior high school English teacher, artist, and close friend of friends named Merilea Megletsch. (I'll drop her last name from here on as she has done, legally choosing to be known now only as Merilea, an artist living in Oakland; see figure 2). In a series of interesting events that all of us were grateful for because we desperately needed someone with an English degree, she left teaching, her marriage broke up, and she joined us at 505. She was pure sunshine (see sidebar 2).

SIDEBAR 2

THE SEA (by Merilea)

People have pivotal moments in their lives, and one of mine was about as good as you can ever get. It happened in 1971. I was caught in a wave of change in my personal life. My marriage was falling apart; I had quit my teaching job in Iowa City to try and keep it going, but that didn't work. I learned about the PDI collective through a neighbor who was dating one of its members. So I ended up on the shores of 505 South Lucas, setting course for a new direction in my life, living in a commune whose members were creating and publishing *Penal Digest International*, a newspaper focused on our prison system.

I was born in Chicago in 1944. I vividly remember riding the CTA in the early 1950s with my mother through the South Side of Chicago. The CTA tracks were built above street level, so riders were able to look down and witness events on the streets below. The train passed through a huge slum area. Even as a child, I was totally shocked at the filth and trash that people in ragged clothing waded through on their way to their destinations. It didn't take long for me to understand the stark relationship between poverty and crime, and that a nation that allows such intensive poverty is the real criminal.

In the sixties I went to college and majored in history, mostly European. History taught at that time was pretty much about the study of warfare, endless wars. What I learned was the criminality of all wars and how the ruling elite of the day used the common people to fight for them. So by the time I found myself at 505 South Lucas among people dedicated

FIGURE 2. Merilea, junior high school teacher and artist before becoming the "first non-offender" to join the PDI staff.

to bringing the reality of prison life from the voices of prisoners out into the open, I was pretty primed up.

My first experience of being near a prison occurred when I accompanied publisher Joe Grant and photographer Warren Levicoff to New York City, where Joe was going to be interviewed on a morning program. It was September 1971, and we arrived in New York City just in time to witness the tragedy unfolding at Attica Correctional Facility. Joe became actively involved in trying to avert a pending showdown between prisoners, who had taken some guards as hostages, and the prison rulers. Meanwhile, outside the prison walls, local people in pickup trucks were having a great time drinking beer and cheering on the prison guards like it was one great circus.

Upon returning to Iowa City, I was anxious to help in whatever capacity I could to get the paper ready to go. I also joined Kathy Dearden in preparing our meals. Our dinners were excellent, carefully planned and primarily vegetarian. During our evening meals, we sat around our large dining room table and shared our stories and thoughts. We had in-depth discussions on the prison system, the war in Vietnam, and life in America as it was at that time.

I developed deep respect for members of the commune. Brother Richard Tanner (a great poet), John Price, Bob Copeland, Kathy and her husband Warren, Randy Knoper, Rebecca Hensley, Joe, and others did much to influence the way I came to understand the criminal "no-justice" system. I especially cherished "Mr. James" Crawford and Becky Evans, two young teens so bright and full of fun. Two people who joined us later to work on the paper were Will Corrado and Walter Plunkette. Will in particular became involved with the Church of the New Song, visiting prisoners at Fort Madison and the boys' reformatory at Eldora, both prisons in Iowa. I came to deeply appreciate the men and women prisoners who provided us with articles and artwork for the paper. Despite being on the "inside," they were very much a part of the PDI commune and one of the reasons why the paper was so successful.

EYES WIDE OPEN

The following year I arranged to get an interview with Cook County Jail's warden Winston E. Moore. Randy and Will came along with me. Cook County Jail, which is located in Chicago, is a three-tiered structure that at the time was terribly overcrowded and viewed as one of the worst jails in the nation. Both Randy and I easily sensed the razor-sharp tension wafting through the tiers of cells. There were so many bars and doors, and doors of bars, that it looked like a Franz Kafka landscape from which no one could escape, a place where justice was a stranger. In the interview, Warden Moore told me that he felt the conditions there were as serious as Attica's, and that it wouldn't surprise him if an Attica-type riot broke out at any time. This was my first time deep inside a jail and it was a real eye shocker.

The warden showed Randy and me the view of the jail from his office. The jail was a holding pen for those too poor to make bail. The vast majority of inmates were black and poor. Many inmates spend years rotting away without being brought to a trial that will determine whether or not they are even guilty of the accusations made against them. As a result of that Cook County Jail experience and my memories of the filthy slums I saw as a child, I came to more clearly understand the thread tying poverty with the prison system.

CRIME PAYS BIG BUCKS BIG TIME

With voter passage of the notorious ballot-initiative "three strikes" law in 1993, California became the flagship for the development of the Prison Industrial Complex. The "three strikes" law mandates that courts impose life sentences, with no parole possible until usually twenty-five years, after third felony convictions. Since 2004, twenty-six states have enacted three-strikes laws, although none are as severe as California's.

As *Prison Nation* noted in 2005, the 1990s were the Golden Age for the Prison Industrial Complex, netting nearly $40 billion for corporations that designed, built, and serviced prisons.[1] In California, one company, the Corrections Corporation of America, realized a 31-fold increase in its contracts with the state in three years, from $23 million in 2006 to $700 million in 2009, "all without competitive bidding."[2]

And, of course, the two million prisoners in the United States are a source of cheap labor, bringing in money to states and corporations. Even our very own U.S. government receives military supplies manufactured in prisons. In 1995, Reese Erlich, a freelance reporter teaching journalism at California State University, Hayward, detailed the rise of the Prison Industrial Complex, and how governments and corporations profited from the growing prison industries. He explained how corporations and politicians subverted laws made in the early 1950s that protected laborers in the private sector from having to compete with prison labor.[3] With the development of privately built and operated prisons, prison industries boomed during the 1980s and 1990s, amassing huge profits by using cheap, exploited prison labor and tax breaks from state governments. Unions such as the AFL-CIO and UAW are now struggling to regain the protection they once had.

LOCKIN' IT DOWN: NEO CON CAPITALIST SLAMS

The National Correctional Industries Association, Inc. (NCIA), formed over sixty years ago, is a major lobby for the Prison Industrial Complex. One of their main goals is to ensure the continuation and expansion of prison industries, in part by lobbying legislators to ensure that prison laborers do not receive minimum wage or legal entitlement to be viewed as employees: "It is important that it be made clear that Congress did not intend inmates to be considered employees under the Fair Labor Standards Act; and it is essential to terminate the numerous and costly lawsuits filed by inmates."[4]

VOICES

In the spirit of historian Howard Zinn's book *A People's History of the United States*, the PDI was the first national publication founded by an ex-con to provide a platform through which prisoners could share their plight with each other, their families, friends, and people concerned about the deplorable conditions of the prison system. The paper circulated in hundreds of state and federal prisons, as well as libraries throughout the United States. In his book, Zinn chronicles the riots and revolts that have occurred within the prison system going back to the 1920s. He describes the momentum building for revolt through the 1950s and 1960s and culminating in the Attica rebellion. He notes how extremely difficult it has always been for prisoners to receive letters from, or send them to, family, friends, and lawyers.[5]

For its brief time in history, the PDI made it a little less difficult.

NOTES

1. Http://www.november.org/stayinfo/breaking3/NWOM.html.
2. Http://www.capitolweekly.net/article.php?xid=yl82yoctf9d1au.
3. Reese Erlich, "Prison Labor: Workin' for the Man." http://www.prop1.org/legal/prisons/labor.htm.
4. NCIA Resolution: Fair Labor Standards Act. http://www.nationalcia.org/?page_id=67; Al Jazeera. http://english.aljazeera.net/indepth/opinion/2011/04/201142612714539672.html. It is no surprise that William Andrews, the CEO of the Corrections Corporation of America (CCA), the largest private U.S. contractor for immigrant detention centers, declared in 2008 that "The demand for our facilities and services could be adversely affected by the relaxation of enforcement efforts . . . or through decriminalization [of immigrants]." Nor is it any surprise that CCA and other corporations have financed the spate of neofascist, anti-immigrant legislation in Arizona and other U.S. states.
5. Howard Zinn, *A People's History of the United States, 1492–Present* (New York: HarperCollins Publishers, 2003).

By now, our first issue was almost ready to print; morale was high, and we were attracting more and more prison writers and artists.

One of the slickest check-passing artists I'd heard of wrote a wonderful article, "CHECK-MATE: The Trade Secrets of a Professional Check Passer." Some of the ex-cons on the staff didn't like it—they thought we were giving away trade secrets.

I had some photographs by John Ricardo, a prisoner from the Florida State Penitentiary who had taught himself photography while doing time. One dramatic photo we turned into a poster that we used as the center spread in the first 24-page section. It showed the electric chair at Raiford, Florida, with the caption "You think speed kills . . ."

Our entire staff participated in an all-day seminar on prisons and corrections at Scattergood, a Quaker school east of Iowa City. Artist Phyllis Lehrman photographed the day's activities for a feature in the second issue. Media coverage of the activities gave us more press. Everyone fell in love with Phyllis.

With the addition of a law section, the best writers in the system—the jailhouse lawyers—began to get involved. The law section in the first issue made public an important ruling: The Arkansas prison system was in such terrible shape that a federal district court judge, J. Smith Henley, had declared it unconstitutional to sentence people to prison there. Of course, the state was given time to make changes, but the decision was an important one that would help us later.

The law section also included another decision that concerned a black man who had been arrested for armed robbery in Cedar Rapids. The man had never before committed a crime. His record was absolutely clean. Further, even though armed robbery by a black man normally meant that he would go to prison for a minimum of ten years, in front of district court judge Ansel Chapman, the accused admitted that he had committed the robbery. An exhaustive pre-sentence investigation report followed. In the end, because the circumstances surrounding the case were so unusual, and despite the severe criticism he knew he would come under from the news media, Judge Chapman gave the man a suspended sentence and placed him on probation. The judge made the right decision. The man never committed another crime. It took a judge with incredible courage to do what Chapman did. Iowa wasn't easy on him, but he weathered that storm.

To ensure that there was no opposition to the PDI when we sent it to carefully selected prisoners, we added a third story to the front page: "Why should any inmate or ex-offender be interested in a college education?" by board member Dr. Magoroh Maruyama.

Jackie Blank, an Iowa City friend, approached me one day and handed me a note. "I think this describes what you are doing better than anything I've read," she said. On the slip of paper was written, "Our life's mission is to be impatient—to push social progress a little faster than it is prepared to go." We placed it on the front page of the newspaper above the title and went to press in June 1971.

It had taken us a year and a half to publish this 72-page tabloid that no one seemed to be interested in. Regardless, we were a nonprofit corporation, we had tax-exempt status, and I was confident that we were going to rock some boats.

Our staff had grown, too. Board member Myra "Mickey" Mezvinsky was taking more time off from the demands of her busy family life to sort through folders of poetry; board member

Bill McDonald was helping us turn our headquarters at 505 South Lucas into a halfway house for recently paroled men, women, and children. To the best of our knowledge, it was the first of its kind. Paul D. Burian, an incredibly resourceful jack-of-all-trades from Westinghouse Learning Corporation and a good friend of John Clark, joined the board of directors.

Within a couple of weeks, subscriptions began coming in from law professors, senators and representatives, prisoners, and libraries. Meeting the expenses of printing on a regular basis suddenly became feasible.

On a trip to New York City, I met with directors of the Famous Artists School, whose home-study courses seemed to be in great demand but were too expensive for prisoners to afford. The directors agreed to donate to the PDI $300,000 worth of art and writing scholarships for us to award to prisoners. In retrospect, I believe that when they agreed to donate the scholarship money, they already knew they were going to declare bankruptcy, but they made the offer anyhow to get good publicity for themselves. As it turned out, the school declared bankruptcy in less than six months, and the prisoners got zip.

A young woman showed up one day with a story that she wanted us to publish. She and her husband had been so jacked around by the correctional system in Iowa that she wanted to share their experience. Although her story was typical, we felt that her ability as a writer would inspire others. "The Guilty and the Fumbling" shared the front page with a story that came up the day before we were going to press with our July 1971 issue.

PDI Stops Extradition of Arkansas Escapee

That second story involved a prisoner who had been picked up in Cedar Rapids after escaping from Tucker Prison Farm in Arkansas. I read in the *Cedar Rapids Gazette* that he had waived extradition. He obviously had not read the first issue of the PDI, I thought.

I rushed to Cedar Rapids and drove directly to the Linn County jail. No one was inclined to do me any favors, so I asked to visit the escapee from Arkansas to do a story on prisons down there. They agreed, but they wouldn't let me bring my tape recorder into the jail. They wouldn't even let me have my notebook. Nothing. Zip. I left all my material in my van, but as I started in I said, "Hell, let me take them a copy of our newspaper. I'll just leave it inside."

The guard said, "Okay."

Roy Daniel Childers was called out. He had no idea who I was or why I was there. I didn't waste any time.

"Why did you waive extradition and agree to go back to Tucker?" I asked him.

"What else could I do? I have no money. No lawyer. Nothing."

"Do you want to go back?" I asked.

"Are you nuts? It's crazy down there. I'm going to end up doing heavy time for running."

I introduced myself and showed him a copy of the first issue of the PDI. I explained why I thought he should not go back to Tucker Farm. Then I told him that I had an attorney who was willing to take his case, and money to pay the attorney. I didn't have either. What I did have was a decision from federal district court judge J. Smith Henley, stating unequivocally that serving a prison sentence at Tucker or Cummins Farm in Arkansas constituted cruel and unusual punishment.

I told him I would have an attorney working on this first thing Monday morning.

"No good," Roy told me. "I'm being picked up at 6 A.M. by Arkansas deputies and taken back to Tucker."

There was no time for lawyers; I had to go directly to a judge. With a black marker I turned the front page of the PDI into a legal brief:

9:20 A.M. 7/31/71. I, Roy Daniel Childers, wish to state publicly that I retract my waiver of extradition to Arkansas on the following grounds: (1) that I was not represented by counsel during my hearing in Judge Maxwell's court on or about July 29th, and that, whether or not I have a right to counsel, I was ignorant of the court decisions that have ruled that imprisonment in Tucker or Cummins prison constitutes cruel and unusual punishment; (2) that I was forced to be a trustee at Tucker which is a violation of J. Smith Henley's U.S. Dist. Ct. decision of Feb 18, 1970; (3) that returning me to either Tucker or Cummins prison will constitute sentencing me to death either at the hands of inmates, or the hands of trustees, or the hands of guards. Let it be known that I wish to appear before Judge Maxwell, or any Dist. Ct. Judge in Linn County on Monday morning, or before, with my attorney Joseph Johnston, of Iowa City, Ia., and (4) I, Roy Daniel Childers, refuse to return to Arkansas and will fight extradition.

It was signed by Roy and witnessed by me. I told him I would do my best to get to a judge.

I called Judge William R. Eads from the pay phone at the jail. He was home and agreed to see me. He issued the following order:

In the matter of the
Extradition of
Roy Daniel Childers

The sheriff of Linn County, Iowa is hereby ordered to not release Roy Daniel Childers to the State of Arkansas, or any legal representative or law enforcement officer thereof, until the matter of the waiver of extradition is set for hearing.

The court shall issue further orders to the Linn County Sheriff subsequent to the time and date of hearing concerning the extradition of Roy Daniel Childers.

Signed, William R. Eads, Judge, 8th Judicial District of Iowa
1:28 P.M. July 31, 1971

The next morning, the deputies from Arkansas were turned away from the jail.

Later that day, Roy's wife called me and we discussed options. I decided to appeal to the judge at the hearing and request that Roy be released on bond. I was advised by lawyers that there were no provisions to allow bond for escaped prisoners. "Face it, Joe, he's already proven to the world that he runs. No one will put up the money. The risk is too great."

I answered, "Let's get him released on his own recognizance." And we did, with help from Joe Johnston. Johnston was the young attorney who had helped me form PHASE IV, our nonprofit, tax-exempt corporation, when I was first laying plans to begin the PDI. Now he came to our aid again. He was incredible. Not only did he stop extradition, he asked that Roy be released on bond. This was unheard of unless the bond was so high that the courts were absolutely assured that he wouldn't run again. But Johnston was eloquent. Not only was Roy released, he was released on his own recognizance—just his and our collective promises that he would stay for whatever was coming up.

The news media picked up the case at once. It was a compelling story: an escaped prisoner, a wife, twin daughters who were seven or eight. Great kids. With signs in their hands that said, "FREE MY DADDY," they captivated the press photographers.

By the time the second issue went to press, we were sending out subscriptions as fast as we could process them. Every time I would check the fast-increasing numbers, I'd catch Becky glancing over at me with a sly grin on her face. Many a time over lunch or dinner, or on the road, we would recall the time we stayed up all night filling out return mailers so it appeared that more than seven people wanted to see the PDI. In this bio of the PDI, I'm sharing this secret for the first time.

Once, many years later, I asked Becky if she had ever mentioned it to anyone. She was bouncing Anna, her beautiful little baby girl, on her knee. She flashed that quiet smile at me and said, "I ain't no snitch."

Success Was Killing Us

With subscriptions skyrocketing, we should have been coasting—but we weren't. The more we received, the more we struggled, because on most we were losing money. The vast majority were from prisoners, who were allowed to subscribe for a dollar down and the rest when they could afford it. Exactly what we had hoped for was now happening, with one exception—we couldn't make it on one dollar per subscription. Or, in the case of prisons where there were no jobs, and consequently no pay, 25 cents for a year's subscription. Each issue we mailed to those subscribers cost us at a minimum the price of postage. In addition, many prisoners who had no money got the paper for free. Fortunately, a large number of supporters began sending in an extra dollar apiece with their own subscriptions to help us out.

We learned that the average number of prisoners who read an issue of the PDI was twelve. Groups were subscribing. The first person would write the names of all the participants on the front page. As each section was finished, it was passed on. By the time the last prisoner was looking at an issue, the next issue would be arriving.

In the second issue, which came out in July 1971, letters to the editor increased in number. The first was from a young conscientious objector from Florida. Robert was more qualified to be running a newspaper than any of us at the PDI. He came from a newspaper family. I think his dad was the editor of a newspaper in Florida. I contacted Bob's draft board and they agreed that he could do alternative service working with the PDI. No other person was to have a greater influence on the development of the PDI into a respected international journal (see sidebar 3 and figure 3).

FIGURE 3. Bob Copeland (*left*), first CO (conscientious objector) to do alternative service with the PDI. From Florida, Bob brought experience as a writer, editor, and all-around everyman when it came to running a newspaper. Merilea (*right*) brought art and high energy to the PDI.

FIGURE 4. PDI cartoon by Bob Copeland: *Hippie Out of Step with the Troops*. Courtesy of PDI Archives.

DRAFTED INTO SERVICE AT THE PDI (by Bob Copeland)

I was drafted into service at PDI, but if Uncle Sam's left hand had known that his right hand had put me there, I would have been moved quickly to a VA hospital and handed a bedpan to clean. I know I contributed more to the greater good at PDI.

As a college junior at Lake Forest (Illinois) College in 1970, I was disgusted by the lies from Washington, the carnage in Southeast Asia, the violence and poverty and racism in American towns and cities. My worldview and plans for my future were radicalized by the ferment of the times. They peaked with the U.S. invasion of Cambodia, the killings at Kent State and Jackson State, and the ensuing turmoil on campuses across the nation. I vowed then to forsake careerism upon graduation, and to find an honest organization through which I could work for peace and social change.

One month before leaving college, I mailed my Florida draft board my claim for conscientious objector status. Shortly after my induction physical that summer, I was amazed to learn that Selective Service had approved my petition on first reading. I was classified as a C.O. and required to perform two years of alternative service.

One afternoon that summer, my father brought home from the newspaper office where he worked a copy of a prison newspaper from McAlester, Oklahoma. I read with interest a back-page ad for the *Penal Digest International*, a slick monthly published in the country's first ex-convict-owned and operated halfway house in Iowa City, Iowa. I thought it seemed the perfect opportunity to apply my journalism experience and revolutionary impulses while working for social and personal changes.

I wrote PDI, and Joe Grant responded by welcoming me to join them. Again I was amazed when my draft board assigned me to Iowa City for my service stint. Selective Service would have been more amazed had they foreseen all that my work at PDI would entail.

From the moment the door at 505 South Lucas Street opened to me, I felt both at home and swept up in a tide of heroic effort, high hopes, and boundless collective energy—pushing, pushing for change, with the dark unknown always lurking around the corner, at the edges, and under the surface.

The living was communal, vibrant, and in constant flux. A core group of people worked nearly round the clock to get out the PDI and maintain its links with prisoners around the world. Other workers came and went. Cross-country travelers stopped by for a night or several months. We were a rainbow of personalities: ex-prisoners fresh from the joint, college professors, teenage runaways, artists, aging alcoholic vagabonds, writers, fugitives, do-gooders, lawyers, con men, and musicians.

Money always was too tight to mention, but we lived well. We took care of each other, ate together, shared dreams and fears, clothes and beds, hopes and shortcomings. We were a family constantly redefining ourselves, our circumstances, and our destination. Personal growth in such a setting was guaranteed.

Then there was the mail. The letters, letters, letters kept our kaleidoscopic free-world lives rooted in the shadows of a separate reality—the prisons of the world. The mail came in torrents, outpourings of hope and rage and suffering and great creativity. Prisoners sensed that our family was open to them, that our founders saw with their eyes, that our voice was intended to be theirs.

We received eloquent poetry, astute legal analyses from jailhouse lawyers, cartoons and drawings, news reports, humor columns, helpful critiques of our own efforts, and harrowing accounts of brutality and injustice behind the walls. The latter were far too numerous, and they kept coming, insinuating their painful details into our psyches, galvanizing our allegiance to our constituents, strengthening our determination to make their plight known, to effect some change in their conditions.

We corresponded with thousands, and we were changed deeply by the exchanges. Talk of prison reforms gave way to essays on abolition. We became *Prisoners' Digest International.* Our editorials took on a sharper edge. Issues of PDI continued to be banned at certain institutions, and we were denied personal access to a growing number of prisons. Friction with local authorities increased. One night we awoke to waving flashlights and cops walking through our house looking for a fugitive their teletype said might stop by our house. Outside, other officers waited, guns drawn.

We saw the American prison as a microcosm of the whole society. In the dynamics of the relationship between keeper and kept were crystallized potent truths about power and poverty, right and wrong, privilege and prejudice, fear and forgiveness in our culture. Ultimately the fundamental questions were spiritual, which led us into alliance with a group of federal prisoners who had forged their own religion, a vision of truth and unity called the Church of the New Song. Once judicially recognized as protected under the Constitution, New Song spread quickly through federal and state prison systems. We assisted the process and became ministers ourselves, finally gaining personal access to the people we had been serving from outside the walls.

I stayed at PDI beyond my required tour of duty because the work and the people had become part of me. We truly believed in the power of nonviolent conflict resolution to create a new approach to criminal justice. We devoted all our energies to living our convictions, and we changed many lives.

When I left PDI, it was to serve as New Song resident minister for the men in the Iowa State Penitentiary. Ultimately, I burned out. What I read of prisoners today is dishearteningly familiar, even more frightening than the horrors we faced decades ago. I hope that those who are working for change there today have access to back copies of the PDI. I know there is enough truth and inspiration in those pages to be of help for generations.

We also had letters from congressmen John Culver and Fred Schwengle; law professor Herman Schwartz (whom we would next see at Attica Prison during the riots, when so many prisoners were murdered); Celeste West of the San Francisco Public Library; Dr. Karl Menninger; Reverend Walter Kellison (whose daughter was one of the university students who helped make the breakfast program a success); and many prisoners.

We were also beginning to hear from political prisoners. Political prisoners were, for the most part, extremely radical. They condemned the prison administrations, advocated the use of force to gain equity, and used such forceful language that in order to avoid the label of "dangerous troublemaker," I had to edit out of their letters any comments about "prisoners rising up" or "prisoners organizing to take control of their lives." Two or three subscribers in the New York prison at Attica were killed when the National Guard stormed the prison. Sam Melville (1934–September 13, 1971) was a prolific letter writer. Citing his opposition to the Vietnam War and American imperialism, Sam was the principal bomb setter in the 1969 bombings of eight government and commercial office buildings in New York City. We were unable to publish his letters—much too radical. Sam's letters would have stopped the distribution of PDIs to most of the prisons. He was a serious radical who advocated violent change. We could not include letters that advocated violence. He started an underground newspaper inside the walls of Attica called *The Iced Pig.* He didn't mince words.

Correspondents joined us from prisons in South Carolina (Gary Addis), San Quentin (John Severenson Watson and Donald Chenault), Wisconsin (S. L. Poulter and Bruce Brandi), Minnesota (Jim Bosley), Virginia (James Williams), Florida (Thomas Winberry), Illinois (Harold Sampson and Dean Hill), Missouri (Earl Guy), and Iowa (Barry McDaniel). Other outstanding writers were taking their places as regulars, including Tom Puchalski (New Jersey State Pen) and Gordy Peterson (Minnesota State Pen).

The Mad Writer from Cell 1616 in San Luis Obispo, James Ralph Williamson, was back again in issue 2 and would continue with the PDI until its demise. I will never forgive the California correctional officials who refused to allow me to visit this remarkable writer and full-time character.

Cartoon panels by an old friend from Leavenworth were back in issue 2 also. "The Concrete Bungle," by Drummond, never failed to entertain.

Stanley Eldridge, from behind the walls of Indiana State Penitentiary, was emerging as an important American poet. His poem "A Tear for Darryl" had University of Iowa Poetry Workshop students hanging around the office reading from the ever-growing pile of poems arriving from prisons around the world.

One complete 24-page section devoted to the Florida prison system was powerful. Written by reporters from the *St. Petersburg Times*, it allowed the voices of prisoners to be heard when few newspapers were listening to prisoners. The series (actually a tabloid section) was probably a circulation builder for them, but it was a sincere attempt to bring change to the prisons of Florida. We picked it up because it was the kind of coverage that appealed to the people in the free world. Wes Graham laid out that section using barbed wire running on, in, and through each page of the section to give it a sense of prison. Unfortunately the barbed wire didn't work. The 24-page section looked like it had come out of a freshman high school class.

We were learning.

The law section of the July 1971 issue provided prisoners with information about the *Palmigiano v. Travisono et al.* (317 F.Supp. 776 [1970]) case. Thomas Ross, assistant editor of *The Challenge,* Adult Correctional Institution, Rhode Island, provided insights and analysis of the case that was pending in the United States District Court for the District of Rhode Island.

In that case, U.S. District Court Judge Pettine, in a 43-page opinion, ordered that prison officials "shall not open or otherwise inspect the contents of any incoming or outgoing letters" between a long list of specified individuals, embracing federal and state officials, court officers, and Rhode Island attorneys. The temporary order also stated that mail inspected for contraband could not be read, and that letters to approved correspondents from prisoners could not be opened and inspected. The order was to stand until a three-judge panel could meet in October for a trial.

Also in the Law Section, Richard G. Singer provided a lengthy article entitled "Censorship of Prisoners' Mail and the Constitution." The article included thirty-one footnotes of cases supporting Singer's views that censorship of mail is dehumanizing, demeaning, unconstitutional, and unnecessary. He closed his article with a thought we all hoped was true: "Prison reform is in the air. Let us hope the humanizing breath will invigorate us all." I also felt that reform was in the air. Unfortunately, the reform never happened. Programs would start, but would be stopped before being given the necessary time to work. Sit down with any correctional officials and they will swear to you that they have tried everything and nothing worked. The facts are that no rehabilitation programs have ever been adequately funded and given time to work.

As I page through back issues of the PDI, reading the articles, remembering the authors, I am struck by the number of contributors I met in the living room of the house where the flag flew upside down, signaling a nation in distress. In this house, I was able to hold meetings when more people were involved than I could fit into my one small room. Here, my friends from the women's prison rested in a manner to which they were most assuredly not accustomed. Frequently I found myself being introduced to people who became significant contributors to the PDI.

One such individual was a young assistant law professor from the University of Iowa. Phillip J. Mause was able to listen to a legal problem and, without moving from his chair, provide endless citations, analyses, and sound opinions.

In our July issue, Mause reviewed two books: *Criminal Law: Cases, Comment, Questions* and *Criminal Process: Cases, Comment, Questions*, by Lloyd L. Weinreb, professor of law, Harvard University. Mause's comments eloquently enabled jailhouse lawyers to better grasp and use the legal tools that Weinreb discussed. Again, the use of footnotes provided prisoners with the roadmaps so frequently denied them in prison—citations and explanations of cases and how they related to points of law. In the end, however, Mause took the books and the law schools to task, pointing out, "Our historic failure to ask and answer . . . basic questions in the law schools has contributed significantly to the current breakdown of our criminal justice system."

Around the time our July issue appeared, *The David Susskind Show* featured a group of ex-prisoners who were working with the Fortune Society, a New York City–based prisoner-support organization that took its name from a play, *Fortune in Men's Eyes*—a graphic description of life inside a maximum security prison. Mel Rivers, Danny Keane, Prentice Williams, Chuck Berganski, George Freeman, and Stan Telega discussed the horrors of prison, and the incredible difficulties faced by ex-prisoners when they were released. The show was originally seen in the New York area, but it was subsequently seen in many parts of the country. Repeated calls to local television stations finally got Iowa a showing of the program. David Rothenberg was the steady, hard-working force behind the success of the Fortune Society. Years later, he would run for a New York city council seat and be narrowly defeated. David's was one of the few political campaigns I personally contributed to. He is a remarkable person who has done a great deal of good for prisoners and ex-prisoners. The Fortune Society, staffed primarily by ex-offenders, is a not-for-profit community-based organization dedicated to educating the public about prisons and criminal justice.

The Kids and the Cons

Rex Fletcher was paroled from prison in Oklahoma in March 1972 and came to live with us as a PDI coeditor. Unfortunately, he was only with us for a few short months. During those months he had a difficult time adjusting to life outside prison. Rex was older than most of us, in his early fifties. He had been locked up a long time—thirty-three years, to be exact. As a young man, according to what I heard, he had been involved in armed robberies. I never questioned people about past crimes, but I knew that he had never killed anyone, nor had he ever harmed any women or children.

Before he arrived, I told my little pal Patrick Holderness (age five or six) and his older brother Lester (ten or eleven) that Rex was coming to Iowa City and he needed a couple of friends more than even he realized. He's got a temper, I said, maybe drinks more than he should, when drinking anything at all could get him sent back to prison, and he tended to believe, like a lot of people, both young and old, that we should go forward and win the war in Vietnam. He thinks pot smokers should be disciplined, and he has great respect for the American flag.

Lester and Patrick sat there looking at me, waiting for more information. I was describing a man who sounded strange to these kids.

Lester said, "Dammit, next thing you'll tell us he drinks Coke."

What can I say about Lester Holderness? Lester was different from most of the kids his age. All the kids who hung around 505 were a little unusual, but Lester was extreme. At the time, we were boycotting Coca Cola products. None of our friends were drinking Coke, particularly the kids. If he saw anyone with a Coke, he would start his rap. I was always reminding him to watch his language. Lester's language when he was upset could embarrass a crew of laborers waiting for work at the union hall. After he learned about the boycott, he went to one of the supermarkets in town and asked to see the manager. When the manager came to the front of the store, Lester asked him why he had all that Coke on the shelf when there was a boycott. The manager told him to run along. Lester raised his voice to about twice its normal decibel level and asked him again. Now some customers had stopped and were listening. The manager told him he wasn't interested in any boycott. Lester was appalled. He started to leave, but about halfway to the door he turned around and said, "You oughta be ashamed of yourself!" He stood there for a moment thinking of what else he could say and obviously could think of nothing, so he simply yelled, "GODDAMMIT!" and stormed out. One of the cashiers told me about it. My kind of kid.

Years later, whenever I bumped into Lester I would jokingly ask him if he wanted something to drink. "Maybe a Coke, Lester?" I'd ask. He'd look at me and say, "I do not drink Coke, Joe."

Lester was a good kid. All his little brother Patrick wanted in life was to be with him.

"Damn kids," Lester would say.

Rex Fletcher needed help to stay out of trouble. Plus, he was a good guy—generous, loved to go swimming, liked to work out. He was a tough guy who took care of himself.

The kids were looking forward to his arrival. When he arrived, it was late at night. We hadn't moved into 505 yet. Joe Johnston, the lawyer who had agreed to take Roy Childers's case, had recently bought a house that he didn't plan to occupy for three or four months, so he was letting us stay there. In those days, one typesetting unit punched the tape. Then the tape was fed into the unit that set the type. Work went on all the time. Some of our typesetting equipment was in the den along with a massive pile of punched paper tape that went with it. Other equipment was scattered around town. With more people arriving to work on the PDI, we needed more space. Joe Johnston's house was a comfortable temporary residence. "I'm living high as an Oklahoma hog," Rex would say.

We showed Rex around the office and took him for a walk around town. We all loved Iowa City and he sensed it. I told Rex that he could start work as soon as he felt ready. I explained that he had two jobs: helping me with a couple of young kids who needed a friend, and relaxing and getting used to life in Iowa City.

Rex received what was to him a strange welcome in Iowa City. In the afternoon he would take a walk and stop in some of the working-class taverns in Iowa City. There he'd meet some of the good old boys, and everything would be fine until the good-old-boy conversations got around to his past and they realized who he was: a dude who had spent thirty-three years behind bars. They were looking at an older guy who was athletic, articulate, and obviously independent. They wanted no part of that potential scene. So the older, working-class conservatives Rex could relate to didn't want anything to do with him. The hippies, the freaks, the peaceniks, and the antiwar activists, on the other hand, were in love with Rex. He had spent more time in a cell than they had on earth. He was a handsome old guy, in great physical shape, and clean. The young women admired him. Some even made serious moves on him. He was uncomfortable in the presence of women who joked about sex or discussed personal relations openly. His politics and sympathies were difficult for people to take in, but they knew his history, understood why he was a conservative, and were forgiving. Rex, on the other hand, was not as forgiving. He thought the hippies and Yippies were un-American. The flag was important to him. He was uncomfortable with them; unfortunately, after he moved into 505 he was surrounded by them.

Every afternoon Rex would go to the Iowa City Recreation Center for a swim. Patrick never missed that trip, even though he couldn't swim. He would flail and fight and churn his way around the shallow end for a few yards as if he had 25 pounds of rocks jammed in his bathing suit. Then he would call to Rex. Rex would swim over to Patrick, Patrick would grab hold around Rex's neck, and Rex would start to swim laps, back and forth, never tiring, for thirty minutes or more. Patrick loved it and so did Rex.

Rex never had a family. Suddenly there were kids who depended on him. Coworkers, who were more family than employees, were around day and night. The large meal gatherings were more festive than crowded, and people worried if you were gone longer than expected.

Walking home late one night, I saw Lester hanging around outside a tavern on the edge of downtown.

"What are you doing up this late, Lester?" I asked.

"Waitin' for Rex."

"Does he know you're out here?"

"I dunno."

I went in. Rex was sitting by himself at the bar. I walked over and ordered a beer. Small talk. He was lonesome. Finally I said, "I'm worried about Lester. It's a school night and I just saw him up the street."

Rex looked worried. "Lester? Downtown at this time of night? Drink up. Let's find out if something's wrong."

And out we went. Lester was checking the coin-return slots on a bank of pay phones.

"Hey, Partner!" Rex called. "What gives?"

"I dunno," Lester responded with a shrug. And we all walked home together. That happened more than once.

But the most serious problem was that the people Rex admired and wanted to be with rejected him, while the people he rejected or wasn't fond of being around loved him. The hippies and the antiwar activists were kind, considerate, generous, friendly. These "outlaws" would gather at 505 for dinner, and Rex was the senior member of the group. He was gracious and had wonderful stories. But Rex wanted to be telling the stories to his peers, to the "good old boys" at the taverns where the older workers hung out, and they didn't want to listen.

Frequently, Rex would find himself one-on-one with one of these young radicals, and his discomfort would show. On one level he was the equal of young and old; unfortunately, thirty-three years in the can had robbed him of exposure to social, political, and cultural changes that these young activists had grown up with, and that were part of us at the PDI. In fact the word "collective" even caused him to scrunch up his face in deep thought as he pondered how to respond to a young man's questions.

Watching the two of them was like living in two different worlds simultaneously. Rex, with a clean white T-shirt and slacks, his shoes clean and polished, always appeared to be fresh from a barber's chair and in great shape physically. The young man wore torn jeans and a ragged T-shirt as he kicked back, bare feet on an old coffee table, hair down to his waist, smoking a joint. Rather dramatic cultural chiaroscuro.

Somewhere along the line, things got distorted. Rex had been too long in prison. He may have been a robber, but he was a patriotic American. The flag was an important symbol of his love of country. It was a symbol that many of the people who were in and out of 505 had little time for. Life was out of balance for Rex: "*Koyaanisqatsi*," as the Hopi say, and as Philip Glass described so eloquently in his music for the film of the same name. When Rex arrived in Iowa City, he was already in an emotional spin from his sudden change of lifestyle. He had read nothing to prepare himself for what he was walking into. His magazine of choice had been *Playboy*. If we had known, we might have been able to find him a few issues of *off our backs*, *The Progressive*, and a few other publications of the Left.

Then we were notified that Rex would have to return to Oklahoma because of a paperwork mix-up. We had lobbied everyone from the federal office holders right down to the warden for Rex, and we were successful; but the paperwork had been pushed through too fast. Rex was convinced they were going to revoke the parole approval and never release him. He discussed taking off. His voice was edged with panic. Rex couldn't sit down and relax. He paced the office, the dining room, the streets. He was like a leopard that was cornered and was looking for a way to avoid the net.

Making a run for it meant he would have to leave the country. "I don't think I can go back," he told me. He had spent too much time in the can already. The thought of going back was more than Rex could deal with.

I sat with Rex and listened to him as he mulled over the choices of the Oklahoma State Penitentiary or a boat to Jamaica, where the extradition situation was fair. I had close friends down there and had occasionally thought of making the move myself, though I never did. There's too much of the North Country in my soul.

Rex asked, "If I run, what will it do to the PDI, Joe?"

"It would be a great feature. We'd defend you and get you a pardon."

Rex laughed and said, "A pardon? How would you do that?"

"I figure if we could get you released, we can do anything." Rex liked hearing that.

"The PDI will be dead in Oklahoma," he said.

"Is, not 'will be,'" I answered.

I called the governor, the warden, and parole board members; everyone reassured me that it was a technicality that would be worked out.

Rex was skeptical, and he knew I had been lied to before.

But running was so serious that I made Rex an offer. I promised him that if the State of Oklahoma revoked the approved parole, I would come to the prison and not leave the front gate until they gave Rex back to us. He was family, and he believed. Rex headed back.

When we next heard from Oklahoma, the news was good. Rex had returned calmly. He just walked into the front office of the state penitentiary and sat down to wait. He was soon back in his cell at night, and in the prison newspaper office during the day. Support for Rex poured in from all over the state and the country. He was back in the slam because of red-tape "screw-ups." It was as simple as that. After a few weeks, he was back on the street and on his way to Iowa City.

The reunion was special for all of us, but mostly for the kids. Unfortunately, the same problem persisted: Rex was lost in the middle ground of two opposing political forces, unable to accept the New Radical Left, whose membership wanted him as a friend, and not accepted by the conservative Right, whose friendship he wanted. After a few weeks, Rex started to miss Oklahoma and his friends down there who shared his politics and accepted his past transgressions.

He finally reached a point where he had to go home for a few days.

One day, a woman drove up from Oklahoma to see Rex. She was an antiques dealer and absolutely striking—short, solid, an Oklahoma Indian who drove her pickup and camper around the country buying collectibles. She and Rex had been corresponding for many years, and when she arrived, we could see that much more than simple friendship was involved here. When they left for Oklahoma, I realized Rex might be on a path that would take him away from the PDI. I wished them the best, assured Rex that this was his home, and told them to be cool. He said they would be back in a week or so, and I think that was their plan. Then they were gone.

If he had applied for permission, the State of Iowa would have let him make the trip, but the process would have taken a few weeks, and Rex was feeling desperate. He had to "go home or go nuts," as he put it.

On the way, they had a minor accident. While checking the car, the police found some guns. The fact that they were civil war relics cleared Rex of a serious possession of firearms charge, but not of the charge of violation of parole. He had some blind spots; we all do. The antiques dealer was once again on the outside waiting for Rex, just as she had been since first reading his columns in the Oklahoma state prison newspaper years earlier.

It was painful watching Rex withdraw into himself over those few months. He was surrounded by friends; he appreciated everything that was happening to him; but his free-world dream wasn't being fulfilled at 505.

I know Rex went back asking himself, "What's the sense of trying?" There were times during those PDI years when I asked myself the same question.

National Lawyers Guild: "Give the Prisoners Their PDIs"

Bad news was arriving from around the country. Some prisoners had been denied the first issue of the PDI despite our efforts to not be seen as "troublemakers." Others were contacting us to say that their wardens were not allowing them to draw money out of their accounts to subscribe to the PDI. Some prisons quickly passed a new rule: You couldn't draw just one dollar out of your account.

Our lawyers went to work at once. National Lawyers Guild attorneys in the cities closest to the offending prisons were contacted. They were in the offices of the wardens the next morning. We had discussed how we wanted them to deal with the wardens. First, they were to find out exactly which articles in the PDI the wardens objected to. Second, they were to have copies of the PDI with them so they could read the objectionable articles.

Invariably the wardens were concerned about some innocuous statement or article they had taken out of context, or something they had been told that turned out to be untrue. Talking about their concerns and looking at a copy of the PDI sometimes was enough to make them change their minds. If they had arbitrarily decided to keep the newspaper out because it was published by an ex-prisoner, they quickly were told what was going to happen if they persisted. No warden relished the idea of the news media following the likes of William Kunstler or Stan Bass or our other heavy hitters into his office bright and early some Monday morning. Looking back, I believe I might have been able to print everything, even pieces by Sam Melville and other political prisoners, if I had used this threat every time there was a complaint by a warden.

Some prisons were set so far back from civilization's road that names like Kunstler and Bass didn't mean anything to them. The administrators of the Florida State Pen at Raiford epitomized this group. Gene Jones was removed from his job as editor of the *Raiford (Florida) Record* because he was determined to write an article for the PDI. Lawyers were notified, and they in turn notified Gene that he would have whatever counsel he needed—counsel to defend him, and counsel to ensure that retaliation by prison administrators against PDI contributors was stopped immediately wherever it happened.

The warden at Statesville Prison in Illinois looked me in the eye and told me the PDI was too radical to be allowed inside the walls. When I asked him which articles he was talking about, he told me, "I forget!" I asked him if any of his prisoners were allowed to subscribe to the *New York Times.*

"That's different," he answered. "The *New York Times* is a newspaper."

Over the next few months, I came to enjoy conversations like this. "That's right. The *New York Times* is a newspaper. But it's a newspaper that has a special privilege: a second-class postal permit that only subscribed-to newspapers can get from the federal government," I answered.

I had with me the page from the *Times* that stated, "Second Class Postage Paid at —— ." Then I opened the PDI and showed him where it said, "Second Class Postage Paid at —— ."

"The fact of the matter is that the only difference between the *Penal Digest International* and the *New York Times* is this: They are a daily and we are a monthly. If you can keep us out because you don't like the idea that a newspaper is concerned about how prisoners are treated, then you can keep the *Times* out because you don't like their editorial policy."

Looking around his office was like looking at a history of oppressive penology in the United States: leg irons and remnants of all that seemed dear to the old boys who ran their prisons with absolute authority. They even thought they could kick newspapers around. This warden still thought that wardens could play God.

There are still wardens like that. And guards. And prisoners, too.

Our lawyers moved quickly and effectively.

With the Roy Childers case taking up more of our time, the question came up about how much energy and time we should devote to free-world issues. To me the answer was automatic: we had an obligation to help prisoners, ex-prisoners, and any members of their families. Decision-making support was always available from Merilea, Richard Tanner, and community friends. Our staff was still growing. The first people released to my custody as halfway house residents were two women from the Iowa Women's Reformatory who had participated as PDI representatives in discussion groups, and as panelists at recent conferences that addressed prisoners' issues. They were right at home at 505. Soon we had others.

A Halfway House Like a Home

This halfway-house business happened quite by accident. I had been critical of the halfway-house programs that the states were slowly developing. Coming out of prison and readjusting to life in the free world was difficult at best. If the period of adjustment was going to be effective, prisoners had to live in an environment that would be as close to real life as possible. It was thus to the advantage of both prisoners and society that halfway houses had men, women, and children living in them. If a person had problems living with children and persons of the opposite sex, then the time to work them out was while he or she was in a minimum custody environment.

Our home at 505 was perfect. The most serious problem we faced was not being able to apply for financial assistance from state or federal agencies that had funds available for halfway houses. Our house was in a quiet residential neighborhood. An application for financial assistance would have meant publicity, which would have brought an end to everything we were doing. For a while people thought of us as just another group of people, no different from the many large houses around town that contained mixes of students.

When ex-prisoners arrived, they had to check in with the local state parole office. As more and more arrived, we attracted the attention of the police. One day the chief of police came by with a couple of detectives. I welcomed them into the house, and we sat in the living room talking about the PDI, the staff, and the number of ex-prisoners who were living with us. He asked me what kinds of rules we had for the people living with us. I said that we had the same rules in effect in our house that he had in his: Respect people's privacy and property, clean up after yourself, and don't break the law.

They had come to 505 to inquire about a young runaway. They had all the information they needed except for a picture of the girl, which was good since she just happened to be serving them coffee.

Hers was a sad case of parental abuse. We were able to verify that she was telling us the truth by contacting a social-service caseworker in her hometown. Anyone who came to 505 could count on help and a meal, but everyone had to be honest with us. We were determined that the respect we were building in the neighborhood not be jeopardized. It's worth noting that this young girl worked at the house for a few months, started back to school, got her high school degree, went on to the University of Iowa, got her college degree, and worked as a counselor helping young kids. Today she is a social-service worker in the Southwest, working with Native Americans.

My most vivid memory of the police chief's visit that day is when he asked if he could look around the house.

"By all means," I answered. "Anything you will let me do in your home you can do in mine."

His look told me that he didn't understand. He was working on it, but it wasn't coming together, so I explained. "What I'm saying, Chief, is you can look around our house any time you want, as long as I can look around your house anytime I want. That's fair, isn't it?"

I gave him credit for seeing my intended humor. He chuckled, thanked us for the coffee, and left. He never came back.

"Go Catch a Rabbit"

The folks at 505 were not impressed by uniforms. Here again, the subject of customary law would come up. A number of men at 505 had done long prison terms in the toughest prisons in the country. They had spent long periods in solitary confinement, they had been beaten, they had been in life-and-death situations. Some, while serving sentences for nonviolent crimes, had been forced to kill while defending themselves from aggressive prisoners. It was not possible to frighten them. They were always prepared to defend themselves. And that, I always pointed out to our residents, is not a laid-back way to live your life. Again and again I stepped forward to defuse potentially dangerous situations when I was out with people from 505.

One night I was walking around Iowa City with a friend who hadn't been on the street for more than a month. We were walking and talking and found ourselves in front of a very active nightclub, Gabe & Walker's. We sat down on some park benches that were built into the landscaped area. We had been sitting there for thirty minutes or so when two police officers came by and started talking to the people who were hanging around. They were part of the new public relations program. Humanizing the police force. Just friendly folks trying to help.

We sat there silently, watching the two officers, and I could see that Freddie was becoming increasingly tense. They were speaking to everyone one at a time, and we were part of the scene, so it was just a matter of time. Finally one officer said to Freddie, "Hi. Sure is a nice night." Freddie looked at him but did not answer. The officer said again, "Sure is a nice night." Freddie was not making conversation.

The officer looked at me. He knew who I was.

"How ya' doing?"

"Fine," I answered.

"Have I done something to alienate your friend?"

"What makes you think I'm Grant's friend," Freddie asked before I could answer. And then, before the officer could answer, Freddie added, "And what makes you think I have an obligation to answer any of your questions?"

At that point I thought the officer would excuse himself and leave. He didn't. His partner overheard the conversation and stepped over. He looked at Freddie and said, "I'd like to see your identification."

Freddie looked up at him and said, "I don't carry identification, and there is no law that says I have to carry identification. And if you didn't already know it, I'll quote you the law that says that you have no right to arbitrarily ask me for identification. I was sitting here enjoying myself when you"—Freddie nodded to the other officer—"and you interjected yourselves into my space, and quite frankly I don't like it. I don't know either of you, have no desire to make your acquaintance, and would appreciate very much if both of you would catch a rabbit"—which means, "Get your ass outta here!"

One of the officers looked at the other and asked, "Catch a rabbit?"

Freddie looked at me. I couldn't hold back the laughter.

A few months later, it became clear to me that I was becoming part of the indoctrination of new police officers in Iowa City. Walking past the cop shop one night, I noticed someone sleeping on one of those same benches by Gabe 'n Walker's. Two cops had also seen the fellow and were walking over to check him out. Just as one of them tapped him on the foot to wake him, I saw that it was Iowa City steel guitarist Dan Keely.

I walked up and told the two cops, "Relax. He's waiting for me. He called and asked me to pick him up."

The body on the bench moved and, still half asleep, said, "That sounds like my friend Joe Grant."

The two cops did a double take. They obviously knew me, or knew about me, but we had never met. I expected some interest by the police in our newspaper and the folks living at 505. The looks from these two rookies were proof enough that they had pictures of me, and probably other staff members, at the station so we could be watched.

We didn't have any rules posted at 505. However I did stress the importance of anyone living at 505 not getting involved in anything illegal. We never had a problem until the state and the feds managed to convince two prisoners to request our help. First the two began acting as representatives of the PDI by going around convincing prisoners to subscribe. We helped in all the usual ways, and they were released and joined us at 505. (More later on these two undercover ex-cons who we accepted and trusted.) They almost destroyed us with a drug-bust setup that grabbed everyone, and sadly, a killing by a "staff member" who was given a pistol by one of the scum working for the feds. A pistol that had been provided by the Johnson County sheriff. But I'm getting ahead of myself.

Arkansas Escapee Told to "Cool It"

PDI lines of communication were being quickly established in prisons throughout the United States and Canada. By the time the third issue was ready to print, we had prisoners subscribing, or attempting to subscribe, from every state and federal prison in the country. Letters of support for Roy Childers and his family were arriving from people and organizations both in and out of prison. But we were discovering an unexpected problem: Roy had a temper. On two occasions he had struck his wife during arguments. He had been drinking on both occasions. We didn't set down any rules about what people did on their own time. We only asked that they not break any laws. We didn't expect more of our staff and residents than we did of the general public. We met with Roy and explained what a serious setback it would be to his case if his family left him, which is what would happen if he didn't learn to control his temper. In the presence of his wife and the twins, he reassured me that it would never happen again and that he would control his temper. Again I explained how tenuous his freedom was. And again he told me how grateful he was for all we had done for him. I knew he was going to fuck up. Every conversation with him elicited an endless string of "I, me, my . . ." and never "we, us, our family, our kids."

Dealing with people who had spent so much time in prison, for crimes that were so stupid they made up records for themselves so they had something to brag about, was exhausting. How often do I overlook unacceptable behavior? was a question I asked myself—one that was being asked by others as well. We were a mixed population of men, women, and kids. Violence was an absolute no-no!

Unfortunately I was responsible for the only case of violence at 505. A young boyfriend of Becky's made a remark about her one day, and my role as "father" got the best of me. He was way out of line, and I jumped him with every intention of kicking his ass, or getting mine kicked. Bob Copeland was much faster than me. He got me in a bear hug and held on. I quickly cooled off and apologized.

George Jackson Murdered in San Quentin

Prison activists were stunned by the news of George Jackson's death on August 21, 1971, during what the California Department of Corrections head, Raymond Procunier, described as an attempted escape. Procunier blamed the increasing prison violence on the access prisoners had to underground newspapers. Jackson had been in the California system for several juvenile convictions. When he was eighteen, he was charged with robbing a gas station and stealing $70 using a gun, and was sentenced to serve from one year to life in prison. He became involved in gang activity, assaulted guards a few times, and his sentence was extended again and again. After five years in prison, he met and became friends with W. L. Nolen, who introduced him to Karl Marx and Mao Zedong. Jackson and Nolen founded the Black Guerrilla Family and based its practices on Marxist and Maoist political thought. Word of his activity spread to the outside world, and his activities were seen as disruptive by the prison system; he spent frequent time in solitary confinement, during which he studied political economy and corresponded with supporters and friends in the free world. These letters would be edited into two best-selling books, *Soledad Brother* and *Blood in My Eye.* I recalled that one of San

Quentin's AWs (assistant wardens) had described Jackson as a prisoner who "didn't give a shit about the revolution and was a sociopathic hoodlum."

After nine years in San Quentin, he and Nolen were transferred to Soledad prison. A year later, Nolen and two other black inmates were shot by guard O. G. Miller during a riot with the Aryan Brotherhood. Jackson called for "selective retaliatory violence." In August of that year, Jackson, Fleeta Drumgo, and John Cluchette were charged with murder for allegedly beating and throwing guard John V. Mills off the third tier of Y cell block. A year later—August 21, 1971—Jackson was murdered when, according to prison authorities, he used a 9 mm pistol given to him by his attorney to take hostages, six of whom were found dead from stab wounds in his cell, and then attempted to escape with fellow prisoner Johnny Spain. Jackson and Spain made it to the yard, where Jackson was shot dead and Spain, with nowhere to go but that proverbial "car trunk in the sky," surrendered.

Again and again, wardens of U.S. prisons laid the blame for their problems on "outside agitators" and any newspapers that were fighting for recognition of prisoners as human beings who deserved basic human rights. Meanwhile, they did everything in their extraordinary power to avoid talking about the overcrowding, absence of rehabilitation and education programs, unhealthy prison diets, and prison employees who lacked the interpersonal skills necessary to work in ethnically and racially mixed environments. When Hispanic, black, and Indian prisoners from inner-city slums and ghettos were supervised by small-town, predominantly poor, conservative white guards, prisoners and guards both suffered from emotionally and physically disabling degrees of stress. Prisons often were isolated and difficult for families to visit; prison industries still manufactured license plates, shoes, and furniture—which taught prisoners job skills that were nonexistent in the free world.

Tragedies like the killing of George Jackson brought the issue of prison violence to the public in splashy headlines and lengthy interviews with wardens and directors. Rarely available to the public were articles by writers who were familiar with the prison systems—writers who had investigated prison conditions, listened to prisoners AND the administrators, and written stories that dealt not only with the violence that took place in prison but also with the root causes of that violence.

What Procunier never mentioned when he attacked underground newspapers was that these same newspapers and others like them had been warning him of impending violence and rebellion that would be built not upon what prisoners were reading, but upon what wardens and administrators were not reading. These incidents would be triggered by what was being done to ensure that "rehabilitative" prison systems were not only punitive, but excessively punitive.

In colonial times, sanctions against people who violated customary or legislated law were purely punitive. The most effective way to deal with crime was "Red Hannah"—the whipping post. It was public, it was swift, and then it was over. Offenders of public norms rarely committed acts that took them back to Red Hannah. The Quakers built the first penitentiaries in Philadelphia because they thought the existing form of punishment was barbaric, and they believed that to punish with acts more violent than the crime was wrong, un-Christian, and lacked the element that would cure the criminal and satisfy the ever-present Christ: forgiveness. "Penitentiaries"—where offenders could be "penitent"—were thought to be more humane methods of punishment. The Quakers believed that a person who had committed a crime—sinned, so to speak—would repent that "sin" if kept in a cell where he or she would be exposed to the Bible and religious teachings and kept reasonably active. This was the beginning of rehabilitation.

Unfortunately, the punishment models persisted within the penitentiaries until well into the 1900s. Prisoners were locked up and forgotten about. There was nothing that served or helped the prisoner. Parole didn't exist, nor did time off for good behavior, education departments, or vocational training that could help a prisoner prepare for his or her return to the free world. Prisoners were being released from penitentiaries in worse shape than when they went in. Having lived in the system and studied its history, I can state, absolutely, that no state or federal prison has ever initiated a program of rehabilitation and allowed it to work.

Theoretically, the forties and fifties saw a change in the way legislators and the public perceived the "criminal." At the insistence of religious organizations and humane groups, some legislators began to challenge the policies of lockstep and silence. The "rehabilitative" approach was to reward a prisoner for abiding by prison rules, for studying, for working conscientiously—for becoming a better person. When rehabilitation programs were started, prisons saw an emergence of education departments where prisoners could get high school diplomas or college degrees, and vocational training programs that actually trained prisoners for useful vocations outside prison. Prisoners were able to "make" parole long before the original sentence was served. Church services, libraries, and recreational facilities were brought into the prisons. Other changes included parole programs, revisions in the sentencing codes, and the awarding of good time, whereby prisoners who did not violate prison rules could have two days taken off the end of their sentences for every thirty days of good behavior.

All these steps toward a more humane, rehabilitative model were accompanied by publicity and a favorable acceptance from prisoners and the public. Unfortunately, the programs were never fully funded, never entered into with the kind of conviction necessary to bring about meaningful change in the system. While the public believed that prisoners were being treated humanely and were being provided the opportunity to rehabilitate themselves, most programs in fact were cosmetic only.

Violence in the prisons was caused by the refusal of correctional administrators to deal with legitimate prisoner complaints. Prisoners learned about demonstrations not from the radical, alternative, or underground newspapers, but from the TV evening news, where they saw the country's youth demonstrating against racism and the war in Vietnam. Demonstrations that began peacefully were quelled with high-powered water hoses, dogs, and clubs. The greater the violence, the greater the numbers of demonstrators. It was a "war" the government could not win, because it was a public war. At the same time, many of these demonstrators and war resisters were ending up in prison. As the prisoners spoke with these political activists and learned of their success in ending racial segregation and then the Vietnam War, they became convinced that the same course of action was available to them.

Little did they know. The wars that erupt inside the prisons are private wars. Outsiders only see and hear what the government allows. During speaking engagements, the first thing I stressed was, "The walls are to keep the public from seeing what is going on inside those walls."

Many prisoners who become students of psychology, sociology, criminology, or penology learn that the number of poor and nonwhite prisoners is disproportionately greater than their numbers in the general population. Murderers from Park Avenue homes are treated differently than murderers from poor families with no resources. When one criminal walks and another faces a lengthy prison sentence simply because one can afford the best lawyers and another cannot, justice is not served. The persons who do the time realize that they are as much prisoners of a stratified economic system as they are of a judicial system.

During the Attica uprising, which happened the month after George Jackson was murdered, one of the prisoners yelled to us, "When both have done the crime but only one does the time, that one becomes a political prisoner." He was right. A day later, when well-armed members of the National Guard and the highway patrol, through clouds of tear gas, charged in with guns blazing, he was dead.

Although the PDI never pinned specific blame on capitalism and the U.S. judicial system for the plight of all prisoners in this country, there is no doubt that many prisoners are indeed victims and have committed crimes because of what society has done to them personally. For many years I have used as my political mentor Eugene V. Debs. Debs was a man workers could talk to and understand. On the subject of prisons he stated clearly, upon his release from a federal penitentiary where he had served a lengthy sentence for speaking out against the United States entering World War I, "As long as there is a soul in prison, I am not free." The reason so few people understand the truth about prison conditions is because the public is not allowed inside the prison walls. In-depth, investigative feature stories that expose conditions and make demands do not find favorable reception in mainstream daily newspapers.

As for the death of George Jackson during the "escape attempt," anyone who has ever been in San Quentin as a prisoner or a visitor knows that what Procunier described was not possible. The idea of Jackson hiding a gun in his Afro hairstyle was preposterous. The "shootout" was a brutal assassination. It was one more act of violence in what seemed to be a never-ending conflict between guards and prisoners.

Playboy Kicks in Cash, Boosts Subscriptions

With circulation growing, publications began calling 505 for interviews. One call came from a *Playboy* magazine editor, who invited me to submit a request for a foundation grant. The application was successful and we were given $2,500. Equally important was *Playboy*'s mention of the PDI in one of their issues. We only rated a paragraph, but with a circulation in the millions, the response from the free world and from prisoners was remarkable.

I visited the foundation's office at *Playboy*'s headquarters in Chicago two or three times and became acquainted with some of the writers and photographers. Three people I remember quite well were Jill Parsons, secretary to the foundation director; Craig Vetter, author and feature writer; and Don Myrus. Jill and her husband Roy became supportive, resourceful friends. Craig introduced me to people in the photography department who helped us out with film, paper, and a variety of supplies that, though dated, were perfectly usable.

Don Myrus was editorial director of Playboy Press. One day I mentioned the sorry state of prison libraries. Not only did they lack books, I pointed out, but almost every book they had was dated or damaged. I was glancing at some of the books Playboy Press had published. In those days the list was small—twelve to be exact: some science fiction, a few horror, and the Bedside *Playboy* Advisors and Readers. Not exactly literary classics, but entertaining. I asked him if *Playboy* would donate a set of the books to any prison libraries that requested a set. Don asked how many prisons might ask for sets. I honestly did not know and told him so. I did mention, though, that such an offer might get more responses than he or I would ever imagine. He liked my idea and said he would get back to me.

On July 27, he wrote me a letter stating that Playboy Press would send three sets of the twelve books to any prison library that sent the request on library or prison stationery. The offer terminated 60 days after publication of the ad, which appeared in our July issue. (During the first year, it wasn't unusual for issues to be published late, as was obviously the case here.)

During that 60-day period, letters arrived from prison libraries not just in the United States but from around the world. The prison grapevine had picked up the news. Dollar subscriptions were flooding 505, and book requests were flooding *Playboy's* Chicago headquarters.

Up to that point in our brief history—the July issue was only our second issue—we had not had a chance to statistically measure our actual impact on anyone or anything. The ad gave us our first opportunity. In the end, it cost *Playboy* somewhere between $80,000 and $100,000. It also cost Don Myrus his job. Don thought it was rather humorous. I was completely bummed. Don had given the PDI a bigger boost than we had ever received, with one exception. August Bergenthal, a Wisconsin prisoner, after seeing a few issues of the PDI, became a serious financial supporter. More on Augie later.

As a result of accepting grant money from the Playboy Foundation, I took considerable heat from colleagues—particularly women. Maybe I deserved it. Although I wasn't a reader of *Playboy*, I recognized that it was not possible to disassociate yourself from the people or organization you accepted money from. They wanted to help, and we needed help. But in a way, accepting a person's money is like saying, "You are okay!" All of the people I met there were okay. They were gracious, helpful, professional, damned interesting, and fun to be around.

A couple of years later, while passing through Chicago around Christmas, Sharlane and I were invited to a party that the photo editor was having at his loft. When we arrived, we found a fellow in a large lot across from the loft waving us into a parking spot. The parking fee for the night was only $2—a real bargain in Chicago. Two hundred cars at least were lined up neatly. Later I found out that no arrangements had been made for parking. Some street dude had seen a vacant lot and cars piling up on the street, had broken the lock on a chain that kept cars out of the lot, and had gone into business for himself. When I asked him later how he happened to get into the parking lot business, he laughed. "Man, this street was a mess until I snapped that lock and helped you folks out. Hope you don't think $2 is high." I assured him that $2 was more than fair.

Playboy helped us, and in a strange way harmed us. The rapid increase in circulation was dramatic, certainly relative to underground newspaper standards; however, 90 percent of the increase was due to prisoners who were taking me up on my offer of "Pay $1 now and the rest when you can afford it." With no financial backing, it was clear that our seemingly successful newspaper would be running on empty much sooner than I ever suspected.

Perhaps the most interesting feature in issue number 3, which appeared in September, was about a Minnesota prisoner. Dick Mitchell arrived at Minnesota State Penitentiary in 1959 and immediately set a record for the number of consecutive days spent by a Minnesota prisoner in solitary confinement—900 days. For months he was told that he would be moved back to the general population if he would simply make the request. He refused. "I didn't do anything to get placed in solitary and I refuse to do anything to get out." Actually, any prisoner who whistled in a Minnesota State prison hallway went to the hole. Mitchell whistled.

No prisoner, until Dick Mitchell was sent to the hole, was ever gassed—had his cell filled with tear gas or pepper spray by the guards—for refusing to eat. Mitchell was gassed so many times that whenever guards were going to punish another prisoner with gas they would move him to Mitchell's cell first.

Mitchell was an amazing man. After his release, he finished school and became a counselor. When his cellmate, Frank Eli, later wrote his book *The Riot*, he based the character of Indian Joe on Mitchell. How many Frank Elis and Dick Mitchells are still around?

Attica, NY

Shortly after issue 3 went to press, I was called to New York City for a series of interviews with radio and television stations. I drove there with Merilea and Warren Levicoff, our photographer, in Elinor Cottrell's Volvo station wagon, which gave us many more miles per gallon of gas than the PDI van.

Our primary purpose was to speak out on behalf of the Attica prisoners. Conditions there were intolerable. Prisoners worked in shops where temperatures were over 115 degrees, the food was vile and frequently inedible, they were allowed one shower a week—the list of complaints was long, and the prisoners were justified in requesting changes. Attica was a small town, far upstate, without a single black resident. The guard force was exclusively white, and the great majority were uneducated. The educational requirement to become a guard in New York and most of the other states, including Iowa, was an eighth-grade education.

On the morning of September 9, 1971, I was on the air at a radio station in Harlem. We hadn't been on the air for long when a group of men who were members of the Black Panther Party entered the station and announced that a revolt was in progress inside the prison at Attica, and that the prisoners had taken over.

We immediately took a break to get the details. What we learned was that the takeover had in fact happened, and that forty-nine guards and civilian employees had just been taken hostage.

Merilea, Warren, and I were facing a dilemma. We were in New York City, and we had to get to Attica—in upstate New York, 350 miles away—as quickly as possible. We had no money, but we had a credit card for gas. One of the Panthers offered to cover the cost of one airline ticket to Attica, and I gratefully accepted. It was critically important to get Warren and his cameras on the scene as quickly as possible, so he got the nod. A member of the Black Panther contingent rushed him to the airport.

The interview continued, and I discussed the PDI and the conditions inside Attica, and called for support for the prisoners.

At 10 A.M., Merilea and I started driving. We opted for the interstates that crossed Pennsylvania. We made a quick stop in Elmira to refill the thermos with coffee and arrived in Attica at 5 P.M.

On the way, we had followed the radio news bulletins. Most of the news was coming from stations in Buffalo. The Mutual Radio Network had no reporters on the scene, so as soon as we arrived I ran to a pay phone, called Mutual, and made a deal to cover Attica for them, via telephone and tape, while we were there. Over the next three days, Merilea and I took turns on the phone.

Warren, thanks to the Black Panthers, had caught a fast ride to the airport and was on a flight immediately. When he landed in Buffalo, the first people he ran into were Herman Schwartz, the law professor from Buffalo, and lawyer Bill Kunstler—both members of our national advisory board and our legal defense team. Warren didn't have to look for photo opportunities; they came to him. He was at the main gate of the prison when we arrived.

With the Mutual Radio contact, I thought we could afford a place with a roof rather than having to live in Elinor's station wagon until the prison takeover was resolved and the hostages released. Across the street from the prison were homes. On the front porch of one was an older couple sitting and watching the action at the front entrance to the prison. I walked over and introduced myself. Not wanting to ruffle any local feathers, I mentioned my need for a room, a table for a typewriter, and a telephone to make collect calls. "Who are you working for?" the man asked me. "Mutual. The radio network for all America," I answered. "Come right in," was his reply. "We have a room overlooking the prison."

I looked at the room. It was perfect. It had a bed and a sofa, and we would sleep in shifts.

We shook hands on it. A few minutes later, while we were unloading the wagon, Fred Ferretti, from the *New York Times*, walked up and asked if he could share the room. The *Times* didn't have a better feature writer than Ferretti. We welcomed him.

The prison had been taken over by the prisoners at a few minutes before nine that morning. During the takeover a guard had been critically injured. He died from his injuries—the first casualty.

By nightfall we had made contact with people at the prison. A negotiating team was forming. The prisoners wanted Bill Kunstler and *New York Times* columnist Tom Wicker. Herman Schwartz became part of the team also, as did Clarence Jones, editor of the *Amsterdam News*; Arthur Eve, a New York assemblyman; David Rothenberg, Ken Jackson, and Mel Rivers, from the Fortune Society; Juan Ortiz and "G.I." Paris, from the Young Lords, the Puerto Rican community group that had first formed in Chicago and now was based in New York also; Lewis Steel, from the National Lawyers Guild; Julian Tepper, another of our board members from the National Law Office; and Tom Soto, from the Prisoners' Solidarity League. Three others on the team were state senators John Dunne and Thomas McGowan and U.S. congressman Herman Baddillo. There were others whose names I have forgotten. This remarkable group was at the prison day and night for the four days between the time the prisoners took the hostages and the time the National Guard and the state police launched their attack to retake the prison.

About one hundred state police had taken back part of the prison and rescued some of the hostages late that first day.

Attica: Racist Inside and Out

By the next morning, family members of prisoners began showing up at the prison. They knew that the lives of everyone in the prison were at risk. Only a short space separated these parents, wives, and children from the parents, wives, and children of the hostages. Late the second day, an older woman, the mother of one of the prisoners, came down to the area in front of the main entrance and asked if there was any news about her son. A state trooper turned and said, "Get outta here, nigger."

The woman was stunned. Merilea ran over to her and walked her back to the group that had gathered waiting for news of prisoners. As they walked back, people in the group who were waiting for news of the hostages were yelling, "Go home, whore!" "Go back to New York City, bitch!" Those taunts accurately reflected the feelings of most of the state police, the National Guard, and the townspeople who had gathered. It was an ugly scene.

Each day, the tension became greater. Each day, corrections superintendent Vincent Mancusi and Walter Dunbar (a deputy director who reported directly to Russell Oswald, New York State director of corrections) answered fewer questions. Each day, the number of guardsmen and state troopers arriving at the prison became greater.

It was clear that the guardsmen and troopers were becoming impatient. Cooler heads were encouraging the negotiators to keep everyone talking, hoping that the discussion would continue and that more newsmen would be allowed into the prison.

From the beginning, objective reasoning would have concluded that this riot, the prison takeover, and the taking of hostages were all the end result of many attempts by the prisoners to get Oswald and the state of New York to initiate changes at Attica.

Requests had been submitted again and again, and always they were ignored. Requests became demands—in writing. Finally, the takeover.

Join Me and Avoid a Massacre

What were the prisoners' demands? On the list of demands by prisoners holding hostages at Attica were the formation of a grievance committee; a doctor to examine and treat prisoners; daily showers; religious freedom; fresh fruit daily; an end to pork every day; more recreation time and recreational equipment; education programs; vocational training; an end to the censorship of newspapers, magazines, and letters; and an end to slave labor.

There were also two demands—amnesty for all prisoners, and transportation to a non-imperialistic country—that the prisoners knew would never be met. Amnesty might have been possible if trust could have been established between both sides, but that was not going to happen. The prisoners had the hostages, but the state had the upper hand. And Nelson Rockefeller's state had no intention of allowing these prisoners to force the state into making basic, humane changes.

Helicopters had arrived with tanks of tear gas aboard. Warren was everywhere with his cameras. His pictures were pure art, his energy unlimited.

Early in the evening on September 12, as it was beginning to get dark, the media were gathered around a flatbed truck. For three days I had been listening to the guards, the state troopers, the national guardsmen, and New York Department of Corrections administrators. I had spoken with Warren and he agreed with me. The guard and the police were preparing to storm the prison. Many people were going to die. The most perplexing puzzle was this: How could an army enter a tear-gas-filled yard, with or without gas masks, and be able to differentiate between prisoner and hostage when the shooting started? They couldn't—and that meant that both hostages and prisoners would die during the raid, and sole blame would be laid on the prisoners. The inhumane treatment that had precipitated the takeover would be lost to history.

With these thoughts, I stepped up on the platform and asked the media to listen for a moment. I explained what I sincerely believed was about to happen: a takeover that would result in the deaths of hostages and prisoners. A slaughter. I told them there was only one way to stop the killing that would surely take place the next day: We, as representatives of the nation's news media, must demand the right to be exchanged for the guards who were being held hostage. I explained that regardless of the rhetoric by the radical prisoners, regardless of the threats to kill the hostages—the solution was for the media to spend the next few days in the prison, on the yard, as hostages. The prisoners wanted to talk. They wanted us to see what it was like, to feel what it was like, to listen to the horror stories about life inside the walls of Attica.

Someone said, "The state wouldn't allow it."

"Nonsense!" I yelled over the noise. "If we do it to free the guards, the families, the town, every cop in the country will say, 'Let them in.' We can demand the right to free the hostages on the front page of every paper in the country."

"Who will join me?" I asked. "Who will join me and help avoid a massacre?"

There was one, then two, then a couple more. Four others were all I could convince. The others in the media turned away. They wanted no part of that story. They refused to believe what I described was about to happen right in front of them. And I'm sure many were simply afraid. John Linstead from the *Chicago Daily News* believed what I was saying. So did Fred Ferretti and a couple more, but not anywhere near the number necessary. From Mancusi I got a curt "Out of the question!" and a look that convinced me I was right. These bastards had no regard for the prisoners, and it was obvious to me that the state of New York didn't give a damn about a few guards.

The next morning, September 13, at 9:45, helicopters dumped the gas canisters, snipers opened fire, and the police moved in. Thirty minutes or so later, ten guards and twenty-eight prisoners were dead. Two prisoners and one guard died before the police moved in.

When the bodies of the hostages were carried out of the prison, Oswald, lying with a straight face, told a group of reporters that all had died at the hands of prisoners who had cut their throats, emasculated them, and stuffed their genitals in their mouths.

"Liar!" Warren Levicoff yelled.

Warren was one of the few people covering the riots who refused to believe that the prisoners had killed the hostages. He followed the bodies to the coroner's office, and he would not leave until the autopsies were completed. He stood out in the cold for hours. When told to move on, he refused and stood his ground. He was the first to let the world know that every hostage had been killed by "friendly" gunfire. Their genitals were all intact, and not a single hostage had been mutilated.

A few months later, an article by Linstead appeared in the November 1971 *Chicago Journalism Review*. In it, Linstead noted that the exchange of newsmen for hostages might have avoided the massacre. More importantly, he pointed out that the establishment press had, again and again, accepted information from the state without question, and printed it as fact.

Almost immediately after the massacre, Bill Kunstler had been condemned by wardens, correctional officials, columnists, and an endless lineup of elected officials. Some wanted him disbarred. Again and again he would raise his voice and cry, "Remember Attica!" He would condemn Rockefeller, Oswald, and everyone who had a hand in the shootout. Few people would ever be aware of how long Kunstler agonized over those deaths. He and a few others understood that as long as people were talking, as long as solutions were being discussed, there was hope for a settlement. As long as there was even a remote hope that a resolution was possible, the talking had to continue.

He and others who tried so desperately to avoid the bloodbath suffered because they had failed all the people who suffered and died because of the inhumane conditions the state of New York forced upon the prisoners in Attica.

Four years after the riot, sixty-two prisoners had been charged in forty-two indictments with a total of 1,289 separate counts. One state trooper was indicted for reckless endangerment. In 2000, after twenty-five years in the courts, New York State agreed to pay $12 million to settle the cases of guard brutality against prisoners. Four years later, the state also made an award of $12 million to the families of the slain prison employees—on top of all the benefits the union members had already picked up.

Charles Dickens once visited the Cherry Hill prison in Philadelphia and remarked that those who had devised the system didn't understand it and did not have the right to inflict such suffering on other human beings.

A society can be judged by the way its members treat its prisoners.

Forty-Year Aftermath to Attica

Investigations into why and how the massacre took place began immediately and continue up to the present, over forty years later. I watched conditions improve, and then slowly, inexorably, return to the conditions that precipitated the Attica riot. Information about what happened after the assault came from several sources, including New York State Appellate Division documents; Court of Claims documents; the McKay Commission; Second Circuit Court documents; *Police Misconduct and Civil Rights Law Report* 3, no. 9 (May/June 1991): 98–104; the Attica Justice Committee; conversations with observers; and letters from prisoners and attorneys.

To begin with, even though Oswald had promised there would be no retaliation against prisoners, and even though he was assured that the huge amount of CS tear gas that would be dropped would totally incapacitate everyone in the yard, he sent in 150 heavily armed state troopers with orders to use whatever force they felt necessary.

Further, even though he had been ordered by the state to exclude all Attica prison guards from the assault force because of their proven record of brutality against prisoners who disobeyed orders, he allowed them to participate. The troopers and guards were joined by sheriff's deputies, park police, and unknown others.

To ensure that there were no impartial witnesses, Oswald refused to allow any members of the *Observers Committee to monitor the retaking of the prison. He even denied access to those individuals Governor Rockefeller had selected to be inside the prison when the assault took place.

The state-mandated obligation to account for every round of ammunition that is expended during any law enforcement action was ignored. No attempt was made to publicly inventory weapons going into the prison before the assault.

During the assault itself, which lasted six minutes, only 450 shots were fired, according to the official report. If we only counted the 150 state troopers, 450 shots in six minutes translates to each trooper firing one shot every other minute. Outside, I heard an endless and continuous barrage of gunfire.

Not until seven hours after the assault ended were the first wounded prisoners treated. Some prisoners bled to death waiting for medical help.

The Second Circuit Court, more than a month after the massacre, ordered that injunctive relief be granted against further brutality by guards. Proof was provided to the court that

- Prisoners—including those who were wounded—were stripped naked and forced to run and crawl through a gauntlet of guards, across floors covered with broken glass, while guards beat them with clubs and guns.
- Both Warden Mancusi and Deputy Assistant Warden Pfeil were identified as being in the yard and cell blocks observing the beatings, yet neither exercised his supervisory authority to stop them.
- Deputy Assistant Warden Pfeil supervised the beating of prisoners in the segregation unit. He personally threatened prisoners with death and prevented doctors and lawyers with court-ordered access from entering the prison.
- All evidence was quickly destroyed by the state. Neither ammunition nor weapons were accounted for; bodies of dead prisoners were moved before being photographed; shell casings and spent bullets were not saved. The entire scene was bulldozed over. Videotapes and photographs of the assault and its aftermath disappeared, were altered, or were destroyed.

At that hearing, the barbarous conduct testified to by witnesses was taken as true by Judge Curtin and ruled as being wholly beyond any amount of force needed to maintain order. According to Curtin, "It far exceeded what our society will tolerate on the part of officers of the law in custody of defenseless prisoners."

Muslims Accused of Precipitating Attica Riots

What few people ever learned was the role the Muslim inmate population played during the riot. Prison authorities claimed that the Muslims were the group that instigated the riot. They were immediately subject to torture and punishment. It took years for the outside world to learn that the Muslims became the protectors of the hostages out in the middle of D-yard. I remember that we received word from prisoners—after we returned to Iowa City—that Frank Smith (his subscription to the PDI was recorded as being sent to Frank "Big Black" Smith) had taken the role of protecting the hostages. Prisoners were so incensed that many were eager to exact retribution for their years of suffering. "Big Black" ordered that if a prisoner attempted to hurt a hostage, the group should kill the inmate. If necessary, they were to die protecting the hostages.

Much later many guards testified that prisoners had helped them, and some stated that prisoners had saved their lives.

Our drive back to Iowa after the Attica massacre was slow and arduous. Physically and emotionally we were completely exhausted. We first returned to New York City to discuss what had happened with other prisoners' rights advocates, and to take care of TV obligations we had made. On one of the network panel shows, I found myself sitting next to attorney Roy Cohn. I asked him if his years as a hatchet man for right-wing Wisconsin senator Joe McCarthy during the Communist witch-hunt years of the early fifties had made it difficult to spend time alone. So that the microphones wouldn't pick up his voice, he leaned close to me and asked, "What's real, Grant? What's really real?" After Attica I had no answers. My complaint that he was even on the panel was ignored. If I hadn't felt that I had important information to share with the New York City TV market, I would have walked off the set. Sitting next to this creep was painful and brought back memories of the HUAC hearing in Boston when they were after a history professor from Boston University. I walked the picket lines in front of the hearings; although I don't have photos, Martin Luther King Jr., at Boston University working on a graduate degree, also participated.

After New York, we stopped for meetings in Columbus, Ohio, and in Chicago. Finally we were back in Iowa City and surrounded by our PDI family at 505.

Tom Murton Leads Rally for Escapee

We were pleased to learn that the Roy Childers case was moving forward. A report from the Hawkeye chapter of the Iowa Civil Liberties Union had "taken a stand behind [the] escaped convict who [was] fighting extradition back to the Arkansas prison he had broken out of last July."

In the meantime, Joe Johnston was devoting much of his time to Roy's case. By the time we got back, he had made arrangements for a meeting with Governor Robert Ray. Since Iowa and Arkansas had extradition agreements, the only way we could keep Roy in Iowa indefinitely was with Governor Ray's help. Ray was a conservative Republican, but we were holding rallies around the state, the national press was showing up, and we had a cause célèbre on our hands.

Tom Murton came to Iowa for a series of rallies. Murton, the first PhD penologist ever and the former warden at Tucker Prison Farm (on his way to being appointed Arkansas director of corrections), had shaken up the state of Arkansas and the nation when he took over and did away with the rifle-carrying inmate trustees (who could win parole by shooting an escapee) and the Tucker telephone (where guards would connect electrical leads to a prisoner's genitals and crank up the electricity—just for fun). He also ended the selling of young men to the wheeler-dealers who used them as prostitutes, and discovered the field of buried prisoners who were thought to have escaped, but in reality had been murdered by guards and trustees.

It was a scandal that was heard around the world. As Tom's reward for cleaning up the prison system, ending the graft, and making one of the most barbaric prison systems in the world a more humane place to serve a prison sentence, Arkansas governor Winthrop Rockefeller betrayed and fired him. Rockefeller buckled under to those who condoned the most brutal criminality and profited by it. Think of this: Murton ended the sale of young fourteen- and fifteen-year-old juveniles to end-of-the-line hard-timers for sexual purposes. These kids were used like whores. It was done openly with the approval of the prison administrators, who received a share of the profits. Rockefeller kept the good old boys, and not only got rid of Murton, he helped blackball him.

Tom wrote a book about his experiences as superintendent of the Arkansas Prison System from February 1967 to March 1968. *Accomplices to the Crime* is not easy reading. Years later, Robert Redford would star in a movie that was Murton's story. To avoid having to pay Murton for the movie rights, Hollywood changed the name of the prison, called the main character "Brubaker," and made a ton of money. Really soured me on Redford. Terrible rip-off of a man who placed his life in jeopardy to singlehandedly clean up one of the most corrupt prison systems in the country.

He tried to teach for a while, but his heart wasn't in it. Later, he moved to a small farm in Oklahoma. We were in contact frequently when I couldn't remember an incident or a name. We spoke for a while. I asked him if I could drive down and videotape a series of interviews with him. His was a serious burnout. He wasn't interested. "I can't do it anymore," he confessed to me.

I know burnout when I hear it. Tom had been in the thick of it for many, many years. He had been marked for death by proven killers and prisoners who were as bad as the worst his adversaries could recruit, assassins who had killed other prisoners and, to save work, cut up the bodies so they could be stuffed into smaller holes.

He had had enough.

But he was a major force in helping us with Roy's case. With Murton describing the Arkansas prison system, and Roy, his wife Jeanne, and the twins standing by for interviews and photos, we generated tremendous favorable publicity. By the time I returned from Attica, we had petitions with over five thousand signatures from all over the United States supporting Roy. We felt confident Governor Ray would bend to the will of the people and refuse to sign the extradition papers.

Roy, however, was still acting up and making life difficult for Jeanne. We met with him and asked him to understand that successfully fighting the extradition was not only keeping him out of prison, it was also forcing Arkansas to rush forward with the changes they had to make in their entire prison system to bring it within the constitutional guidelines that federal Judge Henley had set forth.

Roy was having an impact on corrections in the United States whether he liked it or not. Today, remembering Roy, Jeanne, and the twins, I'm amazed at the inconsistencies of so many of the causes we championed. Roy was a former trustee and unquestionably a bully, a wife beater, and not an easy person to deal with. It helped that I was a pacifist, because again and again I wanted to grab him and kick his ass. We were trying to use his case, his plight, to make a point about all prisons, not just the prisons of Arkansas. A damn good attorney, Joe Johnston, was not only spending a great deal of time on Roy's case and getting no fee, but was also spending his own money on the case.

Subscription Drives inside the Walls

As usual during this period, lack of money was a persistent problem. Subscriptions were still coming in from prisoners—at a dollar each. In meetings to discuss the problem, we would resolve to work harder so that prisoners who didn't have $6 could get a subscription for a dollar.

While we were laying out the October issue—issue number 5—Becky and I were invited to visit the federal penitentiary at Lewisburg, Pennsylvania, by John Wagner, a prisoner who had been the chaplain's clerk at Leavenworth and was now an active Jaycee in Lewisburg. He had lobbied the prison chapter of Jaycees to have a subscription drive for the PDI and wanted me to tour the prison, speak to a gathering of the prisoners, and meet with the chapter members. John left Leavenworth a punk and changed his life in Lewisburg. He surprised me. He was becoming an organizer.

The visit to Lewisburg became the first of a series of subscription drives that would pay the monthly printing bills. That night, Becky and I were the featured guests at a banquet. Jimmy Hoffa presented Becky and me with bricks from the prison wall to commemorate the work we were doing to tear down the walls that restricted prisoners from viewing the free world, and prevented members of the free world from better understanding what was happening inside.

I had met Jimmy Hoffa once, years before, and considered him to be a friend and a remarkable man. Contrary to what most people were led to believe, Jimmy never mishandled a penny of Teamsters Union money. He made many loans that were not his right to make, but they were all repaid. It was illegal, but he was not a thief. Hoffa ended up in prison because certain members of the federal attorney general's office had an extraordinary dislike for him. They disliked him because he was a strong union organizer who had stood toe-to-toe with the goon squads hired by the giant corporations to crush the unions.

Hoffa liked the PDI, but most of all he liked the idea that a group of people had gathered together to work for no pay on a cause they collectively cherished, just as I had been doing years before when our weekly newspaper was the most vociferous pro-union voice in Iowa. He knew about working for a cause. That evening during dinner, he slipped me a note and told me to call the people on the list.

"What do you want me to tell them?" I asked.

"Tell them you are a nonprofit, tax-exempt corporation, and that I asked you to call them."

Later, I would do just that. Every call I made resulted in a contribution from a Teamsters local.

Our visit to Lewisburg was the first of many trips that Becky and I took around the country. She loved to drive and could drive for long periods of time. The seemingly endless energy of youth.

Becky had become much more than my ward. We were together constantly on the road, which means she was with me whenever I was invited into a prison. During those months of getting started, we became used to greetings of "Here's Joe and Becky," and Becky was gaining a following of her own.

We were in the Lewisburg post office after a visit to the prison with Diane and Chris Steckman when the kids saw WANTED posters for two prisoners they had just met. Seeing and reading WANTED posters on two men they had just had lunch with was perplexing them.

"These can't be the men we met," said Diane. "They weren't dangerous."

I could only shrug and add, "Everything is relative, Sweetie."

During that tour of Lewisburg Penitentiary, I noticed that Becky was looking a bit run down. We traveled lightly. Becky had a small backpack with an extra pair of jeans and a couple of shirts. I thought Becky needed to dress up a bit. Jeans, old shirts, and ragged winter jackets were generating some criticism from free-world friends. Becky and I went shopping. She got two sets of matching slacks and tops. I thought she looked wonderful, but she was obviously uncomfortable.

"Do you think these prisoners care what we are wearing when we arrive?" she asked.

I nodded and agreed and tried to make sense of decisions that were as much parental as they were for the PDI.

"Can you imagine me wearing either of these outfits to school?"

She had a point and I listened. Better a happy, slightly run-down Becky than an unhappy Becky.

As a result of John Wagner's efforts, we received $2,000 in new subscriptions. Less than 10 percent of the prisoners had opted for the dollar subscription price. Most had spent $6; some had spent $9. That plus a tour of the prison plus a banquet: I couldn't believe that a prisoner had pulled it off. John had been a super wimp—a sissy—for the better part of his prison life. He had been abused and used. He was weak. But something happened to him when he contacted us after seeing the first issue of the PDI. He believed it gave him a broader perspective on prison life and his social status as a prisoner. Reading about the political activism of other prisoners, and gaining a better perspective of his own position in the pecking order, he decided to make a change. As an inmate editor on the PDI staff (some of the ex-cons from Leavenworth were opposed to naming him an inmate editor, but I prevailed and they relented), John had found himself. He had taken up a cause, and the cause, so to speak, had set him free. Being able to involve himself in something outside himself—and outside the prison itself—had freed him from the limitations of the prison, he told me. His activism increased his stature in the eyes of a respected and responsible element of the prison's population. He was never going to be a fighter in the physical sense, but he became a fighter for prisoners' rights and in that role he became fearless. He wasn't afraid of anyone.

A few months later, during a prisoners' strike in Lewisburg, he emerged as a spokesperson for the prisoners. He would pay dearly for stepping into that leadership role.

With issue number 5, we once again alienated some of the prisoners who felt it was wrong to "blow the whistle" on anyone for any reason. I spoke of what we were going to do when Becky and I were at Lewisburg. Many prisoners were upset.

Here's what happened: The use of heroin had been growing more serious with each passing year. I had seen on many occasions the hell addicts went through when they were locked up with no access to drugs. On a trip to the East Coast, I met two ex-cons I had known at Leavenworth who were involved in some illegal activities that put them in contact with the drug trade. One of them was a courier who, by a variety of circuitous routes, was involved with smuggling. Both had recently been "burned" and asked me what I would do if I had a list of the main heroin processing plants in two of the major port cities.

I had to think about that for a while. When I questioned them and learned that the plants were condoned by the French government, I thought of a way we could bring more information about drug trafficking to the public. Most people know that the great majority of drug sellers who end up in prison are the users who sell to support their habits. These are the people who are the least dangerous and the least important. They are also the most vulnerable, and they receive the most publicity. But people never hear about the protection the processors and large suppliers get from governments. I decided I wanted the list, provided they would vouch for its authenticity. They did, and they gave me the addresses and phone numbers.

In the lead story of issue 5, we called for a boycott of French wines until the labs were closed down. When I broke the news of the soon-to-be-published story at one of the federal maximum-security prisons, some felt that I had violated the code of silence, one of those customary laws of prison behavior that are so damned interesting. Most, however, liked that I was breaking with that tradition. I liked the idea of closing the processing plants, and doing so with considerable publicity.

There was much picketing of liquor stores that carried French wines. In Iowa City the picket lines were made up of PDI staff, college activists, and union members, and the ensuing publicity was effective. The State Liquor Commission, which ran the liquor stores, agreed to empty the French wines from the store. I said I would buy them to destroy them for the publicity. The cases were to be on the loading dock. We would arrive, give them a check for the wine, and then destroy the wine. Actually we were going to drive up, destroy the wine, and drive off. When we arrived, the cases were inside the store. They wanted payment before they moved the wine to the loading dock.

You win some, you lose some.

The processing plants were soon vacant, and the PDI's circulation increased. No one with any knowledge of the drug trade, me included, thought that the closing of the plants would mean anything positive in the end. It didn't. They moved. At the most, our "publicity drive" created a minor inconvenience. That we had any effect was gratifying (see sidebar 4).

SIDEBAR 4

IOWA BOYCOTT OF SOUTH AFRICAN WINES (by Joseph W. Grant)

A few years after inciting the boycott of French wines through my article in issue 5 of the PDI, I would organize another action that would result in all South African wines being removed from all Iowa liquor stores. Our state legislator at the time had married into a South African family and afterwards was responsible for the lobbying effort that caused the State of Iowa to purchase the South African wine. Unfortunately, his South African connection was never investigated, so I planned what I thought was an interesting tactic to get him into court and at the same time make a "joyful" noise about Iowa doing business with a racist country. After all the South African wine was pulled off the shelf, I contacted the commissioner in charge of that department and told him I was willing to buy all the wine. After buying it, I was going to destroy it in a public spectacle that would be part of our educating the public about South Africa.

Actually, I was going to arrive with a truck and a team of "workers" to load the wine, but instead of paying for it and loading it, we were going to videotape the team destroying the wine, which was state property, and then leave. Our video record would be the best evidence against what was clearly a criminal act. The tape also would ensure that the destruction of the South African wine would be seen on TV news shows across the country, with an explanation of why it took place. We would plead not guilty in order to get into court for a trial. During the trial, the legislator would be forced to testify about the lobbying effort and the strings that were pulled to get the state to buy the wine. Once that was done, I would pay for the wine—make restitution, so to speak.

On the day of the action I was called by the commissioner, who informed me that the wine had been moved to a location that he would not reveal until I paid him in advance. Someone who was part of my team of seven had informed them of our plans. One in seven. Bad odds. But the wine was off the shelves, and the state canceled all future orders. So it goes.

Women Prisoners Protest

The lead story in issue number 6 was a letter about the demonstrations that had been taking place inside the Oklahoma State Prison for Women at McAlester. For two years, incident after incident had created a rising tide of anger among the prisoners, which finally led to a riot. A letter from a black prisoner reflected the desperation that the prisoners felt. Fights between blacks and whites, she wrote, were resolved with the blacks being locked in solitary confinement in the cells that Oklahoma used to teach prisoners conformity.

The letter addressed issues that went back to 1969, when a woman died because the prison doctor refused to give her medical care. "She is faking," the doctor had maintained. The woman had spent three days in the "hospital" room—a room with six beds and a toilet. Although she was unable to eat, no attempts were made to provide her with nourishment intravenously or to take her to the local hospital. Shortly after her death, a sister prisoner went before the parole board. Instead of appealing to the board for parole, however, she chose to inform the board of the senseless death. She was labeled a "troublemaker" and denied parole.

While Rex Fletcher was still a prisoner, he attempted to alert the public to what was happening in the women's prison, but to no avail. In the free world, letters from prisoners generate no media interest unless they contain specific information that concerns some sexual aberration. The media generally follow up on such instances by calling the warden for an explanation—which they invariably get. But they never get the truth, because the media have neither the inclination nor the internal channels.

After learning of this death, we drove to McAlester to meet with the warden and personally ask questions. We were called "troublemakers and instigators." He added, "You people cannot come down here and tell me how to run my institution!"

Early in 1971, a woman with a history of two previous heart attacks had another attack in the hall just outside the dining room. The doctor who answered the call said there was nothing he could do for her. He returned to the dining room to finish his lunch. Then he called an ambulance. In November 1971, a woman with epilepsy suffered an attack at 10 A.M. in the same area. She was left on the floor until 5:30 P.M. when the doctor returned from Springtown.

Copies of the letter and copies of the PDI were sent to all the state legislators, the governor, and the elected federal officials. Our Lawyers Guild contacts and the Oklahoma Civil Liberties Union were also informed. As a result of our efforts, the medical facilities were upgraded somewhat and treatment of prisoners showed some improvement. Hardly enough, but it was something.

The staff of the PDI was being called to emergency situations involving prisoners in every part of the country. The stress on all of us was great. What kept people going was the knowledge that fellow human beings were living in situations that made our lives look like dream jobs. We were free, Cathy Kelly was providing us with two of the best meals we could ask for each day, and we had our evenings together, along with a constant stream of visitors from around the country and the world.

And we had a purpose. Fulfilling that purpose kept us on our toes 24 hours a day.

PDI Ends Innocent Indian Boy's Six Years in Prison

I was asked by a prisoners group to speak at the Iowa reformatory in Anamosa. When requests like that arrived, I tried to turn the session into more than me speaking. I'd ask to bring musicians and singers, because prisoners seldom heard live entertainment.

On this occasion I spoke, the band played, and everyone had a good time. As we were leaving, a young Indian approached me.

"Do you have a minute?"

I said I did, and he told me he was nineteen years old. "They are going to transfer me to Fort Madison tomorrow because I will not cooperate with them."

"What's the problem?" I asked him.

"To begin with, I have been locked up since I was thirteen, and I have never committed a crime, been charged with a crime, or been tried for a crime."

As soon as you have any indication that there is a serious problem, you get the person's name and number as fast as you can. Invariably the guards will see you with a "troublemaker" and they will come over and tell the prisoner to "move it on out."

With his name and number safely in my pocket, I asked him what had happened.

He said he had been sent to Eldora, the Iowa youth prison, when he was thirteen because he ran away from home and didn't go to school. He couldn't handle life at Eldora, so he ran away from there. They caught him and brought him back. He ran away again and they caught him again. And again. After three years of this, when he turned sixteen they sent him to Anamosa, the state reformatory. Anamosa was a walled prison but considered to be medium security. In other words, they didn't have armed guards on the walls. He was no more cooperative there than he had been at Eldora. Now the State of Iowa was going to teach him the ultimate lesson. They were going to send him to Fort Madison to do some time with the men. He'd damn sure regret not cooperating at Anamosa.

I asked him my stock question. "Is everything you have told me the truth?" He said it was. "If anything you've told me isn't exactly the way you said it was, please tell me now."

"Everything I have told you is the truth."

He knew what was in store for him at the Fort, and it wasn't going to be pretty. He didn't have a friend to turn to for help. He was trying to save his emotional life when he walked up to me that day.

I told him he would hear from me before the day was over. Or, if I didn't get back to him today, I would be at the prison personally first thing in the morning.

Anamosa is only forty-five minutes from Iowa City. Back at 505, I called around to verify that he had no criminal record or outstanding charges. His record was clean. The kid had never committed a crime and had been locked up for six years. I called the director of corrections and explained to him the young man's situation. I assured the director that I was certain he had been unaware of the problem. However, I said, "Now you are aware of the problem. If you don't place that young man in a minimum security situation NOW, we will drive to your office with a TV crew first thing tomorrow morning."

"Does the prisoner have a lawyer yet?" he asked.

"I'm making arrangements now. What civil actions will be taken I do not know."

The young man walked out of the prison less than an hour later, spent a few days on the farm, and was discharged.

I called the director back that night and thanked him for acting immediately.

"That young man was lucky he met you today," he said.

"No," I answered. "You and I are lucky I met him today, because if anything had happened to that boy, it would have been bad for everyone in the State of Iowa—particularly you."

He agreed. We spoke for a while, and before the conversation ended, he mentioned that he had already set the wheels in motion to determine if any other people were doing time in Iowa who had not committed a crime.

In the PDI's Law Section we ran the complete decision in the case of a Virginia prisoner, Robert J. Landman, who had filed a civil action against the director of the Virginia Department of Corrections, M. L. Royster, et al.—the "et al." in this case being the superintendent of the state penitentiary and the superintendent of the state farm.

This case was important because it forced the state to stop using certain forms of punishment, including bread-and-water diets, chains, and leg irons. The case contained a number of important court orders, but perhaps the most important was that the state had to list the rules and regulations concerning standards of expected prisoner behavior, and minimum and maximum punishments that could be accorded those who violated these rules and regulations. In addition, the court ordered that the rules had to be posted and made available to all prisoners.

That step was an important tool in ending the arbitrary and capricious use of rules and non-rules by guards against prisoners. Now, if it wasn't in the book, it didn't exist.

With the assistance of Steve Fox, a psychology professor from the University of Iowa, we formed the National Prison Center (NPC). According to the NPC's original statement of purpose, which was published in the November/December 1971 issue of the PDI: "The Center's activities would be conducted in a 'closed-loop' manner, with constant cooperation

FIGURE 5. Rev. Steve Fox (*left*) and Bro. John Price (*right*). Steve's position at the University of Iowa was helpful to the collective, particularly as an expert witness in cases against prisons using solitary confinement as a behavior modification tool. Steve died on May 31, 2006. Bro. John resides in Louisiana.

and reciprocation between prisoners, ex-convicts and professionals and paraprofessionals on the NPC staff. Central emphasis [would be] on the removal of barriers between those working for prison change on the inside and their brethren outside the walls." Someone asked, "What about the cistern?"

Response was favorable.

Thankfully, He Didn't Order 1,000 Subscriptions

Early one morning, Merilea found me sitting quietly in the office. I had been up all night trying to figure out how I was going to pay for the January issue. When she saw me, she said, "Is it that bad?" I nodded, and she handed me the morning mail.

As usual the envelopes were filled with cashier's checks and one-dollar bills. One envelope contained a typed letter with the check. I added the check to the pile without looking at it and read the letter. The writer, a lifer at the Wisconsin State Penitentiary in Waupon, was more articulate than most prisoners in his praise for the PDI. When I got to the final paragraph, I looked up at Merilea, caught her eye, and pointed to the check on the top of the stack.

"What is it?" she asked.

"I think I know, but I'm afraid to look."

Merilea reached over and picked it up. The look on her face told me I was right. "How about an early morning walk to the bank?"

"Exactly what I was thinking." I handed her the letter.

These are the final two paragraphs of the letter from August "Augie" Bergenthal:

If we expect meaningful reform within the prisons of this country, and help for our wives and families, we can't just sit back, as most of our brethren outside the walls seem to be doing these days, and "Let the other guy do it." If ever self-help is God's help had any meaning, it does in the instant case. We gotta put our money where our mouths are.

Your publication must not fail. It is with pleasure and with hope that I have instructed Mr. William Konkel of the Marine National Exchange Bank to place a certified check made out to the *Penal Digest International* along with this letter in the sum of $1000, as my contribution toward your fine efforts. I only wish at this time that it could be more.

Good wishes and good luck,
August K. Bergenthal

Merilea, Sam, and I walked to the bank, dropped the deposit in the night depository, circled back by Hamburg Inn #1, and returned to 505.

Sam had been a resident of 505 for the past few months, since he was dropped off there by a fellow who had lost an appeal. "Would you take care of him until I get back?" the fellow asked. We couldn't say no, and Sam became Iowa City's best-known dog. Actually Sam was more hobo than dog. Every day Sam would leave 505 to have breakfast with Margie Staack and Sharlane across town, after which he would make the rounds of the construction sites looking for handouts. He'd begin on the north side of downtown, where he'd visit the sites during morning coffee breaks. Then he would hang around the downtown sites for lunch. Afternoon breaks would find him in the area of Blackhawk mini-park. Drive by the park after 3:30 and Sam might jump through your car window for a ride back to 505. Whenever I saw him sniffing around downtown, I expected him to pick up a cigar butt, get up on his hind legs, and ask for a light. Hobo Sam.

Sam's fearlessness could send the biggest, most aggressive dogs running for their lives. Ranging ahead of us to check for strays, he'd suddenly make a quick turn and race past us to check the rear. If a dog was within 100 feet, Sam would charge. Dogs always turned and ran.

Groucho Marx once said, "Outside of a dog a book is man's best friend. Inside of a dog it's too dark to read"—or something to that effect.

When we got back to 505, I called the warden at Waupon and arranged for an immediate visit with Augie Bergenthal.

Augie was a tall, thin man in his sixties. I never ask prisoners what they're serving time for; however, early in our conversation Augie told me he'd been found guilty of murder one. I believed him when he insisted he was innocent—not because he had given us a thousand dollars, but because as I came to know him I became convinced that he was not capable of taking a life. A few years later, after many years in prison, it was learned that evidence had been suppressed and witnesses had perjured themselves in his case. He was released.

We spent our time together that day talking about the business end of the PDI. He was bright and alert, an astute businessman and a natural teacher; I had no business experience and was becoming discouraged. People were responding to the PDI, but they all had no money. Still, when I spoke to him, I expressed enthusiasm and recapped our fairly successful track record.

After our talk, he shook his head and offered a sad appraisal of our chances for survival. "You have wonderful ideas, Joe, and the PDI is probably the single most important tool to help prisoners that has ever come along, but you'll never make it without foundation help or government help. You'll never get government help, because government is the cause of the problem and you'd have to get in bed with them to get their money. If the foundations haven't rejected you yet, they will. They rarely give money to radicals. You can't ask for money for your halfway house, because as soon as you do, the public will know who the people at 505 are and they'll chase you out of town. You're wise to reject advertising, because no one would advertise with you anyway. If you don't already understand how serious your problem is, I'm going to regret having given you a thousand dollars."

I was completely amazed. Through my forced enthusiasm, he had seen the weak foundation upon which the PDI had been built.

"What should I do?" I asked him.

"Do you want the truth?"

I nodded.

"Unless you can find a business manager and someone who knows the magazine business and someone with the financial ability to fund a subscription drive, you won't make it."

"How come my board of directors hasn't seen what you've seen?"

"Because they haven't been looking," he said.

One thing I liked about Augie—he gave us money first and advice second. I was quick to admit we needed both.

We talked for the full three hours we were allowed. When we parted, he invited me back and said he would be thinking of ways he could help us.

Back in Iowa City, the PDI staff was busy with issue number 7. With the $2,000 from the Lewisburg subscription drive, and now the donation from Augie, we were solvent again, possibly for as long as two months. A benefit concert was being planned. As I recall, Country Joe and the Fish and five or six other groups wanted to help.

Having money to pay bills was a great feeling. I hated to part with the money, of course, but I loved the act of paying bills. I detested the collectors, but I would walk in with a smile, a handshake, and a good word for everyone. They didn't care as long as the money was there. The most critically important public-relations plan you have to develop if you are barely solvent is with the companies who can shut you down. In our case it was the printer, the utilities, and the bank where we made our house payments. Their collectors were people who had heard every story, knew all the scams, and had sat through the tears, screams, and curses.

For them, I worked hard to choreograph a production number. I made it a point to always pay our utility bills a few days late. Whenever possible I'd pay them in person. It cost a little extra, but I got to know the staff. After a few months it became a standing joke. I'd be late, but they knew I would show up and they'd get their money. I'd write out a check that was a few dollars less than the bill, and make up the difference in cash and change. I'd even show up if I didn't have money. Showing up to talk to a creditor before the creditor showed up

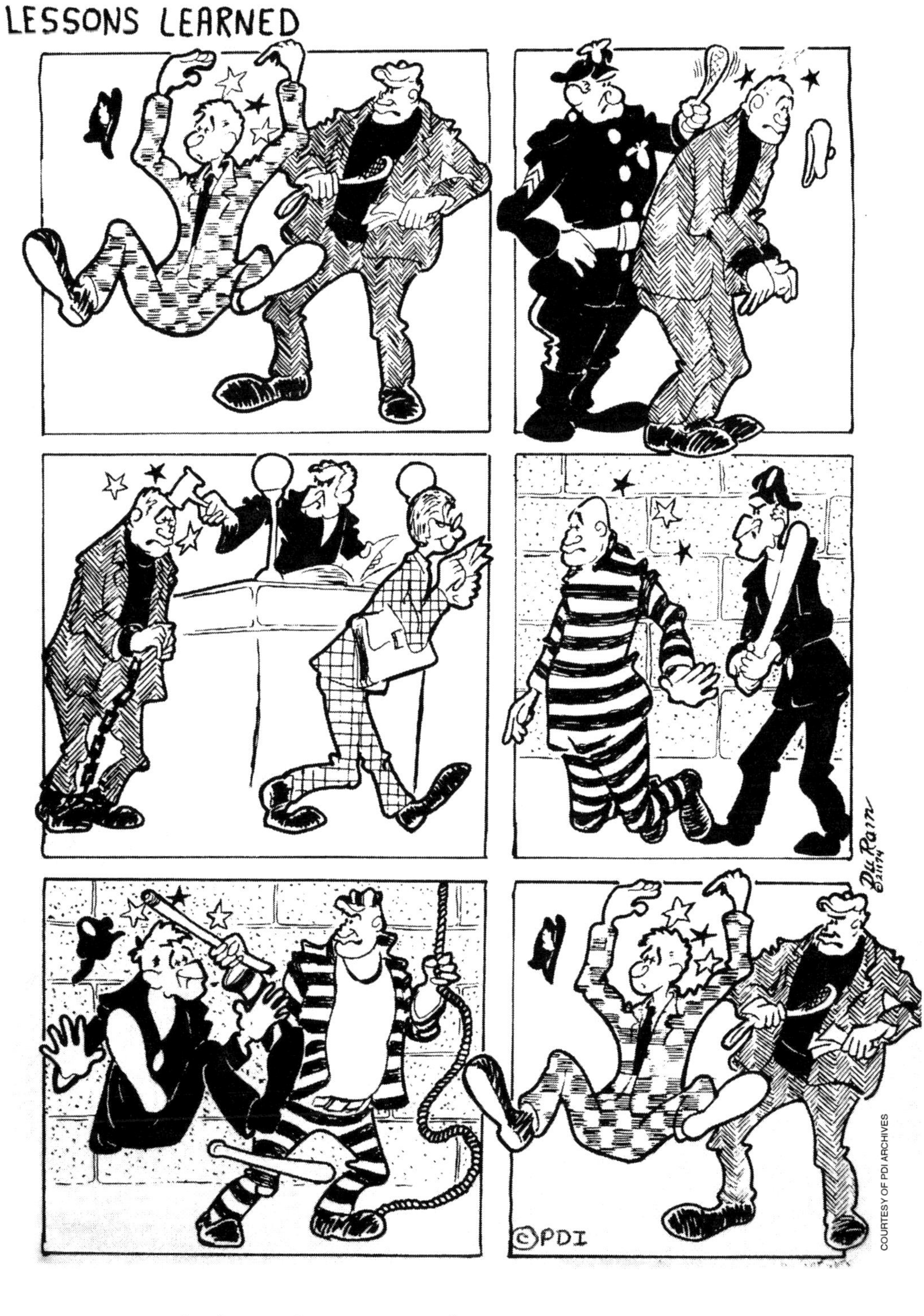

LESSONS LEARNED

FIGURE 6. PDI cartoon by Chas DuRain: *Lessons Learned.*

FIGURE 7. Three PDI cartoons by Drummond, artist and friend of Joe Grant from Leavenworth. *Racial Disunity* (this page), *Prison Reform*, and *The Longest Stretch* (opposite).

to talk to me was a MUST. At times, I was able to keep the utilities turned on even when we had gone far past the point when they normally pulled the plug.

The front page of number 7 was a powerful photograph by George Armitage that showed the silhouette of a prisoner in his cell, his hands on the bars. That photo would be used by publications all over the world. It was one of five or six that I thought were award winners. This issue also included more of Warren Levicoff's photos from Attica.

The cartoons included many more by Chas DuRain, editor of the newspaper inside the Kentucky penitentiary. DuRain and Drummond, from Leavenworth, had become favorites with prisoners. Both were talented artists who had that unique ability to spot unusual incidents and render them as editorial cartoons. By using humor, they were able to comment on many of the ugly, painful situations inside the walls and get by with it.

In this issue, John Severenson Watson took the journalism department at Southern Illinois University (SIU), in Carbondale, to task for the awards they handed out as part of the 1971 Penal Press Contest, which SIU sponsored. He started off by pointing out that Joe Milani, editor of the *Joliet-Statesville TIME*, "had been screaming for years about the inequities of the Urbandale [sic] thing." Topping Watson's list of complaints was that the *Presidio*, from Iowa State Penitentiary, came in third in the magazine category but was awarded the Charles Clayton Award, which is the highest prison journalism award SIU gives. Watson wrote that the "Sweepstakes Divisions" included printed newspapers and magazines and mimeographed publications that pitted weeklies against monthlies. "The time element alone concerning deadlines makes it two different worlds."

Watson complained further that the judges must wear blindfolds to choose the *Weekly Scene* and the *Vacavalley Star* over the *Advocate*. He also took exception to the fact that Donald Chenault, cartoonist for the *San Quentin NEWS*, only received an honorable mention. Since Chenault was reprinted in more prison publications than any prison cartoonist and restricted his themes to prison, Watson wrote, he deserved better.

Finally, Watson pointed out that only fifty-one institutions in 27 states submitted material to SIU for judging, an indication that many other editors shared his views.

A couple of longtimers at PDI believed Watson was right on all counts. The outstanding journalists within the walls were starting to question "the Urbandale thing," and the PDI had plans for a prison press awards program. Unfortunately, the lack of financial resources made it impossible to develop. Still, Watson was correct in his appraisal of the Penal Press Awards program from SIU's journalism department; not only were improvements needed, but there should have been more input from committed prison journalists behind the walls who were award winners.

Judge Leo Oxberger Rules for Prisoners

A news article in the PDI noted that Judge Leo Oxberger, from the Ninth Judicial District of Iowa, handed down a decision that took the most important step yet to end censorship in the prisons of Iowa. It started in the Polk County jail when an attorney for an inmate brought the prisoner his personal books, including many by Chairman Mao. Quoting those cases that made prisoners slaves of the state (*Price v. Johnson*, 1948; *Ruffin v. Commonwealth*,

1871; *Fortune Society v. McGinnis*, 1970; *Younger v. Gilmore*, 1971; and *Sostre v. Otis*, 1971), Judge Oxberger cut through the crap and told the Polk County sheriff to give the man his books.

Our staff was growing. Augie had agreed to become our corporate consultant even while he was still in prison. Authors Kitsi Burkhart, Jessica Mitford, and Diane Schulder joined our national advisory board. Al Cloud and Jill Donaldson joined the staff. Becky Hensley (see sidebar 5), with guitar in hand and a heart full of original music, joined the staff, too, and promptly fell in love with Brother Richard Tanner, and who could blame her? Connie Klotz joined us as editorial assistant and became a critically important right hand woman to Bob Copeland. Merilea took on the position of assistant to the director. Richard Tanner, in charge of circulation, was training Shirley Randall and Jody Hinds to take over while he was on the road. Soon we would add Dick Hayward of the *Joliet-Statesville TIME* and Donald Chenault of the *San Quentin NEWS*, two award-winning artists.

SIDEBAR 5

LOCKED INTO THE LOCKED UP (by Rebecca Hensley)

I remember the first time the subject of prisons and prisoners was presented to me. It was 1971. I was in San Francisco, working on an underground newspaper, the *San Francisco Good Times.* Black Panther Huey P. Newton had been released from prison the year before. George Jackson had just been gunned down in cold blood by guards in California's San Quentin Penitentiary during an alleged "escape attempt" that nobody believed. And former prisoner "Popeye" Jackson of the United Prisoners Union dropped by our collective to engage our interest. I spent that afternoon listening to his tales of what was really going on behind the prison walls. But it would be another few months before I locked into what I call "the prison abolition movement."

I was living now in Iowa City, Iowa, recuperating from a broken jaw I received while riding in a BMW that managed to wind up under a snow truck during a blizzard. Thanks to what I had learned in San Francisco, I was quick to pick up on a conversation in a bar that soon led me to the *Penal Digest International.* When I arrived, the collective was busy fighting efforts of the administration at Attica Prison to keep a special 90-page Attica uprising edition complete with photographs out of the hands of the prisoners inside; the courts eventually said otherwise, and we shipped hundreds of copies into the institution.

Initially I helped to paste up the paper, but it became rapidly apparent that the collective had a much more dire need. There was no organization to the daily process, which had reached crisis level regarding degree of complexity. As many as seventy letters per day were arriving from prisons and jails across the United States representing a gamut of concerns. Prisoners would be looking for penpals, free subscriptions, legal guidance, and jobs. They'd report in detail on conditions that were invariably unconstitutional and sometimes horrifying. They'd send transcripts of their cases, articles or poems for the newspaper, and occasionally even money—which we needed desperately. They'd report that they were about to be or had just been moved from one prison to another and that no one knew where they were, so they were terrified, and begged us not to let them disappear in a system where that was not only possible, but typical.

Such correspondence, stuffed into envelopes of all sizes, filled two huge cardboard boxes and overflowed onto two large office desks. We were drowning in paperwork with no one "assigned" to the task of making sense of it all. So I picked a desk and waded in. It took months and God knows how much postage to catch up, and only then because I relegated the legal questions to their own cardboard box to wait for the coming of an ex-prisoner legal whiz who'd gotten one hundred men released from prison in Connecticut over a 25-year period of incarceration. He was released on parole to work with us under our umbrella organization, the National Prison Center. And he was crazy as a bedbug, but he knew his law.

By the time I finished the task, I had written a song out of the many zip codes of prisons I had accidentally memorized. Prison abolition (not reform) and the prisoners who made this movement necessary were now officially a part of my psychological and emotional DNA.

Over time, I started writing a column I called "At Large" (as in "You're doing time for me—I'm at large for you"). The logo was an icon showing a star-filled night sky since the point had been made to me a number of times that many prisoners never got to see the stars. When I wrote my first attempt, fellow collective member Richard Tanner (a brilliant writer himself and my lover by this time) told me it wasn't good enough to publish, and that I didn't say what I really had in my heart to say. A second attempt got the same treatment, and now I was livid. The emotion his rejections generated in me propelled me to write as I had never written before, and the style that was birthed in me that day is the style I have been using ever since.

Referring to Richard Nixon's line, "Let me make one thing perfectly clear . . . ," I wrote in part:

> Let's take all the walls, real and illusionary, and make them clear as glass so the people can take a look around and see the truth of what has been happening. What is happening in this country behind the locked doors of bureaucratic convenience and individual lack of responsibility? We have been looking through a glass darkly, beloveds, and it is time to draw aside the veils. We have nothing to hide but our own sense of humanity, nothing to fear but our own slowness in seeing and speaking the truth. . . .
>
> And the prisons, ah, the prisons, my friends—pitched for two hundred years in the deepest darkness of our perverted conditionings. What will they yield up to the unsuspecting viewer through those fine clear walls? Go to Springfield, Terre Haute or Butner. Or look through the walls at Marion. See the life. See the humanity caged against itself. See the bleeding faces with no more tears left to shed. See the broken bodies and struggling spirits. See the desperation, the loneliness, the fear, the courage and the faith. See the people staring back at you through that clear glass wall.

The column was a hit, and, at least partly as a result of it, I became something of a hero to some prisoners (a "madonna," one said, though I was never that) because, while others were giving them the knowledge they needed to survive, I was feeding their souls.

When the Church of the New Song was ruled in federal court to be as official a religious body as any other, most members of the PDI collective decided to join. Soon after, we agreed to be the outside headquarters for the Church, which otherwise was completely made up of "purlieus" (branches) inside prisons and jails, where it had been established and spread rapidly. There is little question that this decision, though absolutely necessary, spread us much too thin. In addition to bringing out the newspaper and trying to support the collective financially, we now had to appear at court hearings, take actions to make legal suits possible all over the country, *and* provide chaplaincy services to our members of record inside.

In the maximum security men's penitentiary at Fort Madison, for example, on a given Sunday when the Catholic and Protestant services would have seventeen and twenty-three in attendance respectively, more than four hundred prisoners (out of a population of seven hundred or so) would fill the auditorium for the Church of the New Song service. By court order, we had an office and prisoner clerk in the education building, access to all of our members (even in solitary confinement), and we were (despite administrative denial) important to the peaceful running of the institution.

One night, while allowing Bob and Melissa Copeland, Church of the New Song chaplains at Fort Madison, a break from a year of seven-day-per-week duties, I was called on the phone at home by the officer on duty that night. He said the prisoners were threatening mayhem because one of them was not getting medical attention, and they were afraid he was going to die.

I told him to take the sick prisoner on a stretcher to the downtown hospital without delay. I instructed him to make sure the prisoners saw this happening and to tell the inside leader of the Church that I had been called and was asking the Church members to maintain their "cool" in the face of the officer's humanitarian actions. The next morning, I was thanked by the officer and told that everything went off without a hitch.

Like many other activists from the period, I finally burnt to a crisp after three years. One afternoon, I said to a National Lawyers Guild lawyer that I just sometimes felt like going to Marion Federal Penitentiary and setting myself on fire. "You need a break," he laughed. I didn't listen, but in time, I did walk away from the PDI and the Church of the New Song—though not far.

I wrote letters to Jerry Mack Dorrough, one of the Church founders, while he spent five years in solitary confinement in an effort to win the legal right for all prisoners to grow their hair if it represented a religious or cultural commitment. It was because of his eventual victory that Native Americans can now wear their hair long as an expression of their spiritual/cultural heritage. The Federal Bureau of Prisons had previously claimed that long hair was a security issue because if a man can change his appearance he might be able to sneak out of Leavenworth—though, of course, the same claim was never made where women prisoners were concerned. When Dorrough ultimately won and they *had* to let him out of the hole into the general population, they released him from prison in a ridiculously short period of time—they didn't want folks inside to get the message that The Man had been beaten.

I wrote letters to the editor, newspaper columns, and articles, and I spoke at every opportunity on what prisons are and what they represent in a country that uses them to rationalize white racism while making money by disproportionately locking up black men and women. I created a workshop for ex-prisoners called "How to Stay on the Street—Without

Going Back Up the Wall." I consulted, conducted trainings, and did research on ex-prisoner employability. I worked with adjudicated teenage boys in a facility in Miami. I designed programs for poverty-stricken African American kids, many of whom were already involved in the system on the fast track for prison. I counseled women in a maximum security penitentiary in south Florida (eventually earning myself a never-gets-to-come-back-in-here stamp of disapproval when I purchased $300 worth of new books for the prison library). Eventually, I taught college courses in juvenile delinquency and the sociology of the correctional system.

Today, in addition to everything else, I blog regularly on criminal justice issues. And I am deeply committed to the campaign to release the remaining two members of the Angola 3, Black Panther Party members who have been in solitary confinement since 1972 because of their politics. Both of my children were fathered by men I met while they were in prison. And the last man I dated seriously served twenty-seven years for a robbery that netted $70 and involved no physical injuries.

When I first found this road I've been on these past four decades, people—especially prisoners—would ask me why I cared enough to do what I was doing. I care because, as I read somewhere, the criminal code is the line of demarcation between the individual and the state. A society that can remove *all* the rights from *one* group in that society can remove *all* the rights from *any* group in that society. This society has made an art form out of assaulting the rights of people of color, especially African American men. I am only too clear that anyone can go to jail in the United States if the authorities want them there—for whatever reason. So when I question my longstanding commitment, I always think to myself, "If I was locked in a cell, what would I hope someone would do for *me?*"

And the PDI was getting better. The layout was more attractive, the editing was better, and Bob Copeland carefully scrutinized every detail. With each issue, we had more to be proud of. Every month the numbers of subscribers increased.

A Birthing at 505

Meanwhile, the long-awaited event finally took place, and life at 505 would never be the same. Cathy gave birth to Nimblewill Makalani Dearden, a 6½-pound, 17-inch baby girl.

For weeks Warren and Cathy had been poring over books on home childbirth. They felt confident they could handle a normal birth. If an emergency arose, they were five minutes away from one of the top medical centers in the country. The rest of us continued our normal level of activity. On March 10, 1972, Bob and Brother Richard were at Lake Forest College for a speaking engagement. Richard had been calling in regularly to check on Cathy; when late that afternoon he was told that Cathy was in labor, he ran to the auditorium where Bob was speaking and announced that they had to leave. They thanked the folks for their hospitality and promised to return another time, jumped in a borrowed wreck of a car, and were in Iowa City four hours later. No one complained. They knew Bob Copeland at Lake Forest.

FIGURE 8. Rebecca Hensley, already a seasoned activist when she arrived at the PDI. With her skills as a song writer, singer, and guitarist, she was a critically important link to prisoners and to prison support organizations around the country. She presently teaches at a college in Louisiana.

FIGURE 9. Brother Richard Tanner, eloquent poet and dreamer. He was Joe Grant's comrade and confidant, inside and out, until his death in Oklahoma in 1992.

FIGURE 10. Papa Warren Dearden holding new addition to the PDI staff, daughter Nimblewill Malakani.

When Bob and Richard arrived at 505, Warren, Merilea, and local artist/photographer Connie Hanson were on the third floor attending to Cathy. Throughout the night they sang, held hands, toked, timed contractions, and got themselves into the spirit of the occasion.

Early the next morning, March 11, at 6:40 A.M.—with Bob, Richard, and Merilea as official greeters, Warren as catcher, and Connie as official photographer—Nimblewill was born. One of Connie's extraordinary photos of Cathy holding her little Nimblewill Makalani, backlit against the west window, was used in issue 7, which, because we were running late as usual, was the January issue. Brother Richard described the occasion and the birth:

> Suddenly there was a body bathed in juices and already abuses from the journey just begun from there to infinity as the cord reached from the child back into yesterday and was cut away leaving only the present and the delicate administerings of Father Warren working with seven hands across the body of his and her woman-child taking mucus from the mouth and nose that grows like a button there on the face which has already opened its eyes to the world to greet we five with the flash of blue from the waters somewhere and the child was looking for somewhere to hide away from today while Mother Cathy's sobs subsided into a soft blues-song of begging for her child to lay upon her breast to feel and see and smell and hear the senses of nature played lively upon the instrument of good faith and good vibes and . . . good morning, Sister Nimblewill.

One paragraph from a page of paragraphs with picture—Cathy and Nimblewill, our 505 people, a beautiful little child—a birth. What incredible good fortune for us all.

The next day Becky and I returned home from Washington, D.C., to that new, special feeling. The birth of Nimblewill was a magic moment that lingered long after she, Cathy, and Warren moved to Maui.

The Church of the New Song

Another article that was to take on a growing significance informed prisoners all over the world that the Church of the New Song (CNS) had held its first church service on March 6 inside the federal prison in Atlanta, Georgia. Six hundred prisoners attended. Prisoner church ministers who spoke at this first gathering were cofounder Jerry Dorrough (fellow cofounder Harry Theriault had been transferred to an undisclosed federal prison and was in solitary confinement, where he would spend over eight years) and Herbert E. Juelich. Church members referred to themselves as Eclatarians, from the French "éclater," meaning "to break forth with brightness." Eclatarians were to live naturally, avoid loneliness, and strive for inner peace. Part of this "living naturally" was interpreted by the group that had gathered as never having to shave or to subject themselves to haircuts.

In the middle of the meeting, a black prisoner stood up and asked why there were no black members on the CNS Central Committee. Dorrough pointed out that blacks had been invited to sit on the committee. Another black prisoner stood and said, "As long as we got conflicts with one another, we're doing what the administration wants."

At the end of the brief article, prisoners were invited to send requests for information to the church's prison address.

This was the first time prisoners had been asked to respond to another group of prisoners. With the exception of married couples who were locked up, such correspondence was against the rules of every prison in the country without special permission. After the invitation appeared in issue number 7, every state and federal prisoner in the United States and Canada knew about CNS. The response would send a shock wave throughout the federal and state prison systems. The PDI became the free-world headquarters for CNS. Allowing that to happen was one of my major mistakes.

On the Road with the PDI

In the February 1972 issue, John Wagner emerged as a man who was much more than a huckster who could promote a successful subscription drive within the walls of the federal prison at Lewisburg. John had come a long way from his days in Leavenworth, where he was involved with the choir, the chaplain, and the Trailblazer Jaycees. He had probably heard the words "prisoners' rights" prior to picking up his first copy of the PDI, but he had never given it a second thought. That he had obligations to other prisoners had never crossed his mind. His was a life of "doing his time" with as little pain and discomfort as possible.

When he became involved with the PDI, he did so to help promote what he thought was a good idea. What he didn't understand then was that many duties and obligations came with the job. He learned that truth in the best way possible by getting into the thick of the Lewisburg prison strike when it started in the spring.

With the peaceful strike in progress, the population was split down the middle. You were either with the strikers or against them. Many prisoners headed for their cells and stayed there. John spoke out for the strikers. In the February issue, we published his first of two articles in a series called "Anatomy of a Prison Strike." Two months later, on April 14, he was awarded with "the road trip," the famous punitive transfer gig that the Federal Bureau of Prisons gives to any prisoner whose refusal to cooperate is deemed serious.

First PDI Associate Editor Wagner was forced to don travel coveralls. Then he was placed in leg irons, chained from his ankles to his waist to his wrists, handcuffed, and seated on the bus heading west. His worldly belongings were thrown into a box. His mail would never catch up to him during his solitary life on the road. Every night he stayed in solitary confinement in a different county jail or federal prison. It wasn't enough that you were a prisoner. The bureau wanted more. They wanted to make examples of people who wouldn't lie, cheat, and steal for the man. They wanted these carefully selected prisoners to spend hours chained to the seat of a bus that was either freezing cold or sweltering hot. No letters, no showers, no toothbrush, no decent meals. Just hour after hour of pounding down the highway toward another solitary cell, eating cold burgers and greasy fries twice a day, and arriving at each night's scheduled destination too late to even get a county jail meal.

Many have made the trip, and many more will.

During that road trip, John spent time in solitary confinement in Terre Haute, Indiana; Leavenworth, Kansas; El Reno, Oklahoma; La Tuna, Texas; Tucson, Arizona; Terminal Island, California; and Lompoc, California, as well as in some county jails along the way. Five weeks after he began, he arrived at the federal penitentiary on McNeil Island in the State of Washington.

There are ways to communicate in the jails and prisons—even from a solitary cell. Along the way he spoke to prisoners and shared information about the PDI, the folks at 505, and the strike. In return, prisoners went out of their way to bring John a cup of coffee, something to smoke, and news from the prison grapevine. In Terre Haute, he met Nat Warden, a frequent contributor to PDI, Pun Plamondon of the Rainbow People, John Maybery, Jay Vidovich, Johnny Sullivan, Tamie Sargis, Billy Silvers, and Rocky Bijeol. Billy "Duchess" Thompson paid him a visit in Leavenworth, as did Arthur Rachel, the PDI associate editor and former tier boss in the Cook County jail. John would be gone the next morning, but the prisoners would contact us by mail, by phone, through family visitors, and even through guards who had not bought into the system. According to the prisoners, John told them to "Contact the PDI and tell 'em I'm working on a series." He didn't have pen and paper, so he was writing the series in his head. His third and final article for PDI—his first called "On the Road: Time on the Transfer Circuit"—would appear in our June 1972 issue.

Richard Tanner and I contacted the Bureau of Prisons in Washington, D.C., and were given permission to visit with John when the bus got to Leavenworth. We were there when the bus arrived, but the warden overruled the bureau and would not let us visit with John.

Instead, we sat in the van in front of the prison and wondered at the warden's enormous stupidity. Every prisoner knew why we were there. They knew we had permission from the bureau to enter and visit. Half the cells from A and B block were faced out to where we sat, so hundreds of prisoners saw us being turned away. John's status inside, and ours outside the prison were both enhanced. Such arbitrary acts by prison administrators gave prisoners a hook to hang their anger on. With the PDI, however, the message was, "Don't react with violence—sell subscriptions, share your copy of the PDI, help your Brothers and Sisters."

When John arrived at McNeil Island, our attorneys greeted the United States marshals and the warden with legal briefs. However, before we could stop the harassment, they had John back on the bus for a return trip to Lewisburg, Pennsylvania.

John's response was, "Let's go." He wasn't going to give them the satisfaction of thinking he was having anything but fun out there on the road. The first five weeks hadn't softened him up. He was a model prisoner, a PDI associate editor we were proud to have on the staff. At every stop, he talked about the right of a prisoner to subscribe to the prisoners' newspaper. After every stop, prisoners would send us the news about John's "visit" and their conversations with him from his solitary cell at the other end of the tier.

Our lawyers met that bus a few more times with legal briefs, and just about the time they were going to drop him back in Lewisburg, the bureau decided it would be in their best interest if they let John settle down a few miles from home to finish his sentence. The long journey ended in Sandstone, Minnesota, seventy-five miles from his home. It was a good place to finish a sentence, if you didn't mind noise, bland food, giant bloodthirsty mosquitoes in the summer, and unimaginable cold in the winter.

I Find a Religion and Challenge
Contemporary-Prison-Normal

A few weeks after the article about the Church of the New Song (CNS) meeting in Atlanta appeared in the January issue, Richard Tanner and I were invited to join the church, become ministers, and address prisoner members in Atlanta.

I can't speak for Richard, but religion didn't, and doesn't, hold much interest for me. While at Leavenworth, Frank Sepulveda and I had formed a Unitarian Universalist Fellowship, because they are an organization more concerned with improving the human condition on earth than sweating out life to get a seat in heaven. I found them and their brand of religion acceptable, more acceptable than they ultimately found me. A few years later I would become the first UU to be formally excommunicated by the Unitarian Universalist church in Iowa City, after I let the Air Force know what I thought of an F-86 jet fighter that was being turned into a shrine at the Iowa City airport.

Still, I welcomed the invitation because, while CNS was looked upon by prison administrators as a religious "con job," I saw it as the safest means of getting us inside the prisons under the U.S. Constitution's guarantee of religious freedom, so we "clergy" could discuss the rule of law with prisoners.

When we arrived at the federal prison in Atlanta the administrators refused to allow Richard inside. Prison administrators frequently did this to us. They would approve a request to speak at, or visit a prison and then change their minds at the gate and leave us standing in the parking lot, where we were not allowed to stand for very long. I was allowed into the auditorium, but I was searched first, and all my notebooks were taken away.

Before the prisoners were allowed into the hall, a row of guards lined up and formed a complete semicircle around the stage. When the doors opened to this Free Exercise Seminar, as the organizers referred to the gathering, over 1,200 prisoners, more than had ever attended a church service in a federal prison, poured into the hall to share with me three of the most memorable hours I have ever spent in prison. Many others were turned away because there wasn't even standing room.

With the help of friends from Atlanta's underground newspaper, the *Great Speckled Bird*, I had arranged for some musicians to appear with us that day. The musicians were sensational. They rocked that auditorium like it had never been rocked. Then it was my turn.

Earlier, at the gate, Richard had written and given me a note to the prisoners when he learned he was being barred from entering the prison. Somehow when I was searched, his note had been missed. I read Richard's message to the prisoners. Then I asked them to let Richard know how much they appreciated his coming all the way from Iowa City only to be refused admittance.

The roar so exceeded my expectation that I was stunned. The guards in front of the stage damn near turned and ran. They were nervously glancing at the prisoners, then at each other, then at me, and all the while trying to speak to each other, trying to be heard over the deafening roar of the prisoners. The solid stone and steel surfaces caused the sound to ricochet back and forth across the hall. Whistles and screams bouncing off the floor, the ceiling, and the walls magnified the sound. Brother Richard, standing outside, not only heard the roar, he felt the ground shaking.

After eight or ten minutes, when the prisoners were back in their seats and quiet, I spoke about the obligation we as prisoners and ex-prisoners had to bring the rule of law into the prisons. With my outline gone, I simply shared with them what we had been writing about in the PDI and planning back at 505, ideas about how to negotiate conflict in this violent environment that prisoners had been forced to believe was contemporary-prison-normal.

I talked about the concerns prisoners were writing us about, and told them how legislators were sitting down with us to discuss the beatings and killings and violence that could be controlled only by prisoners. I shared the discussions that went on late into the night at 505, and mile after mile on the road as we drove from prison to prison to prison.

I could hardly believe what was happening. There were no divisions in the crowd, no cliques. This spontaneous "coming together" of 1,200 hearts and minds and shared concerns seemed to generate its own revolutionary energy. You could actually feel the ground and walls move.

Outside, Richard heard the roar slowly building and the ground beginning to shake. He watched as tower guards called security to find out what was happening and picked up their rifles in preparation for what sounded like trouble.

"I thought it was time to circle the wagons," a guard told me a few hours later.

The cordon of guards lining the front of the stage locked their arms and tightened up into a human wall, but as the band picked up the rhythm of the crowd with a closing song, the prisoners simply walked through the line of guards. No one was pushed or hurt; they just walked through.

The stage was suddenly packed with prisoners. As a result of the front-gate shakedown, my pockets had been emptied. Suddenly I had eight or ten letters, some of them dangerously thick, and many small, folded notes stuffed in my pockets, socks, and belt. The guards couldn't possibly see what was happening, but then it didn't matter. I had been searched coming in and would probably be searched going out. If I was caught with signed letters, there would certainly be trouble for the prisoners who had written them, and trouble for me. By the time the guards cleared the stage, I was standing there with my pockets loaded, holding five oil paintings that prisoners had also given me along with a half dozen books and a large walnut plaque that proclaimed me head of the church in the free world.

The guards surrounded me before I could get rid of the letters, and they led me out a side door. Once we were outside the auditorium, I was able to understand what had been happening. The roar from the crowd had not diminished. I leaned close to one of the guards so he could hear me. "These paintings have been cleared by the AW. Security has cleared the books, but you guys will have to take them through the gate for me. I came in with nothing and that's the way I'm leaving."

It was a gamble. They nodded, and I divided all of the paintings, the books, and the plaque between them while we stood in the hall waiting for the band and their prison guard escorts. As soon as they joined us, we were escorted to the front gate. But the guards stopped him from leaving. Instead, they told me the warden wanted to talk to me in his office. I was convinced that I was in big trouble. I was still on parole. They could grab me and slap me in a cell, and it could be months before our lawyers got me out.

I was one distressed ex-con, but I showed nothing. As soon as the guard got me to the warden's office, I mentioned that I had to piss and he pointed me to his personal toilet. Once inside, I checked for cameras and dropped my pants. Then I gathered all the notes and letters, tucked them into my socks and shorts, and stepped out, thanking the warden for allowing the church service. We chatted about nothing for a few minutes. Finally I excused myself, shook the bastard's hand, turned, and walked toward the door. A guard opened it and escorted me to the front entrance, where other guards had the paintings and books.

I walked out with a tremendous sense of relief. I made it out without a search. I was so sick with the anxiety and fear of the anticipated search that I damn near threw up.

Richard was pacing up and down the sidewalk at the base of the long flight of stairs. When the door swung open and he saw us, he ran up the stairs and helped me with the paintings.

"I thought there was trouble, Bro. It sounded like a riot was starting." Richard chuckled at the thought. "We do not need a riot!" He didn't seem surprised at all the paintings I was carrying, but then again Richard rarely showed surprise.

Later that night, we sat with friends from the *Great Speckled Bird* and talked about what had happened. The musicians had never had that kind of experience. They speculated that it was going to be happening right across the country. These were remarkable people with a killer publication. (See *Insider Histories of the Vietnam Era Underground Press, Part 1*, in this series.)

"Let's call Reidsville and see if we can do this down there," one of them offered.

"And then on to 1600 Pennsylvania Avenue," I said. "The White House will be easier than Reidsville."

Certainly we had the means and we had the message, but Reidsville, where the Georgia State Prison was located, would later refuse to let the PDI inside.

We talked about elections inside the prisons—not just of representatives on an inmate council, but of tier bosses, real representatives, elected on ability and merit to head negotiating teams that resolved conflicts in their immediate living areas.

We would develop teams of "ministers" who were serious about opening up the prisons and bringing the rule of law to the prisoners. We'd need access to educational programs for prisoners who wanted to help. Conflict resolution must become as important as showers. If the prisoners could keep the prison clean, keep it organized, and keep everyone fed, they should be able to work out a way to keep the environment peaceful. With teams from the free world coming into the prisons on a regular basis, there was a good chance that we could counter the ongoing efforts by administrators and guards to fragment the population along racial lines.

We were positive that the means had been handed us to bring the issues and the solutions directly to the prisoners. On the drive back to 505 we stopped in Chattanooga, Nashville, Evansville, St. Louis, Jefferson City, and Leavenworth. We couldn't get into any of the jails and prisons, but we always parked the van where the prisoners could see that the PDI was there trying to get back in.

When we got back to 505, we learned that the Federal Bureau of Prisons had issued an order that I was never to be allowed back into a federal prison as a speaker. A year later I would be allowed into Leavenworth to watch prisoners get GED certificates, but I had four guards with me at all times. If twenty-five prisoners had shown up at the church service in Atlanta and we had given them all gift prayer books and hummed a few bars of "Onward Christian Soldiers," we would have been welcomed back into every joint in the country.

Our experience in Atlanta was reported in the March issue. The entire trip had seemed too good to be true. Prisoner response to the idea of having their own religion was greater than we had even dreamed it would be. Other prisoners would learn of it through the PDI. The power of the newspaper was apparent. We had to use that power carefully. As it turned out, we wouldn't be careful enough.

Peter Breggin, MD wrote the front-page article, "Psychiatry in the Prisons." As a faculty member of Washington School of Psychiatry, he had campaigned vigorously and extensively against psychosurgery. His book *After the Good War* reflected his political concerns and his ability to tell a great story.

Another article, by Dr. Richard Korn, a professor from the Berkeley School of Criminology, was built around Korn's testimony before the Senate Judiciary Committee. Dr. Korn was an energetic man with a keen sense of humor and an eloquent voice, which was frequently raised on behalf of prisoners and other underdogs. In Cleveland one afternoon, he gave me a copy of a poem he had written about his father. The poem had been enlarged and silk-screened on heavy, poster-sized paper. Later, framed and matted, it was too much of a temptation to someone and was ripped off.

CREATION: The Arts in Prison: The Total Participation Publication

The April/May issue had 56 pages and two supplements. In the January issue, we had informed our prison readers that Tom Murton was planning to publish a monthly journal, *The Freeworld Times*, under the sponsorship of the Murton Foundation for Criminal Justice. To inform prisoners that the new publication was available, our first supplement was a 12-page insert edition of Tom's first issue. At the time, Tom was a criminology professor at the University of Minnesota. For some reason the prisoners never accepted *The Freeworld Times*.

This was a painful time for Tom. He had challenged some of the most dangerous, most corrupt politicians, and had won the battle while losing the war. He had stood up to assassins with pens, assassins with knives and guns, and the elected assassins with the power to legislate. I remember Tom saying that his newspaper would "pierce the façade of reform and shed some light on the efficacy of prison reform efforts." He never had a chance. In Arkansas he proved that he was a reformer who could not be bought. For thanks, he was thrown out on his ass and blackballed.

I had not missed a single move the establishment made in their treatment of Tom Murton. When people in the Federal Bureau of Prisons, in the courts, in Des Moines around the capitol, and in many a foundation office told me that I would get financial assistance from funding agencies if I would be less outspoken, I knew they were wrong. They may have believed what they were telling me, but I knew that if a legitimate reformer and now university teacher like Tom couldn't get help, there was nothing anyone could do to get help. We'd proceed as originally intended. We'd be the free-world voice for the imprisoned for as long as we could. We were not going to modify our message or refuse to print the letters and articles from our prison editors and contributors for any reason.

CREATION: The Arts in Prison, a slim little magazine of poetry, art, and fiction by prisoners, also premiered in this issue. In order to add *CREATION* to this press run without busting our budget, I had to come up with some way to cut the costs without offending our subscribers. Here's what I did:

CREATION started out as a 12-page tabloid with a quarterfold. The gutter of the quarterfold was glued on each page, and the other sides were untrimmed, giving us a 24-page magazine that couldn't be opened. Trimming would have cost me more money—and I didn't have it. To read it, the subscriber had to do the trimming. I drew a dotted line across the top of the cover left to right, down the right edge, and across the bottom to the bottom left corner. Printed along this dotted line were the instructions: "Cut along dotted line and become the final participant in a total participation publication."

As soon as some of our graphic-designer friends at *Playboy* saw *CREATION*, they called us to say it was the first really original idea they had seen in many years. I told them there wasn't much originality in having your readers slice the pages ("instead of each other," as someone at my elbow offered). It was just an interesting way to get them to participate in the creation of *CREATION*.

The next time I saw Don Myrus, he was holding an uncut copy of *CREATION*. "This is a great idea, Joe," he said. "I wish I had thought of it."

"Yeah," I said, "but you also thought it was a great idea to offer a set of *Playboy* books to prison libraries, and look where that got you. Or was that another one of my ideas (*groan*) that blew up and ended with a friend getting burned to the tune of seventy-thou plus?"

That boon to the prison libraries was a catastrophe to the Playboy Books division. Adding Don's $70,000-plus salary to the $100,000 the books division lost, I could only sit there shaking my head in disbelief—not because of the amount, but because Don was sitting there all smiles, seemingly without a worry in the world. Later, to my great relief, one of his assistants told me, "Don't worry about Don. He's a pro, and there are organizations who would grab him in a second if they could. He's only out of work when he wants to be."

That was a consolation. I shook Don's hand, thanked him, and reminded him that the

PDI would love to help him out if there was ever an opportunity to do so. He responded with that great smile and said, "How about signing this first issue of CREATION: The Arts in Prison for me?" As I did so he added, "Stay in touch."

That made my day. The first time someone other than a booking officer had asked me for my signature.

Another article in the April/May issue contained the results of a special survey on county jail conditions. Extensive, very detailed information had been gathered by prisoners who had spent time in the surveyed jails and was published in the issue, which was picked up by many free-world dailies from cities whose county jails made the survey. Because the results of the survey were so shocking, the article showed up in U.S. dailies and, translated, in dailies in Mexico and Denmark.

We were contacted by state legislators whose districts were home to the jails. Responding to their questions was easy. We were able to support many of the revelations with photographs. I was also able to question the representatives about what they really knew about jails in their districts. Unfortunately they never got back to me. No aspect of the conditions of county jails and prisons was ever on the table for discussion. The representatives were invariably strong on law enforcement and weak on what happened after an arrest and conviction. Every aspect of custody was a foreign territory to these politicians.

We began getting letters from people in the free world, and an occasional subscription. We rarely printed these letters, since space was always a factor and the prisoners came first. The exception was when ex-prisoners wrote. They had a voice, as did the families of prisoners.

The PDI Buys a College

The next issue, June, marked our first anniversary. It was an exciting anniversary for us all, despite our financial strains.

The two months leading up to the June issue had been one of the busiest periods in the life of the PDI. We were involved with all the day-to-day work, and we were helping with the development of the Church of the New Song. A few weeks earlier I had been in Clinton, Iowa, for some reason, being shown around the town by a fellow some of the folks at 505 called White Man—not because he was a racist, but because he was so absolutely Mr. Average, straight, American male that he just didn't appear to fit in with the 505 crowd.

Clinton is a working-class river town with a rich political history of supporting labor and regularly electing Socialist mayors. On the drive through town that day, we passed a beautiful old campus that had been John Neumann College for many years and then, for a while, a Catholic girls school, Our Lady of Angels Academy. Now it was closed and for sale by the Redemptorist Order. I asked my friend to stop so I could explore my sudden inspiration for a home, a printing plant, a college, and government funding.

The college sat on a hill overlooking the Mississippi River. The main building was a huge old mansion with rooms for about three hundred students and faculty. It had two cafeterias, a large chapel, an auditorium, and an endless number of furnished rooms. A caretaker told me that it was heated with water and that one of the boilers needed some work done on it.

The college was on nine of the most expensive residential acres in the town. Most of the land was lawn, but there were also tennis courts and a small stream. Scattered around the grounds were typical Catholic college statuaries of Jesus and a few of the saints. The entire place was pure art. I spent the rest of the day, that night, and the next day studying every inch of the buildings, the boilers, the electrical systems, and the kitchens. It crossed my mind that some developer was going to buy this place, tear the building down, tear up the trees, and build ticky-tacky. At the end of the second day, I drove back to Iowa City and picked up Sharlane. We returned to Clinton to look at the place together.

Finally I called Bishop Lowery, who was head of the Redemptorist Order, and made plans to see him the next day to discuss purchasing the college.

We found the Redemptorist Order with no trouble and were welcomed into the bishop's study. There, I told him about the PDI, our phenomenal growth, our lack of money, and my belief that with the college I could attract top teachers and a student body who would live together, work together, teach together, and learn together in this ideal environment. In doing so, I added, we could attract the attention of private and government money to run the college. The PDI was already tax-exempt.

The bishop was genuinely excited about the idea. He even asked if he could join the faculty to help get the college started. He had a graduate degree in sociology and all the theology a bishop of the Redemptorist Order needed. I told him he would be joined on the faculty by Dr. Richard Korn, from the University of California at Berkeley, and Dr. Steve Fox, neuropsychologist from the University of Iowa's psychology department.

Bishop Lowery and I discussed price and down payment. We agreed on $63,000 for the entire property. He took $1,000 as a down payment. I had three months to arrange financing for the remaining $62,000. Meanwhile, half of our staff moved to Clinton immediately, and half stayed at 505.

Artists from Ohio State University donated paintings and sculpture, and everything went into a large room just inside the front entrance: our New Song College art gallery. One wall of the art gallery I reserved for a display of crosses with a crucified Christ; however, since there was never a lily-white Jesus, I painted him a rich mahogany—closer to the skin color of the real carpenter from Nazareth.

I thought of the irony. Here I was in a college—our college—opening the New Song Art Gallery. Two-and-a-half years earlier, I'd left prison with a station wagon packed with years of accumulated paintings. After a month of painting in a large downtown room that Eli Abodeely had provided, I was ready for an art show at the People's Unitarian Universalist Church in Cedar Rapids. Notoriety was helpful, and large crowds and good sales provided the money to move to Iowa City, enroll at the university, rent a room, and get busy with plans for an underground newspaper.

So far, so good. The College of the New Song was beginning to feel like a home.

In the June issue, we devoted more space to the Church of the New Song than to any other single topic or organization. My purchase of the college in Clinton dominated the front page and two pages inside, while individual articles from prisoners spoke to the effect the PDI was having as it spread the CNS story to prisons across the country and in other countries. I had corresponded with cofounder Harry Theriault and asked him to try to simplify the religion rather than make it increasingly complex—page after page after page of doctrine and new names to describe women, men, titles, and positions of church officials flowed from his solitary cell. I wondered if it might not save us time if individuals could become members simply by assuming an obligation to respect and cherish all living things.

In the brief time the church had existed, prison administrators were already committed to breaking it. To do so, they attacked anyone who stepped into a leadership role. Each issue from this point on would be dominated by CNS, its court cases, meetings, and prison ministers.

At the time, I did not see the adverse effect this would have on our financial situation. Even the number of dollar subscriptions began to fall off drastically. This issue had only 44 pages. Bob Copeland reduced the size of the type. Still, the PDI was the only place to find the kind of information prisoners had come to depend on.

Jailhouse Lawyers: That Special Group of Prisoners

One of the most interesting articles in the anniversary issue involved the establishment of Buddhist services within the Texas prison system. Frederick Cruz, PDI associate editor and a competent jailhouse lawyer, had been ordained as a lay minister by the Buddhist church while he was an inmate there. After being released from prison, he accompanied the Reverend Calvin Chan Vassallo and two nuns on an official visit, during which Buddhist services were held in Goree Unit and at the Walls Unit (the Texas State Prison is referred to as the Walls). At the completion of each service, a number of prisoners signed a request that the services continue on a regular basis, and that they be allowed to learn more about Buddhism, and even become members.

Prison officials responded angrily to the appearance of their four visitors, especially the Texas state penitentiary ex-prisoner with the Buddhist minister ID card. Barring Cruz from future services directly violated a U.S. Supreme Court decision that had concluded the case of *Cruz v. Beto*, which Cruz himself had initiated and won while in prison. Nevertheless, according to Cruz, assistant director of treatment W. Dee Kutach and warden Bobby Morgan vowed that they were prepared to spend the rest of their lives in prison before they would allow Frederick Cruz to enter any unit of the Texas Department of Corrections in his present capacity.

It was interesting to me that our man Cruz elicited such a violent response from prison administrators. The possibility of Buddhist services attracting much interest in the Texas prison system was certainly remote. But, as with CNS, Buddhism provided prisoners with a means for stability in their lives that administrators could not control.

Anyone can enter a prison to preach the traditional Christian message of "forgive sin, give yourself to God, be born again, and dig down deep to help us spread the word"; however, arrive with the literal message of Jesus—sharing, rejecting violence, being your brothers' and sisters' keeper, living the message through actions that help the poor, finding a closet to pray in—and you are out on your ass. The theologian and philosopher Paul Tillich once wrote, "All institutions, including the Christian church, are inherently demonic."

The actions by Frederick Cruz further convinced me that the freedom-of-religion clause in the Constitution—and a battalion of ACLU and jailhouse lawyers—was going to provide us with the means to get our message into the prisons. A message stressing unity would attract the leaders and ultimately the rank and file. The Christians I most respected—Phil and Dan

Berrigan, Liz McAlister, Dave Dellinger, and the thousands of activists from Catholic Worker houses across the country, the Unitarian Universalists, Mennonites, Church of the Brethren, the Quakers—all understood that equity and the peaceful resolution of conflict were the foundation of Jesus of Nazareth's teachings. Suddenly we had a Buddhist challenging a prison system as the Muslims had challenged the system in the sixties. The Muslims exemplified the kind of discipline that enabled their members to prevail over the most brutal treatment. The body and the mind had to be clean and well exercised to measure up to the expectations of their God. Individuals understood that to be looked upon favorably by God demanded full-time commitment, a communal approach to belongings, and recognition that the condition of the least able member reflected the whole.

The Church of the New Song stressed peace, freedom, and justice and was attracting thousands every month. Whether or not its spiritual leaders would provide inspiration and stability was yet to be seen. Whether or not CNS would attract members disciplined enough to stand up to prison administrators and hold with their own religion was also a test that was coming.

Carlos Porras Jr., chairman of La Causa de La Raza, El Reno (Prison), Oklahoma, provided us with an excellent article, filled with information about the disproportionate number of Chicano soldiers who had been killed in Vietnam. He wrote, "For a people who comprise six percent of the population, we represent 18 percent of Viet Nam's casualties. An equally astonishing statistic is that roughly 22 percent of La Raza is behind bars in prisons throughout America. After arrest we do an average of 23 months more than the Anglo . . . one out of every five Chicanos is incarcerated . . . in La Tuna, where the Chicanos comprise roughly 80 percent of the population all of the policy makers are Anglo."

After writing a letter documenting and formally requesting an investigation into a savage beating of a Chicano prisoner by Anglo guards, Carlos was transferred, along with the inmate who was beaten, the witness to the beating, and the chairman and vice chairman of the Americans of Latin Extraction (ALE), a self-help organization within the prison. It was a typical response by prison officials from all the states who were faced with demands by intelligent, articulate prisoners. Transfer them. Keep them moving. Hide them in the dreaded county jails, where uneducated guards earn their jobs through political favoritism and hold their jobs by following orders.

A lengthy report detailed the formation and development of the National Prisoners Coalition (NPC). After the initial meeting in Washington, D.C., it was agreed that Richard Tanner would complete a white paper on the concept of the coalition and the history of past efforts to organize; Hy Cohen would draft the constitution and bylaws; Dan Karger would prepare a position paper on prison industry and labor; and Becky Hensley would correlate all information coming into 505 from members of the committee. Mary Jean Erickson was to prepare a white paper on social services as they affect prisoners, ex-prisoners, and future prisoners, while David Miller, PDI's man in Washington, was checking federal and state legislation that could affect the NPC. Ron Daigneault was being sent to Providence, Rhode Island, to check out the Prisoners' Reform Association.

John van Geldern provided us with an extraordinary article about prison lawyers, that special group of prisoners who take up the study of law from the confines of a cell. Attorney Fay Stender, a friend and ally of van Geldern, provided him with encouragement and sisterly legal advice when he needed it. John was himself one of the most highly respected prison lawyers in the country, particularly in California. He had locked horns with the best and the brightest lawyers the state and federal governments had, throughout a career that had included the days when a jailhouse lawyer would be thrown in the hole for helping a fellow prisoner. John recalled the skills of his friend Willie Hill, a black prisoner with a fifth-grade education, whose remarkable memory enabled him to cite from over 5,000 cases.

John wrote, "[Mr. Hill's] phenomenal legal recall has helped to unravel the ineffective representation afforded to prisoners by numerous graduate lawyers. Many an indigent California prisoner owes his freedom to Willie Charles Hill, Jailhouse Lawyer extraordinaire."

To give readers some idea of how effective John was as an attorney, a partial list of his accomplishments in 1970 included the writing of some 176 briefs relating to eight prisoner class-action cases and ninety-six individual cases. His work resulted in the change or repeal of a number of unjust, unlawful prison rules, and relief for forty-seven of the ninety-six individuals. The relief ranged from outright release to modified sentences. He ended the article by pointing out that he was proud to be a member of such distinguished company as Willie Hill, Chuck Warnocks, Tony Citrinos, Rodney Nunes, and Frenchy Martins.

In the July issue we printed our second *CREATION: The Arts in Prison.*

Jose, a former Leavenworth prisoner, wrote:

> Go
> to the ghetto.
> A garden where
> talons
> grow and
> harden
> and the whetstone
> of
> hate
> is much used.

This poem, that one line, was cemented in my mind. As each year passed and the politics of prison deteriorated, those few words would describe what I remembered about prison and surround me as I watched life in the free world become more stratified—the increasing number of homeless veterans, the racism, the poverty—and watched resources being poured down the sewer that was the Vietnam War.

A number of poems by "Wilkerson & Williamson" appeared also in this issue. James Ralph Williamson was one of PDI's most prolific writers. We never met, but his and Wilkerson's letters arrived regularly at 505, and we always had space for the comments of these remarkable writers who shared a "View from Cell 1616" at San Luis Obispo. Wilkerson and Williamson were an inspiration to many prisoners. Either would have been an excellent addition to the PDI staff.

Alex Kulikoff's art should have earned him the top awards from Southern Illinois University. The two drawings he sent us for this issue were reprinted in newspapers around the world.

The number of poetry and art submissions increased for this second edition of *CREATION*. The isolation of prison life and being forced into the emptiness of the prison environment leads, I believe, to an individual's need to express himself or herself. With rare exception, that expression arrives as poetry.

It seemed that women, particularly those in youth prisons, were the most prolific. I remember Merilea saying, "If we run out of money and have to stop printing *CREATION*, it will disappoint a group of prisoners who are devoting more of their time to poetry."

Attica Massacre Remembered

The next month, we dedicated a full page to the memory of those who had died at the Attica Massacre the year before. The prisoners had been responsible for two deaths. The guards had gone in shooting and left forty-one dead. It was noted that a memorial had been placed outside the gates of Attica, but that no prisoner's name was on the memorial.

Hanging from the front of New Song College was a huge banner: 1971 Prisoners Dying, 1972 Prisoners Trying. The entire staff gathered in Clinton for a staff picture in front of the college.

A small group of people from the neighborhood around the college complained that I was responsible for a population of killers, rapists, child abusers, and people who were a threat to the safety of their women and children. Petitions were circulated. The fact that nothing in the petition was true was ignored.

The number of non-offenders who joined us in Clinton outnumbered the ex-prisoners. The children from our breakfast program in Iowa City visited us in Clinton and had the time of their lives. In short order, the kids were more familiar with the huge building than I was. A favorite pastime was running up three stories, racing across a large recreation area, and diving into the tube that was the fire escape. I joined them. Lester asked if he could sell rides to kids in the neighborhood.

Dr. Schein's Behavior-Modification Tactics

Also in that issue, we published an article by PDI Associate Editor L. A. Ramer, a prisoner in Marion who had gathered information to document the Federal Bureau of Prisons' commitment to brainwashing and the modification of prisoners' behavior. When he submitted the material to the PDI, he sent it also to the United Nations Economic and Social Council in New York. Responses to the article came from readers around the world.

The federal prison in Marion, Illinois, housed those who were considered to be the most dangerous prisoners: political prisoners, prisoners who had developed organizing skills while in prison, and prisoners who had assaulted prison guards and/or administrators. Beginning in 1962, the Marion facility had been a youth prison. During this time, the experts had developed a system where prisoners could be moved from one part of the prison to another without the need for guard escorts. Every move could be monitored with television cameras. Some of the cameras were stationary. Others were mounted on tracks that could follow individuals or groups as they were being moved. This constant monitoring, plus cells with barred doors backed up with solid steel doors and a highly trained guard corps with a SWAT team mentality, made this prison the most secure, escape-proof, dehumanizing prison in the United States.

On the first day that adult prisoners were transferred into the institution in 1968, two men were being escorted to their cells by cameras mounted on tracks. One of the men flipped a tightly rolled-up piece of a matchbook cover onto the track and jammed the camera. Suddenly two high-risk prisoners were missing. Actually they had walked a few steps and then, out of sight of the jammed camera and not in range yet of the next, they had simply stopped. They could not be seen or heard. As far as the control room was concerned, they were gone. While the whistles blasted and the horns hooted and the guards scrambled, the prisoners stood calmly waiting for the emergency teams to arrive in their SWAT outfits. When the teams arrived, neither prisoner would admit responsibility for jamming the cameras. Instead, they maintained that they knew nothing. The videotapes of the prisoners were studied, and neither could be seen throwing the wad of paper; neither had made a move that could have been construed as throwing or flipping anything. When the Bureau of Prisons is faced with a quandary of not knowing who to blame, the bureau's behavior-modification policy is to punish everyone who is in a position to do whatever was done. Thus, the prisoners had the distinction of being not only the first to get cells, but the first to get solitary cells. Since all the cells were solitary cells, solitary confinement became the norm.

A few years before these first adults were transferred to the Marion prison, Associate Editor Ramer learned, James V. Bennett, director of the Bureau of Prisons, had sponsored a three-day seminar for all senior staff and administrators in the federal prison system. The main speaker was Dr. Edgar H. Schein, associate professor of psychology, Massachusetts Institute of Technology's School of Industrial Management. His theme was "Man against Man: Brainwashing." Intentionally or not, Dr. Schein gave the bureau a powerful weapon. The message he delivered from his treatise was, as quoted in the PDI: "In order to produce marked behavior and/or attitudes it is necessary to weaken, undermine or remove the supports to the old patterns of behavior and the old attitudes. . . . It is often necessary to break emotional ties. . . . This can be done by . . . preventing communication with those [the prisoner] cares about, or by proving to him that those he respects are not worthy of it and . . . should be mistrusted."

Then the seminar participants were given a list of tactics that he considered to be the most effective in modifying behavior in the prison setting. These tactics (see sidebar 6), which were officially adopted by the Bureau of Prisons (BOP), marked the official beginning of allowing doctors, psychologists, and prison authorities to engage in sanctioned torture. Here is how officialdom on the federal correctional level approached behavior modification.

SIDEBAR 6

DR. EDGAR SCHEIN'S LIST OF BEHAVIOR-MODIFYING TACTICS

1. Physical removal of prisoners to areas sufficiently isolated to effectively break or seriously weaken close emotional ties.
2. Segregation of all natural leaders.
3. Use of cooperative prisoners as leaders.

4. Prohibition of group activities not in line with brainwashing objectives.
5. Spying on the prisoners and reporting back private material.
6. Tricking men into written statements which are then shown to others.
7. Exploitation of opportunists and informers.
8. Convincing the prisoners that they can trust no one.
9. Treating those who are willing to collaborate in far more lenient ways than those who are not.
10. Punishing those who show uncooperative attitudes.
11. Systematic withholding of mail.
12. Preventing contact with anyone unsympathetic to the method of treatment and regimen of the captive populace.
13. Building a group conviction among the prisoners that they have been abandoned by and totally isolated from their social order.
14. Disorganization of all group standards among prisoners.
15. Undermining of all emotional supports.
16. Preventing prisoners from writing home or to friends in the community regarding the conditions of their confinement.
17. Making available and permitting access to only those publications and books that contain materials which are neutral to or supportive of the desired attitudes.
18. Placing individuals into new and ambiguous situations for which the standards are kept deliberately unclear and then putting pressure on them to conform to what is desired in order to win favor and a reprieve from the pressure.
19. Placing individuals whose will power has been weakened or eroded into a living situation with several others who are more advanced in their thought-reform and whose job it is to further the undermining of the individual's emotional supports which has begun by isolating him from family and friends.
20. Using techniques of character invalidation (e.g., humiliation, revilements, shouting to induce feelings of guilt, fear, and suggestibility) coupled with sleeplessness, an exacting prison regimen, and periodic interrogational interviews.
21. Meeting all insincere attempts to comply with cellmates' pressures with renewed hostility.
22. Repeatedly pointing out to the prisoner, by cellmates, that he has not in the past lived up to his own standards and values, and that he still is not in the present.
23. Rewarding of submission and subservience to the attitudes encompassing the brainwashing objective with a lifting of pressure and acceptance as a human being.
24. Providing social and emotional supports which reinforce the new attitudes.

At the conclusion of the seminar, BOP Director Bennett gave his staff the go-ahead to experiment with methods of behavior modification. In his own words, as quoted by Ramer in his article "The Bureau's Brainwashing Tactics":

We are a large organization with [many] thousands [of employees] in 31 different types of institutions and we have a tremendous opportunity here to carry on some experimenting to which the various panelists have alluded. We can manipulate our environment and culture. We can perhaps undertake some of the techniques that Dr. Schein discussed. What I am trying to say is that we are a group that can do a lot of experimenting and research and we can change our methods, our environments, and perhaps come up with something more specific. What I am hoping is that [you] will believe that we here in Washington are anxious to have you undertake some of these things. Do things on your own—undertake a little experiment with what you can do with the Muslims—undertake a little experiment with what you can do with some of the sociopathic individuals. . . .

If there is one thing that you can get out of this visit to Washington, let it be that you are thoughtful people with lots of opportunity to experiment. There is a lot of research to do—do it as individuals, do it as groups, and let us know the results.

In 1968 and 1969, Dr. Martin Groder, the psychiatrist at Marion, introduced the U.S. Bureau of Prisons' behavior-modification program there by semantically camouflaging the language and goals so that the public and our elected officials would think they were reading about transactional analysis, encounter groups, marathon sensitivity sessions, and psychodrama instead of what it was: brainwashing.

The August 1972 issue of the PDI contained more documentation of inhumane treatment of prisoners than any single document I have ever been able to find. Ramer's article and others, such as "The Manifesto of Dehumanization: Neo Nazi," "The United Black Front vs. Brutality in Atlanta," and "Myth and Reality in Walla Walla," documented a lifetime of suffering and made this issue one of the most important we ever published.

Behavior Modification and Eddie Sanchez

Perhaps our best example of how the behavior-modification programs of the federal government were used is the case of my friend Eddie Sanchez. Eddie was, in many ways, typical of many prisoners in the end-of-the-line prisons. He had been arrested first as a young teen, spent his formative years in a juvenile institution, and graduated to the reformatories and then to the penitentiaries. His case was a classic example of what poverty, lack of education, and racism do to a child. Eddie was one of many prisoners placed in the S.T.A.R.T. program, a program based on the theory that behavior desired by the prison administrators could be strengthened by rewards, while inappropriate behavior could be modified and ended with carefully administered degrees of punishment.

Eddie's case was unusual. To begin with, he was not a troublemaker. He was more of a loner. He listened and politely refused to participate in the program.

Doctors placed him in solitary confinement for a few days. The program they had designed for Eddie began. He was denied showers, recreation, exercise, mail, books, and magazines. After a couple of weeks he was asked if he would participate. He still refused. Then all of Eddie's clothes and bedding were removed from his cell. Now he was in a cell totally stripped of everything that was considered necessary. Nothing remained. He was naked. He still refused to participate.

At every meeting with the doctors, he made it clear that all he wanted was the right to do his time   he wanted to be left alone.

The final step in their plans to change Eddie, to modify his behavior to meet the expectations of designers of the program, was to place him, stripped, spread-eagled, face down on the metal bed, with handcuffs on each wrist and ankle attached to each corner of the metal bed and stretched tight so he could barely move. For seven days and nights, for over 168 hours, he was secured in this position. He was not allowed to use the toilet or to wash. No urine or fecal matter was cleaned up during the seven days and nights, so he was forced to piss and defecate on himself and lie in it. He was force-fed a minimum of liquid food and a small amount of water—just enough to keep him alive. He was allowed no cleanup for the entire time he was subjected to this torture. The actions by the doctors and prison authorities were torture pure and simple. It was an illegal, inhumane, barbaric system of torture, and Eddie toughened up, refused to relent. He had reached the point where he was willing to die rather than give in to the experimenters.

The doctors and prison authorities finally released him. It took him a day to regain the use of his legs and arms. When he was able to stand, he was able to clean himself—in his cell, no shower. He sat and waited.

That night he managed to break the light bulb behind the heavy mesh screen in his cell. With a thin sliver of glass from the broken bulb, he methodically sliced through his Achilles tendon. He was quickly transferred to the Federal Medical Center at Springfield.

What he had gone through was impossible to cover up. We were the voice of the prisoners. We were trusted. When a prisoner was being abused, that information would get to us.

Months after I finally met with Eddie and got the story, he ended up on the bus making the tour from jail to jail, prison to prison. Later I received a letter from Eddie that turned out to be the last I heard from him. He was doing his time and being left alone, but the tone of the letter and the fact that he was no longer communicating with us was troubling.

Shiloh Harry Theriault

Meanwhile, on August 22, 1972 , Merilea stuffed 35 pounds of belongings into a backpack and hitchhiked to La Tuna Federal Prison in Anthony, New Mexico, on the Texas–New Mexico border, where she had been given permission to visit Shiloh Harry Theriault, Bishop of the Church of the New Song.

This was not an easy visit to arrange. Shiloh had become a significant thorn in the side of the Federal Bureau of Prisons. While being transferred to La Tuna, riding in a regular sedan, he was the brunt of remarks by the federal marshals, and when the constant demeaning comments reached a point where he'd had all he could take, an interesting phenomenon took place. The sky clouded over and the weather became threatening. There were flashes of lightning, and suddenly a gigantic cross formed in the sky. Both marshals saw it when Shiloh pointed it out to them and told them it was the spirit of Eclat speaking to him, and it was time to stand and acknowledge the presence of the divine spirit. They laughed at him. He promptly kicked the back and side windows out of the car and went to work on the marshals. The driver lost control of the car and it flipped. The back doors flew open. Shiloh stepped out, stood there looking at the cross in the sky, and waited. Shiloh was a big man. He could have made an escape. When the marshals extricated themselves from the car—it had rolled and ended on its side—Shiloh was standing there waiting for them to join him.

When Shiloh reached La Tuna, he wasn't placed in solitary immediately. Once the cuffs and chains were removed and he'd finished with the routines in Arrival and Orientation he was allowed to walk around the yard. He walked over to the chapel. The door was locked. He kicked the doors in, proclaimed the chapel a Church of the New Song, walked up to the front of the chapel, and waited for his congregation. He didn't have a long wait. The guards arrived, led by the "goon squad" of the big boys who always led the charge when there was a *prisoner problem.* He was quickly removed from "his" church and placed in solitary.

Merilea had recently returned from a visit to the federal prison at Sandstone, Minnesota, where she had met with John Wagner. In the August issue, which was not printed until close to the end of October, we published a collage of stories about the wardens and the prisoners and how a remarkably mellow PDI staffer was able to slip into and out of a prison that had systematically barred the PDI since we began publishing. Merilea was unaware of it, but her hitchhiking travels around the country by herself just scared the hell out of all of us. Merilea's trip to visit Shiloh was unique, because it was the first time a member of our staff had been allowed to visit him in solitary. Merilea had sewn a long cape for him that put to shame any cape worn by any bishop in any other religion in the world. He looked great. When she returned, a collective sigh of relief was breathed. This diminutive young teacher with her shock of tightly curled, kinky hair had become as important to the prisoners and PDI as our second-class permit.

Clinton, Iowa, Neighbors Play Hardball with the PDI

I had thought that buying a college was going to get us some press. I wasn't prepared for the kind of press we were going to get. It didn't take long before we discovered that the folks living in the neighborhood were not pleased to learn that a group of people associated with prisoners had purchased a college. Our neighbors were getting ready to play hardball.

In September, the community laid siege to the college. An organized effort was under way to gather hundreds of signatures demanding that we be driven out. Petition leaders were charging that wives, mothers, and little girls were no longer safe while the killers, drug addicts, perverts, and rapists were living across the street.

The petition circulators convinced many people, but they didn't convince everyone. We had immediately opened a drug counseling service staffed by people who knew how to help substance abusers. I was quick to point out that, if anything, we had gathered many of the people Clinton considered to be problems and were housing them under one roof and keeping them busy. Not that they needed my direction. The great majority of the people who joined us at the college were innovative, intelligent, family-oriented mothers and fathers who just didn't have the resources to survive being out of work for two or three months. These were the forerunners of the tens of thousands who would end up on the streets during the Reagan and Bush I and II administrations. As a way to protest the treatment our people were getting from many of the people of Clinton, I went on a fast. After three weeks without food, I felt great. I was thinking more clearly and feeling better than I had in a long time. Unfortunately,

FIGURE 11. Defense team prepares to fight eviction from New Song College, Clinton, Iowa, 1972. *Front row:* Joe Grant, Sharlane Grant, Judy Levicoff with daughter Lisa, and Brother John Price, jailhouse lawyer in the free world. *Back row:* Ruth Harty is on the left.

the few bucks we saved on food that I didn't eat during that period did little to boost our ailing budget, and in September I missed the first deadline on partial payment for the college.

At the time, I didn't panic, because I was certain that in our negotiations I had discussed the possibility that this might happen, and believed the bishop had indicated that he was flexible with the dates set forth in the contract. Unfortunately, at the time we discussed "flexibility," the bishop wasn't being bombarded with letters, phone calls, and petitions from a very Catholic Clinton flock.

As soon as it became clear that Bishop Lowery was going to start eviction proceedings, I raced across town to retain attorney Donald Seneff. When Bishop Lowery beat me to him by minutes, I resolved to defend myself. I spent the next couple of days researching the Redemptorist Order's beginnings. I learned that the order's founder, St. Alphonsus, had established his "new institute" in Italy in 1732. In his day, he had gathered the beggars, drifters, and thieves around him. If St. Alphonsus had been living in Clinton in 1972, he probably would have taken one of two courses of action. He would have joined us, or he would have convinced us to join him. The good St. Alphonsus would certainly have quoted scripture to the city of Clinton and to the members of the Redemptorist Order about what the college should be used for.

FIGURE 12. Joe Grant, Clinton County Courthouse, representing the *Prisoners' Digest International* and the Church of the New Song, 1973. Grant was stating that the handshake between him and the Bishop of the Redemptorist Order, owners of the college Grant had made a down payment on, was as good as a written contract. When the Bishop then testified that there had been no handshake agreement, Grant said there was no reason to continue and asked for the judge's verdict. The judge went to his chambers, returned in less than five minutes with a five-page typewritten decision, and ordered "Joe Grant and his followers to leave Clinton, Iowa, by sundown."

We divided up the defense. Anne Garza, a staff member from the Iowa City community who had moved into the center with us, was defending herself. John Price, a PDI staff member who also lived at the center, was defending himself and five others. I was defending PDI, CNS, and approximately twenty other individuals.

Although the odds seemed to be heavily against us, we had a good case. Verbal agreements between the bishop and me did not follow the letter of the written contract. However, I believed that under oath, the bishop would have to admit that we had agreed on flexible payment deadlines; in our talks, we had concluded that the most important item on the college agenda was to get the college started. Being in court would also give me a chance to set forth our goals under oath, and answer the many questions I had not yet been able to address. I knew that the city would feel much better about the PDI purchasing the college when I finished testifying.

A short way into the trial, with the bishop on the stand, I asked him about our conversation concerning the deadlines. He said that the only agreements he had made with me were the written agreements in the contract.

That finished us. I believed he wasn't conveying the whole truth, but I had nothing in writing; it was just my word against his. For a while I wasn't sure how to proceed. One part of me wanted to go after him, to really dig into him about the Commandments. I wanted to have him re-sworn to make sure he understood. I wanted to tell him he was going to fry for his lie. But there was no reason to grandstand. I'm convinced to this day that everyone in the courtroom knew what he had done. I think I asked him if there was anything about our conversations that he wanted to share with the court. He said there wasn't. I said I had no more questions. The bishop left the stand, sat down next to his attorney, folded his arms, and put his head down so his forehead was resting on his forearms. He didn't look up for the rest of the trial.

Annie and John presented their cases, and then I called myself as a witness.

Normally, when you are in front of a judge who you know is on the "other side," you wait for him or her to make a mistake that will give you grounds to appeal the decision. With this judge, it happened as soon as I got on the stand. I had already been talking for a while, so when I began questioning myself, my throat became very dry. I asked the judge to call a brief recess so I could get a drink of water.

The judge replied, "Why don't you have one of your cohorts bring you a drink, Mr. Grant?"

Ruth Harty, a Clinton resident who was living with us at the center, was on her feet instantly. "Where do you get off labeling us 'cohorts?' We are sisters and brothers!"

I was prepared to move for a mistrial and walk out of the courtroom. Doing that would have given us another couple of weeks—if nothing else, we might have gotten the ten acres of grass cut again.

But then the judge did the unexpected. He apologized to Ruth and to everyone in the crowded courtroom. Since there wasn't a jury, we had to live with his apology.

I continued questioning and answering myself. I have never been involved in such an emotional courtroom experience. I'm certain everyone in the courtroom believed that the sadness in my voice and the tears in my eyes were based on the conflict between the bishop and me about the college. Not so. I was watching four years of work slowly come apart. I didn't have any less money in my pocket than I had two years earlier. We never really had any money, but we had always had enough to keep the bills partially paid. Now we were close to the end of the rope.

I had a difficult time answering my own questions because I was talking dreams. The college was to have been staffed by faculty and their families, the students were to have been ex-offenders, and all participants and their families would have lived at the college. Everything was to have been shared—the teaching, the cooking, the cleaning, the maintenance. We would have had room for daycare, art, counseling, the PDI, the National Prison Center, a publishing operation. We only needed time and cooperation. And money.

Part of my appeal was to the community to allow us to save the Redemptorist Center, which had been rezoned for single-family dwellings and was sure to be destroyed if someone didn't take it for the school it was meant to be.

The bishop's face was still buried in his folded hands. He couldn't watch. I realized that his hands were tied. Making him suffer would accomplish nothing. The city wanted us out, the police were standing by with a SWAT team to evict us, and the only thing that would have saved us was cold, hard cash.

On the stand that afternoon, I learned that I could no longer generate hatred—not for the bigots, the liars, or the racists. I saw what these people were doing—through their campaign of hate mail, petitions, obscene phone calls, trespassing charges, breaking-and-entering charges, court orders, legal notices, constant threats, and through it all, lies by people from whom you do not expect lies—to keep a small group of ex-prisoners from buying a vacant college in their neighborhood. That the Redemptorist fathers could turn their backs on the teachings of their founder was disappointing. I would think for many years about the kind of pressure Bishop Lowery had to have been under to deny us the college.

The karma was bad in Clinton, and if we had had a hundred of our best, it wouldn't have made any difference. We had certainly shown greater restraint than our neighbors. We could leave the courtroom, the college, and the city of Clinton knowing that we had harmed no one and had helped many.

I asked all of our people if there was anything they wanted to add, and we rested our case. John Price, Ruth Harty, Ma Jones, and others had been eloquent. The judge commended us for our presentation and mentioned that our grasp of the law and our knowledge of court procedure had surprised and pleased him. This comment by the judge is stock. They all use it when someone is defending himself. With those few words, the participants all feel better about themselves. Of course, it was all bullshit. I knew what was coming.

The judge retired to his chambers to reach a decision. I figured he would have the good sense to relax in his chamber for thirty minutes or so for the appearance of thoughtful judicial decision making. I was exhausted. The judge surprised us. Less than three minutes later, he emerged with a five-page typewritten decision with multiple copies. He had ruled against us. His final words were, "You have until sundown to get out of town."

The headline in the *Clinton Herald* boldly proclaimed: "Grant and Followers Given until Sundown to Leave." Talk about the bench shooting from the hip.

That night we sat together at the art gallery and discussed our options. In the end, we narrowed them down to two. Everyone had a vote: Should we barricade the entrances and fight eviction as nonviolently as we could, and in so doing create a media event that would have the networks there in helicopters? or should we just leave? We smoked some Iowa pot that someone had brought, then contemplated quietly as we thought about what the next few days would be like if we stayed. Three of us had witnessed Attica a year earlier. We knew how brutal the police could get. No one was frightened, but we discussed what to do. I wasn't worried that there would be serious rough stuff, but heads would get busted if we stayed, families would be separated, paroles would be violated.

The College Is Stormed

It was during a period of extended silence that we suddenly realized we were being raided. We could hear dozens running in the halls. They were coming in from the back entrances, and we had damn little time to do anything except slam two doors shut and move some desks to block the doors. The noise became louder. It sounded like fifteen or twenty police in riot gear thundering down the hallway. I said, "DAMN! We should have nailed the back doors shut earlier."

Suddenly the entire building was shaking, and the floor of the art gallery was moving us ever so slightly up and over and down and back to where we were. "Hang on," someone yelled. I think Ma Jones had the presence of mind and the wit to offer to hide a small baggie of herb deep in her ample bosom. Jerry Samuels and Ma Jones headed for the second-floor auditorium where Jerry had his bags and music. By the time they were steady enough on their feet to run for the stairs, the noises of the charging police had stopped.

It was very quiet. We felt two more bumps and realized we had just experienced our first earthquake. It was a rather frightening experience. Someone said, "I wonder if it means that God wants us to stay or to leave." Nikki and Lisa Levicoff, two youngsters who were wise beyond their years, looked at each other and broke up laughing.

I couldn't resist giving thought to using the earthquake to our advantage. Since we were leaving, perhaps we could return to court, demand another hearing, and claim we were only doing so because God wanted it, and the proof that she wanted it was her tipping over the statue of her son Jesus and a couple of his pals who became saints. Outrage sells, and the staying power of an underground newspaper depends as much on what others say about you as what you say about yourself.

Brother Richard said, "I like the idea, but only if we can take the statues with us and drop 'em off at the Fort."

Soon everyone was laughing. A short time later, we gathered for our last dinner at "New Song." There was some wine, a little smoke, and eventually consensus. We were tired, in no mood for another siege, more confrontations, and lengthy court actions. We decided to stay one day past the deadline, just to let them know that we were not impressed with ultimatums. Our Clinton brothers and sisters proposed that we camp on the edge of town for a few days to relax and get organized.

"There's a place a couple miles north of Clinton on the banks of the Mississippi River called Bulger's Hollow," said Stan Mortenson. "Legend has it that the place is haunted."

Sounded like a perfect place for a vacation.

Ghosts on Our Side in Haunted Bulger's Hollow

Some forty-five men, women, and children gathered in Bulger's Hollow the next day. Spirits were high as we moved into the small park. Everyone had a job. Tents were pitched. We arranged logs for seating and positioned the tripod so that the huge cast-iron cooking pot filled with rice and vegetables hung directly over the fire. Small smudge fires circled the hollow to discourage mosquitoes as children played and others lined the bank with rods and reels to see if there were any fish for the big pot. Ma Jones was organizing dinner, and someone was planning a family concert for the evening. All our problems, including our uncertain financial future, were set aside. We were free of Clinton, the courts, and creditors for at least a few days. As I watched everyone settling in, I was struck by our group's resemblance to the family outings I had enjoyed as a young child on a farm in Northern Minnesota.

Warren Levicoff was busy with his camera documenting our activities.

FIGURE 13. Joe and Sharlane Grant taking a fishing break after camp was established in Bulger's Hollow, just a few miles north of Clinton, Iowa, 1973.

My hope, as I told reporter Harley Sorenson, who had been sent down to Clinton from the *Minneapolis Star Tribune* to write a series of feature pieces about our attempt to buy the college, was to find a place with homes for everyone, enough space to raise our own food, and a central location to publish the PDI and maybe do job printing to help raise additional revenue.

That evening, storm clouds began to gather over Clinton. Warren wondered if we should take the tents down and prepare to crowd into the cars. Most of the kids were already asleep in the tents, so we packed up loose items and tied down everything else. We could quickly take the tents down later if the storm hit us and it appeared that we were in for a drenching.

Sitting around a central fire with our eyes on the storm building over Clinton, we could look south at the wall of black clouds that were low and rolling our way. The lightning was getting closer. Suddenly the lights of Clinton disappeared as a black wall of water rushed up from the south. It reached us so fast we had no time to wake the children and take the tents down. But just as suddenly, the rampaging storm parted and passed us by. We stood there watching rain pour down on all sides of us like it was happening on a movie screen. The storm lasted for almost an hour. We speculated that Clinton must have suffered from the incredible downpour. The only thing like it that I have ever witnessed was when our destroyer, the USS *Clarence K. Bronson* DD668, ended up in the center of a hurricane off the coast of North Carolina. As the weather went from slight wind to hurricane-force winds, our ship took a 62 degree list, righted itself, and was suddenly in the eye of the hurricane, where it was calm. Our camping area ended up in a similar zone of calm.

I went over to the fire for another plate of rice and veggies. While standing by the cast-iron pot, I glanced downriver and saw a line of cars slowly driving up the river road from Clinton. I pointed to the caravan and told people to get ready for trouble. We knew they were not coming out to invite us back. A few of us walked over and stood blocking the small road leading into Bulger's Hollow. The rest stayed back with the children, most of whom were still sleeping.

When the caravan stopped at the lineup of men and women, the passengers in the first car rolled down their windows. We walked over and asked them if there was something they needed.

"We came out to help," the driver said. "We had such a terrible flood in Clinton that many cars were washed into the river. Clinton is a mess. We figured you folks would have lost everything, and figured we might be able to help."

The visitors yelled down the line of cars, and people walked over, perplexed that the storm had harmlessly passed us by.

Of course, Ma Jones walked over to check the cars. As soon as it became apparent that they posed no harm, she invited them to share our food; they eagerly accepted.

The people started getting out of their cars. As they joined us and looked around the camp, they shook their heads in disbelief. The tents were up, fires were blazing, enough smoke was being generated by the smudge fires to keep the bugs away, pots still hung over two of the fires, and people were walking around as if nothing had happened.

The last car on the line left and soon returned with a couple of cases of Linies beer. The one question that was asked again and again was, "Do you have any idea of how much damage the storm did to Clinton?" We fed our guests, enjoyed the beer, someone from Clinton fired up a joint, and everyone relaxed.

It was a perfect evening—considering.

The next morning, when Harley Sorenson checked in with his editors at the *Minneapolis Star Tribune*, he learned that a Larry Johnson was trying to get hold of me. I called Larry and was offered a couple of houses, some property for more houses, all the land we needed for gardens, and a large two-story office building up in west central Minnesota, all of which represented a good section of Georgeville, a small town that had gone broke during the Great Depression. He wanted $400. Good things come to those who are impatient.

Late the next day, Sharlane and I left for Iowa City on our way to Minnesota with Jerry Samuels, Judy and Warren Levicoff, their daughters Nikki and Lisa, Ma Jones, and Bill Smith.

They're Coming to Take Us Away, Ha Ha

505 had always been home to a musician or two. Becky Hensley was an accomplished singer, guitarist, and composer. Bob Copeland, when he finally found time to concentrate on music, played guitar, sang, and composed like he wrote—which was extremely well. Over the brief time we were in business, we hosted many musicians who had been booked into Iowa City. Biff Rose was a 505 favorite. However, the person who stayed for the longest period of time was Jerry Samuels. Jerry had an international following as a result of his recording "They're Coming to Take Me Away, Ha Ha," which he recorded under the name Napoleon XIV, and "The Shelter of Your Arms," which many musicians recorded. Jerry called us when he learned that he had been booked into the Carousel Lounge on the "Coralville Strip," which everyone except folks living in Coralville referred to as Iowa City's "garbage can" because of all the fast food outlets crowded in between motels and gas stations and restaurants just outside of town. We invited him to stay with us during his three-week appearance in Coralville.

Jerry was always on the move, a speed freak without the chemicals. The day he arrived, he announced that we were going to eat "Chinese" for dinner that night. He had already driven off and returned with wine for dinner, so we figured he had also been grocery shopping and was planning to take over the kitchen and prepare one of his specialties.

At dinner time, Jerry announced that dinner was ready. On the dining room table, completely covering it, were carry-out containers from one of the local Chinese restaurants. Jerry was busy opening them. On the table were all of Cathy's wooden serving spoons, most of which would not fit into the containers. While we crowded around our long dining table filling our plates, I noticed a shocked look on Becky's face. I asked her if she was okay. She didn't say anything; she just handed me the food receipt Jerry had tossed in the trash. That dinner had cost Jerry almost $200, which was more than we spent on food in a week. When we explained that to Jerry, he explained to us that he spent 80 percent of his time in recording studios and control rooms or on stages, none of which came with kitchens. When he was hungry, he reached for the phone.

The dinner was a surprise and it was fun, but I took Jerry off to the side and requested no more surprises. He was asked to clear any food purchases with Cathy so we wouldn't be spending more than was necessary.

After dinner Jerry asked if anyone was interested in dessert, and promptly pulled out a small bag of what he called Lamb's Breath. "This is the best Jamaican pot I have ever tasted," he said and began rolling joints.

In those days, it was not unusual to see marijuana around town. Hard drugs were never tolerated at 505, but pot was lumped together in the same category as beer.

After enjoying Jerry's "dessert," someone asked Jerry if he had ever tried Iowa pot. Jerry laughed and pointed out that he had been seeing tons of Iowa pot, or ditch-weed, on his drive in from Chicago. Of course, this wasn't the same brand of marijuana that had been grown in Iowa during World War II and harvested for the fibers that made great rope. This was the amazing end result of many years of genetic manipulation by local botany professors. Jerry tried it and couldn't believe its potency. He touched it, smelled it, tasted it, and smoked a little more. Then he just sat there with his feelings and thoughts until finally he got up, walked to the piano, and wrote, in about twenty minutes, "I Owe a Lot to Iowa Pot."

> Oh I owe a lot to Iowa Pot,
> Iowa grown and grand
> I never knew what beautiful Boo
> Grew in this groovy land I'm in
> And I'm indebted indeed to wonderful weed
> Iowa grown and grand.
> Oh I owe a lot to Iowa pot . . .

And on and on.

Over the next three days, while he was waiting to begin his Friday night gig, Jerry spent all his time at 505. By the time Friday arrived, he had learned much about prison. He opened his first set at the Carousel with a medley of sixties protest songs interspersed with his own compositions. At the end of the evening, the Carousel manager told him he was not to sing any protest songs or political songs.

"Get your act together, Mr. Samuels," he was warned, "or tomorrow night will be your last night at the Carousel."

Jerry didn't threaten well. He returned to 505, told us what had happened, and informed us of what he was going to do. The next night Jerry opened to a packed house. In every seat was someone directly or indirectly involved with the PDI. A couple of musician friends had driven over from Chicago to sit in with Jerry, including Warren Levicoff's eighteen-year-old brother Steve, who had collaborated with Jerry in the past and who, twenty years later, would write his college dissertation on the history of the Church of the New Song for a doctorate in theology and law (see sidebar 7). The most difficult task for each of us in the audience was sitting there for the evening nursing one beer. Never had the Carousel had such a crowd or made less money. A memorable evening—Jerry's last in that club.

The next day Jerry called his manager and told him to cancel the rest of his bookings. He'd decided to move in with the PDI.

SIDEBAR 7

REFLECTIONS ON *PENAL DIGEST INTERNATIONAL* (by Steve Levicoff)

The prison reform movement that was active from 1960 to the early 1980s saw more success than at any other period in the nation's history. Civil liberties advocates enjoyed success in the judicial system and generated a public awareness that has not been matched since. *Penal Digest International* played a strong role in that public awareness.

PDI was a publication written by a group of ex-convicts and social activists and circulated not only within federal and state prison systems but also in the outside community. More than anything else, PDI was a vehicle for communication, ensuring that those who were inside the prison walls did not lose touch with the reality that they were not alone, that men and women in other penitentiaries and correctional facilities were going through the same oppression that they were, and that people in the outside world were willing to put themselves on the line to do something about it.

As a voice of the prisoner, PDI had qualities that were both advantageous and detrimental. It was brazenly honest about conditions inside the prison walls, unabashedly angry about the fact that those conditions could exist, and forthright in its demands for immediate change. PDI often challenged people by offending their sensibilities, shocking them into the reality of knowing that prison was not a pretty picture.

At the same time, there is another reality: Anger tends to overcompensate for conditions as they exist, and expressing too much anger often has a reverse effect in terms of the goals that are sought.

The Church of the New Song (what could have been an accidental acronym with an appropriate touch of tongue-in-cheek, CONS, had it not been more generally known as CNS) provides a striking example. Founded in 1969 by prisoners, for prisoners, CNS was originally formed as a tool to gain prisoners' rights through the freedom-of-religion clause in the First Amendment to the Constitution. Its proponents raised a plethora of concerns about freedom of expression and effectively addressed the religious rights of prisoners for the first time since the Black Muslims had done so in the 1960s. The constitutional issues addressed by CNS were legitimate, regardless of what one thought of the tenets of their faith system.

PDI, as the most visible voice in the nationwide community of prisoners, provided a voice of communication that spread the CNS message. Yet along with that message came expressions of anger at the traditional religions that CNS members felt oppressed them. As CNS "minister of political correspondence" Norman Gorham wrote in PDI, CNS was "a faith, not of Christ, a dude who may have existed in 33 A.D., or his invisible, pound-of-air Father, but of people—convict people . . . a bastard group of hard-core cons who were sought for various crimes that never took place by the forces of Caesar." CNS, another member wrote, was a church that "does away with the bullshit, the mysticism, life hereafter." And therein lay the problem.

There was never a doubt that members of CNS had the right to hold or not hold whatever religious tenets they chose. But in their often self-righteous anger, they ended up offending many people who would otherwise have defended their rights.

So it was with other issues addressed in the PDI by those who were being burned in the prison system. Hands were reaching in to help ensure the rights of those behind bars, but when those hands were bitten, they retreated. By the time the anger began to subside, society as a whole had changed.

During the late 1970s and into the 1980s, society's desire to effect positive change was replaced by what Tom Wolfe would call the "Me Decade." Liberal social causes that had been emphasized in earlier years were replaced by a conservative political ideology that remains with us today. In the 1990s, a war that would earlier have generated peace protests and resistance resulted in resurging pride and a plethora of yellow ribbons.

Penal Digest International served a purpose in its time that may not be duplicated for another decade or more. The late Lenny Bruce once reflected, "One generation saves up to buy their children galoshes. When the storm finally comes, the kids are outside barefoot, digging the rain." When the new generation comes that has a higher priority in terms of human rights for those who are behind bars, let's hope that a new PDI exists to act as a voice in the wilderness.

FIGURE 14. Words and music to "Prisons and Prisons and Prisons" (*this page*) and "Children, Oh Children" (*following page*), written by Jerry Samuels and donated to Joseph W. Grant, 1972.

Jerry was to stay with us for a while in Iowa City, join us in Clinton, and continue on with us to Minnesota, where we established the Georgeville Community Project. During his stay he also composed "Children, Oh Children," "Prisons and Prisons (My Daughters and Sons)," and "Sing a New Song." Before he left, he gave me the songs to copyright and told me to use any revenue for social action. I have included the music (figure 14). I hope these songs will be sung and recorded. If the PDI is ever to rise from its ashes, phoenix-like, money will be needed.

Following the Activists into Georgeville

During our meeting with the staff in Iowa City, we learned that only 10 copies of our August issue had been allowed inside Leavenworth. Issues for our approximately 140 other subscribers in that prison had been destroyed. Lawyers Guild supporters were contacted, and the legal work began.

Late that night we left for Minnesota to look at the property in Georgeville.

Georgeville is located in Sterns County, about 90 miles northwest of Minneapolis. In *Zen and the Art of Motorcycle Maintenance*, Robert Pirsig describes the area's most distinctive feature as being its lack of anything distinctive. The book begins as he and his son, on a motorcycle, pass through Georgeville on Highway 55, which runs from Minneapolis to Fargo.

Sterns County was unique for a number of reasons. In our area, the distinction was low swampy land, poverty, and damn few resources. It was home to some of the largest granite quarry operations in the country.

According to a University of Minnesota doctoral study, it also was home to more mentally retarded residents per capita than any county in the United States. He attributed this to its concentration of German emigrants who had come to work in the quarries and then had intermarried for a number of generations. Finally, Sterns County had one of the largest turnouts for George Wallace when he ran for president in the seventies. I never researched these "unique" characteristics, but I saw enough quarries and met so many impoverished, emotionally disturbed, conservative racists of all ages that I never questioned the hearsay evidence.

The property in Georgeville had been owned by Larry Johnson, a Minneapolis investor and real estate speculator who had taken a critical look at his life in the late sixties. What he saw was a successful middle-aged man who was getting more than his fair share of the profits while others were getting zip. Upon closer examination, he saw that his substantial taxes were supporting a U.S. military that was on a rampage of death and spending in Vietnam. Having two draft-age sons helped him with his nonviolent coming of age and inspired him to get rid of all his income-generating property. One month he notified his tenants that beginning with the next rent payment, they were buying the property at a bargain price. When the checks rolled in the following month, he realized that he was still in a high-income ballpark — so he signed the properties over to the tenants, threw away his razor, cleaned the polyester out of his closet, and started concentrating on greens from the garden instead of greens from the bank.

Larry had originally rented the Georgeville property for $100 a month to a communal group that included Eddie Felien, editor of *Hundred Flowers*, who recently had become the first avowed Marxist to be elected to the Minneapolis City Council. Larry ended up spending considerable time with the group; subsequently his life became washed in the purifying waters of their democratic socialist politics. His son had taken the same political bath and had changed his name from Alan Johnson to Foster Goodwill. A few months later, Larry would change his name to Ernest Mann. He had cut his income so drastically that he did not have to pay taxes.

As a means of sharing his conversion and economic philosophy, he began publishing a small underground newspaper called *The Little Free Press*, with a you-pay-the-postage subscription fee. He lived in a small one-room house trailer just down the road from where Bonnie Raitt's brother had a recording studio. Unfortunately, a few years later, Larry was accidently shot by a nephew and died. It was a great loss, but he had redeemed himself. After a lifetime of investing in property around Minnesota, and especially in Minneapolis, he took the socialist route to Nirvana and sent the renters the paid-in-full deeds.

Walking around Minneapolis in the winter with his toes sticking out of ragged, worn-out shoes, he told me he had never been happier.

The original Georgeville Commune had been settled by a small group of antiwar activists from the Twin Cities who were approaching burnout from the intensity of their antiwar protests. Three couples needed a quiet "nest" where their soon-to-arrive babies could be born far enough away from the chaos to afford peace and quiet. The two primary "movers" were Keith Ruona and Suzy Shroyer. Suzy's three sisters were also part of the group. Stephen Mickey was a master potter and pottery teacher whose oil-fired kiln produced income-generating pottery that attracted visitors from the surrounding area.

After a couple of years, with the babies born and energies replenished, the core group moved on. As Eddie described it, they had experienced the "rural thing," but had no intention of spending their lives there. Without the productive energies of a few far-sighted, hardworking people, the garden became overrun with weeds; the lethargy of cheap wine and pot soon had the remaining "trippies" ("hippies" who spent most of their time looking for a place to get a handout) crossing the tracks to Highway 55 in search of easier digs.

The commune wasn't Georgeville's first major closing. According to old-timers, the bank had gone broke during the Great Depression, and the post office had closed soon after when the majority of residents left to seek work elsewhere. Georgeville was an end-of-the-line, economically deprived town now, made up of people with no resources and no place to go. I had read about rural poverty, but had not witnessed it or lived this close to it. Later, when I came to know the remaining twenty-five or so residents, I was surprised to find ex-offenders making up the majority of the population. To some residents in the area, however, the commune was a bad memory. Many local farmers were quick to help with plowing our large gardens.

The communes that sprang up around the country never had it easy. Georgeville was never easy. Not back in the thirties, and for damn sure not in the sixties.

Directly behind the large two-story building was the pottery works. Across the alley was a Phillips 66 gas station that was owned and operated by an elderly man who lived next door to the station with his wife. The wife had considered members of the Georgeville Commune to be so sinful that when she walked from the house to the station, she would cover her eyes with her hand. When I asked Pete Wendt, a local farmer, why she shielded her eyes, he told me that the women in the commune would work in the garden wearing miniskirts with no underpants on. When they weeded, they would bend from the waist with their rear ends facing the gas station. Pete said that the gas station owner and his wife didn't like it, but lots of folks would stop, buy gas, and stand around taking in the sights while a soft drink got warm in their hands.

The only other business in the town was a small frame tavern that catered to a few locals.

After carefully checking the various structures and the property, I believed that we would never find a better opportunity to fulfill our needs. The two houses and the large building where the bank had been needed insulation, electrical wiring, plumbing, and a heating source, but the building was open and solid and large enough to support a printing plant and shops. Where the bank had been located, a large bank vault remained. The front door to what was once the general store led to an area that could easily seat three hundred people.

Thanks to farm sales and a weekly auction in Belgrade, I had the houses habitable within a month for less than $200. By Christmas, we had furnished the former bank area with a stove, an antique pocket pool table, and a pinball machine someone had given us. I bought the last two available wood-burning Ashley stoves in Minneapolis for $86 each. We became the tax-exempt Georgeville Community Project.

Jerry Samuels spent most of his time writing music. He also performed briefly at the Sunwood Inn in Morris, Minnesota. With the money he earned, he bought chicken feed, people feed, and a 1942 Model B John Deere tractor that Pete Wendt said would run forever.

We had hoped Jerry would spend the rest of the winter with us, but he met Petronella "Pete" Ludwina Vesters, a North Country woman with a flawless complexion and a keen mind; together they headed for Los Angeles, where Jerry enjoyed some relaxing moments with his friend from New York, studio engineer/musician Jeff Cooper, and Jeff's Roto-Rooter Goodtime Street Band. Jerry tried to sell some of his recent compositions, but was told the new material was too political. This was a disappointment to us because we held the copyrights to three of the best songs. Jerry and Pete sang their way across the country—Jerry doing the singing, and Pete providing him with inspiration. Eventually they settled in Philadelphia.

Also during this period, Warren, Judy, Nikki, and Lisa Levicoff returned to Chicago. Shar and I remained along with five others.

First Issue of *Prisoners' Digest International*

The September/October 1972 PDI was our first since being given "until sundown to leave" Clinton. It also was our first issue to come out under our new name, *Prisoners' Digest International.* The name change was not merely an afterthought to a busy layout session. It was the culmination of an evolutionary change that had been taking place in society and on the staff. Fresh out of prison, I had pondered over a name. I wanted to keep the publication free of gimmicks. If there was a publication I had in mind as an example, it was the *New Yorker.* Clean and straightforward. "Penal" only had one meaning to me: "Prison."

> **pe-nal** *adj* 1. relating to, forming, or prescribing punishment, especially by law. 2. subject to punishment under the law. 3. used as a place of imprisonment and punishment

But to many people, "penal" reminded them of penis or prick and had unacceptable sexual references. They began complaining.

I couldn't believe it. Yet, once the penal/penis "problem" began to insinuate itself into our lives and become part of ongoing discussions, I finally understood the problem. There was no reason why "penal" should not be changed to "prisoners.'" Initially I had steered away from words that caused discomfort. The days of getting inside the prisons were past. We were in, and even moneyless we now had some clout.

Prisoners' it would be.

As Becky Hensley recalled years later:

The paper morphed and the shift was monumental in its formative and reformative nature. The sixties and seventies were, if anything, a period when self-criticism, practical dialogue, and dedicated commitment often gave birth to developmental unfolding in ways not always entirely predictable and sometimes downright cataclysmic. The move from "Penal" to "Prisoners'" was one such developmental unfolding and, believe me, it was not lightly done. It was a public move to a declared position standing unapologetically with (and even beside) the prisoner (both inside and outside institutions) rather than just talking about or even advocating on behalf of the prisoner. There were very specific costs for this shift and I suspect those of us who have survived do not yet fully comprehend what all those costs were. But the process was life-changing for me and probably for others.

In that first issue of *Prisoners' Digest International*, we carried my article about our move and the Georgeville Community Project. In that article, I outlined my plans for an expanded PDI operation that would work within a community and be the watchdog for the rights of all prisoners—economic, political, and criminal. My primary goal was to make ourselves self-sufficient by cutting our expenses and finding a means to generate income. By this time, we hadn't published an issue during the month that was printed on the front page for a long time. The September/October issue was mailed shortly before Christmas.

One way we cut back on our expenses was by traveling less. Our lone exception was National Prison Center board member Dr. Stephen S. Fox, a professor of neuropsychology from the University of Iowa. Because his specialty was sensory deprivation, he was with increasing frequency being called as an expert witness in cases where prisoners, with the help of PDI and the National Prison Center, were filing legal actions against state and federal authorities. His travel expenses were covered by the fees he was being paid to testify. Fortunately, since we were a collective, all earned income went into one fund. This fund was to be used to find a place where the ex-prisoners working on the PDI and our other projects could go when the PDI came to an end. The fees Brother Steve was generating as an expert witness were invaluable.

Also in this issue, we reprinted a lengthy article that Rev. Anthony Mullaney, one of the Milwaukee 14, wrote for the *National Catholic Reporter*. The Milwaukee 14 were a group of antiwar activists, including five priests and a minister, who on September 24, 1968, liberated some ten thousand draft files from Milwaukee's Selective Service office and burned them with homemade napalm. Mullaney was a Benedictine monk with a PhD in psychology who had taught at Boston University. He wrote, "Chaplains . . . play an important role in the

FIGURE 15. Jeanne Schneller, staff member of PDI and registered nurse who went on to work extensively in the Far East.

machinery of control presided over by the [authorities]." Then he methodically pointed out how they were used by wardens to keep other religious leaders out of the prisons in order to deprive political prisoners, and prisoners in general, of the right to be served by religious activists who were sympathetic to their plight. What he wrote echoed what Frank Sepulveda and I had said four years earlier when we broke into the chaplain's office inside Leavenworth to liberate the literature the Protestant chaplain had illegally confiscated from our Michael Servetus Unitarian Universalist Fellowship.

Another article covered the protest over inadequate food inside the federal prison in Marion, Illinois, in October. The protest was ultimately put down with Mace, beatings, and solitary confinement inside solid, windowless cells that had the psychological effect upon some prisoners of being welded inside a steel box without a cutting torch. When an attorney from the People's Law Office in Carbondale arrived on October 17 to visit prisoner Eddie Adams, he was shocked to see two guards dragging Eddie down a hall. The constitutional right of an attorney and client to meet privately was violated in the Marion prison that day when attorneys and clients were separated by a thick glass in the visiting room and permitted to communicate only by means of monitored phones. By the attorney's next visit the following day, Eddie had been beaten so badly he could only get around in a wheelchair.

We carried the full decision by federal district court judge Edward Weinfeld regarding the injunction to lift the ban on the newsletter published by the Fortune Society. Stanley

Bass, legal counsel for the NAACP Legal Defense Fund, and Stephan Shestakofsky represented prisoners Roger Campen and Nathan Wright, and the Fortune Society. This decision was important because it prevented individual wardens from arbitrarily seizing and censoring publications that had been approved by the state department of corrections.

A letter to Senator Quentin Burdick from Federal Bureau of Prisons director Norman Carlson, dated October 13, 1972, stated that all solitary-confinement prisoners in the Leavenworth prison had commissary privileges and hot and cold water in their cells. In this issue, we also published a note by PDI Associate Editor Joseph Harry Brown to Carlson in which he wrote, "Really, Norm, you've got to be kidding."

With this issue, Walter Plunkett took over circulation, John Price moved to prisoner affairs, Jeanne Schneller became editor of *CREATION*, and editorial assistants included Becky Hensley, Ruth Harty, John Honeywell, John Adams, and Annie Garza. Our National Prison Center board of directors included Richard Tanner, Penny Baron, Robert D. Bartels, Jane and Steve Fox, Joseph C. Johnston, Donald Mazziotti, Thomas Renwick, Mark E. Schantz, William Simbro, and me.

Members of the PDI Prisoner Advisory Board (PAB) represented state prisoners in California, Colorado, Florida, Georgia, Indiana, Iowa, Kentucky, Minnesota, Missouri, New York, Ohio, Oklahoma, Oregon, Pennsylvania, and Texas. Federal prisoners came from Allenwood, Atlanta, El Reno, La Tuna, Leavenworth, Lorton, Lompoc, Marion, McNeil Island, Sandstone, Terminal Island, and Terre Haute. S. J. Delaney was a PAB member from Leicestershire, England. Our national associate editor was John Wagner, in Sandstone. These prisoners were constantly harassed by guards and prison administrators. Signed articles by PAB members reporting assaults on prisoners by guards got some of them weeks in solitary confinement. Many were confined simply because of their association with the PDI.

PDI mail came to Georgeville and to Iowa City. An artist I remembered from Leavenworth wrote and asked if he could come to Georgeville to do nothing but paint after he was released: "I have saved enough money to support myself for two years while I concentrate on my painting and I'll save money with your folks in Georgeville." I had hoped that *CREATION* would get the attention of serious artists. It seemed to be happening.

A Difficult Existence

All during this transition, Jerry Samuels was with us. He was remarkable in so many ways—composer and entertainer, great sense of humor—and he adapted to the almost primitive conditions in Georgeville with no problem. He was pure city, but I considered him "down home" most of the time.

One of the young fellows who helped build a greenhouse on the front of the old post office where Shar and I were living asked Jerry about a song he had written. He told Jerry he could sing it, but he couldn't write it down.

Jerry asked, "Would you sing it for me?"

The kid sang the song. Jerry picked up his notebook and in a few minutes handed him his song with all the musical notations and chord structures for guitar. "Do it right and register it with the Library of Congress," he explained to the kid. "You have a good song. Protect it."

Jerry Schurr, a Philadelphia artist, once said that Samuels was a genius. He lived off his music, so he had to be good, but he was able to do things with wire that were equally remarkable. He could take a wire coat hanger and create toys, play pistols, roach clips, decorative wire jewelry. Two attractive pieces of jewelry—a Christian cross and a Star of David—were both disguised roach clips.

He took a gig in a club in nearby Morris and bought us a John Deere Model B tractor, the exact same model my uncle had when I lived on the farm in rural Minnesota. At that time, total school enrollment was thirteen. I was the only kid in eighth grade. Unfortunately, they didn't grade on the curve.

One day, Twin Cities attorney Richard Oakes visited the Georgeville Community Project. While he was there, we discussed a proposal that would allow prisoners with children to be sent to Georgeville instead of prison so the families could stay together. A few weeks later, our first prisoner/probationer arrived with a one-year-old daughter. By spring, we would have seven probationers living with us. Our most serious problem was that we were given no financial assistance from the state, even though we were saving the state around $10,000 a year for each person we kept out of prison. During our first year, we would save the government over $200,000.

Elsie Gustofson, an elderly retired woman who lived in a small house up the street, came to me one day and asked if I'd look at her new kitchen floor. She had purchased expensive linoleum from a Belgrade, Minnesota, merchant. He had sold it to her at $7 a square yard and installed it without preparing the old floor. A few days after the installation, the old nails that had fastened the old linoleum to the floor were coming through the new linoleum.

This was a perfect example of how merchants treated the poor, rural people who were living hand-to-mouth on Social Security and had trouble standing up to the merchants. They would complain and nothing would be done. I didn't see carpeting on a floor until I was discharged after the Korean War. When I was growing up, a family was lucky to have linoleum. Installing expensive linoleum was simple: You tore out the old, pulled all the old nails out, made sure there were no "lumps," and you installed the new.

I had the small-claims forms and helped Elsie fill them out. Then I filed with small-claims court and took the bastard there, where he was ordered by the judge to replace the linoleum after cleaning and refinishing the floor. Elsie didn't even have to drive to St. Cloud for the hearing. It wasn't a big deal to us, but it damn sure was to poor Elsie. It showed the community that we were not a bunch of outlaws or old hippies. We lived there and were not only willing to help our neighbors, we were eager to do so.

During our time in Georgeville we were frequently in small-claims court.

Another time I was in the Belgrade bank and overheard one of the bank managers giving a woman and a ten-year-old girl hell over a check that had been cashed at a local tavern. I didn't know them, but I knew the banker. I walked over, introduced myself to the woman, and, over the objection of the banker, sat down and asked the woman to explain to me what the problem was. She said she had sent the kid to the tavern to buy a pack of cigarettes. In the process, she had overdrawn her account by $2 and she was being humiliated in front of other customers.

Of course, the banker was sternly informing me that I was out of line. The little girl was crying and the mother was sitting there taking the crap.

I asked her if I could take care of this for her, and she nodded. I grabbed a bunch of Kleenex off the "man's" desk and handed half to the girl and the rest to the mother. Then I reached over and grabbed the check the banker was waving, saw the amount, tore it up, and gave the woman $10 to cover the overdraft. I waited for her to make the deposit and took them next door for a talk.

The lines of demarcation between the haves and the have-nots were no different in rural Minnesota than they were in East L.A. or anywhere.

The November 1972 issue was published in early 1973. This was the smallest issue since the PDI was founded: one section of 12 pages, two of which were CREATION: The Arts in Prison. The front page and much of the issue were devoted to articles by Hans W. Mattick, codirector of the Center for Studies in Criminal Justice, University of Chicago Law School ("The Prosaic Sources of Prison Violence"); and Daniel Glaser, PhD from the University of Southern California ("Causal Processes in the Development and Control of Prison Riots").

All income that came into the PDI was being used by the staff in Iowa City. I was supporting the Georgeville Community Project and the growing number of participants—which by now included approximately fifteen adults and children—by accepting speaking engagements and participating in seminars. In the PDI, I wrote: "For the past three months it has been what some would term a difficult existence. I have been on the move constantly. Sleeping on the ground, in the van, in the back seats of cars, on floors in mansions and shacks. It has been cold, wet, hot, bug infested, dirty, windy and sometimes downright miserable. And through it all, right there and not complaining, has been Sharlane. An independent human being, a woman, a partner and a mother-to-be, who values truth above all else."

We had taken up residency in the old post office building. Two rooms down and one up, if you were okay with a ladder for stairs.

The Iowa City "Lynching" of Mike Roe

While I was caught up in my dream of the PDI bringing change to the prison system of the country, and trying to swing a college, an incident took place in a junior-high school in Iowa City that should have become a national issue. Michael Roe, a teacher at South East Junior High School, was assigned to teach a class in Human Relationships and Family Living. One part of the course dealt with human sexuality. Since the class of eighth graders were asking questions about all the different areas of human sexuality, Mike invited two members of the Iowa City Gay Liberation Front to come to his class to discuss their lifestyles and interaction with the straight society. A gay man and a lesbian answered questions, and the class was functioning well until some parents heard about who had been invited into an Iowa City junior-high classroom.

A small, vocal group of conservative parents jumped on the members of the board of education, and Mike was suddenly suspended. Joe Johnston took the case on Mike's behalf. A committee was organized to ensure that a legal defense fund was established to support the concept of academic freedom for all teachers, and for the right to discuss controversial issues.

Some of the complaining parents were saying that homosexuals could be soliciting children while they were guest speakers. The charge was ridiculous, but the response from the general public was lukewarm. I couldn't understand why the gay community didn't rise up and participate in demonstrations to generate more news. Here was a young, straight teacher who was being crucified because he believed in education and understood that homosexuality had to come out of the closets so that students could understand who the members of the Gay Liberation Front actually were. Considering where it was happening, in radically liberal Iowa City, it didn't make sense. The Stonewall riots had taken place two years earlier and had made international news. This young teacher was being kicked around and out of the job he loved and at which he had excelled.

Negotiations dragged on; one hearing followed another. In the end the court ruled that Roe's firing would stand. It was tragic, and I was shocked when I finally heard the entire story. Many supported Mike, and benefits were held to raise money for his legal defense fund, but in the end, this young man, whom I knew and respected, who loved teaching, whose students loved him, whose academic record was without a blemish, was out of work and no one would hire him.

Being denied a teaching job where he had lived and worked for years was a blow that took much out of his life and left a stain on Iowa City's reputation as a blue spot in a sea of political red.

Mike Roe was never mentioned in the PDI. The prisoners had a right to this news, and we had an obligation to print it. I believe that if the PDI had jumped on this outrage, the way any responsible newspaper should have, we could have saved Mike's job.

All the while, what had happened to Mike Roe was slowly happening to the PDI, but from the inside.

I was looking for printing equipment, tools, supplies, seeds for spring planting, anything that could be used to improve the houses and the property. I built a greenhouse across the front of the old post office where Shar and I were living. On sunny days during the Minnesota winters, so much heat was generated that we didn't burn wood in the house on those days.

Our financial problems were not looking any better when a young parolee who had helped us in the past called me in Georgeville. Eight or ten months earlier, Tommy Terrill had stopped by 505 on his way to spending the $500 he had saved on work release. Before he left, he graciously loaned us the $500 to help pay printing bills. Now Tommy needed it back. He was married. He and his wife had just had a baby boy. Medical bills were mounting. Tommy simply said, "If you have it, we need it, Joe."

We didn't, but as luck would have it, the University of Wisconsin called and asked me to chair a panel discussion during a two-day seminar on corrections. I accepted, and we were able to pay Tommy and fix up a frightening-looking one-ton pickup that would carry us all over the country when I finally returned the PDI van.

In the January and February 1973 issues of PDI, we began reducing the size of the type to get more news into the 12 pages of each issue. In the February issue, the Iowa City group pointed out to readers that we only had money for one more issue. They also explained that the Georgeville Project and the Iowa City group were totally separate entities, and that some of the Iowa City group believed more energy had to be directed to the Church of the New Song.

Four pages were devoted to defining the new language of the new religion and explaining how a group could organize a *purlieu* (local "church" headquarters) where the *redactor* (preacher) or *sealed revelation minister* (member of the CNS clergy) could meet with the *mavorites* (men) and *sporades* (women), who could learn how to accept their *candid functions* (responsibilities) and ponder the *exigenic missives* (letters) from the Bishop of Tellus (Shiloh Harry Theriault), who was located in the *fountainhead seminary* (ministerial school of Eclarianity) and was busy explaining the *inverse crucible* (basic Eclatarian belief) to CNS members from a solitary cell.

Although I believed too much energy was being devoted to complicating the language of the Church of the New Song, I did open a church in Georgeville. We were located in Crow River Township, so I called it the Crow River Church of the New Song. All of my community service there was performed as a CNS minister because I believed that the fastest way to "gather a flock" (so to speak) was to become a community resource and let them see the tangible results of my work. If I couldn't inspire them to donate enough food and/or money to allow the ministry to survive, it simply meant that I hadn't become an indispensable resource to the community.

Georgeville Project Finds Outside Funding

Soon after the legal hassles began in Clinton, I was contacted by Dr. Alan Green, director of the Irwin Sweeney Miller Foundation, a nonprofit organization funded by Cummins Diesel Engines in Columbus, Indiana. His interest, he said, was in finding out what I was planning for the community and how I planned to tie it into the PDI. He asked me to contact him when I found a home. When we settled in Georgeville in early fall, Sharlane and I wrote a description of our plans, mailed it off, and forgot about it. Then one day in the early weeks of 1973, we were notified that he was flying in to discuss financial support for the project.

We met Dr. Green at Minneapolis International Airport. There, over coffee, we discussed the proposal, and he offered the foundation's help. Dr. Green told us they would give us enough money so Shar and I could pay ourselves a modest salary with a little left over for the project, if we abided by certain conditions—namely that Shar and I had to attend a week-long Transactional Analysis seminar in Lynchberg, Virginia, and that we had to account for all the money, none of which could be used for the Church of the New Song. When I asked him about the second condition, I was told bluntly, "Because it's bullshit!" Unfortunately the foundation had seen the February issue. Although I saw more potential in CNS than he did, I could see he was a knowledgeable man, and so I had no problem with his conditions. I accepted on the spot. When I asked him why the foundation was supporting us, he said, "This money is an investment in Sharlane and you. It will help you do the things you are doing. Our foundation is interested in seeing where you are going." On our drive back to Georgeville, Shar and I discussed Dr. Green's proposal. We tried to be positive about the PDI and the project, but we were not generating much excitement with the folks at 505, who felt I should be living in Iowa City and concentrating all my energy there.

A few days after the support from the foundation began, I was contacted by someone at the Good Thunder, Minnesota, weekly newspaper. The longtime owner was selling the entire printing plant so he could retire, but the owners-to-be wanted no part of the old equipment. I drove immediately to Good Thunder, a few miles south of Mankato, and was met by the newspaper's owner, the mayor, and members of the town council. They questioned me about the PDI and the project in Georgeville and asked me to consider moving to Good Thunder. "We have a vacant building for any business you might want to start," I was told. "Plus, there are many vacant homes. We can work with you and your team. You will be good for our community, and we can be good for you."

They said they were willing to help us with promotion and fundraising while providing cheap rent. They had a library and proximity to Mankato State University. They also mentioned the potential for community-development funds that might be available from the federal government.

That comment really got my attention. Good Thunder was a beautiful, traditional small town in southern Minnesota, similar to the one near where I had grown up. But now Good Thunder was a depressed area, and they were looking for help and were willing to help us.

I drove alone to Mankato to think about their incredible offer. Then I called Sharlane and we discussed our options. Together we decided we didn't want to be responsible for what might happen if we relocated all our people to Good Thunder. In the end, without talking to the staff in Iowa City, I decided to turn down the offer. Hindsight would prove it was the correct decision.

Instead, with all the foundation money being used for the community project—Shar and I did not pay ourselves a cent in wages—I made the fellow an offer for everything in the plant, which included a 17′ × 22′ Harris offset press and two huge Linotype machines. The townspeople obviously were disappointed to be losing the only printing equipment in town. Nevertheless, he accepted my offer. I returned with a borrowed truck and hoist and removed three printing presses, one hundred drawers of type, two Linotype machines, and all the odds and ends of "stuff" that had accumulated in a printing plant that had been serving the community since the turn of the century.

One month later, we were completely set up to print in Georgeville. I found out that it was much easier going from hot type to cold than from cold to hot. My plans were to have both—letter press and offset.

It was now almost spring. The fifteen of us were living in four homes, along with a regular stream of temporary residents who were sent to us through corrections agencies in Minnesota. We were set up to raise our own food on our own land. A coop full of chickens provided us with eggs. The five windows needed for the bank, each seven feet by three feet, were donated to us by a Minneapolis window company. We were in business.

Goodbye, 505; Goodbye, PDI

One day I was shocked to find out that payments at 505 were many months in arrears. I had purchased the house with my GI loan from the Korean War. The payments were only $225 a month, but by the time I became aware of how many payments had been missed, I had already bought the Good Thunder printing plant. It was too late now to stop foreclosure, and I didn't have any money anyhow. Still, I called Iowa City and told them we would be down within a week.

A few days later I received a letter from Merilea telling me that the Iowa City staff had given her the job of investigating our books, because some of the staff were convinced I had embezzled money from the PDI.

Our books were never in the best order, of course, but after several weeks Merilea discovered nothing was missing, because there was never an accumulation of any money. We had always lived month to month. The staff were amazed to find out that there never was any money. Her letter informed me that "the investigation has cleared you of any wrongdoing."

It freaked me out to learn that they had even believed such crap.

By the time we got to Iowa City, 505 was gone, and the staff had moved to a large house on Linn Street, where they were paying considerably more rent than the $225 monthly payment at 505.

Our meeting there was interesting for a couple of reasons. First, many new people I was unfamiliar with were present. Richard Tanner had called Georgeville to warn me that some of the new staff members were dangerous, and that I should consider staying away from Iowa City. For that warning, I later learned, he was rewarded with a vicious ass-kicking by a couple of the new members. At the time I wasn't worried.

At the meeting, which was attended by the entire staff, I outlined how the PDI could be saved and shared what I had put together in Georgeville. There was some concern about being so far away from a city, but I pointed out that the mail was delivered to Georgeville just as regularly as it was to Iowa City.

I asked staff members if any were interested in moving to Minnesota. A new staffer named Jack Kime saved everyone the trouble of answering by telling me, "If you move any part of the PDI to Minnesota I will personally guarantee that you will not live to see that baby born," and he pointed to Sharlane, who was sitting next to me and was unquestionably very pregnant.

We were all sitting on the floor in a large circle. I looked around the room to see if there was consensus. Jane Fox, a board member at our National Prison Center as well as a CNS jurisconsult and sporade, said nothing because of her commitment to CNS; no one else did either. Richard had warned me about several CNS members, including Kime, who had recently joined the PDI staff after being released from Fort Madison. I could see now that he had been correct in his warning—PDI decisions were now being made by the Church of the New Song and by people I did not know.

One lesson I had learned in the can was this: When someone said he was going to kill you if you did something, you had two choices: you could kill him first and then do what you were going to do, or you could say screw it, chalk one up for the killers, and walk away.

"Looks like you folks have yourselves a newspaper; when you close down let me know." I took Shar's hand and helped her up. We walked out of the house and that ended our contact with them.

When we got in the van, Shar said, "Good riddance."

I agreed.

We had one more stop to make before we returned to Georgeville. The three-year lease on our van allowed us to drive 10,000 miles a year. In two years, I had put 100,000 miles on its odometer and had only made three or four payments on it. For some unknown reason, the company had never billed me. I wondered why, but I had an idea. With that idea, I devised a plan. There had been an electrical fire in the wires under the dash a couple of months earlier. The body was in good shape and the engine burned less than a quart of oil a month, but the wiring was a problem.

When we got to the company, I said to the sales manager, "I want you folks to rewire the van and give it back to me, and then I'll start making payments on it."

He looked at me like I was nuts and told me my proposal was the stupidest thing he had ever heard.

I raised my voice. When I did, he got a panicked look on his face, motioned with his hands to "please keep this quiet," and looked around nervously to see if any other potential customers were listening. Then he ran over to his boss's office and shut the door.

As I watched him, I thought about the fact that I had never received a payment-due bill or a warning about possible repossession. His need to keep this discussion from his boss indicated to me that he and possibly others were leasing vehicles and pocketing the payments. It was an old scam. I was only guessing, but I thought they were dirty.

When he sat back down, he looked at me and said, "How are we going to get this worked out, Joe? You owe us over $4,000."

I took a chance. I spoke as seriously as I could under the circumstances and said, "I think that everyone, including you, is going to be much better off if you take the van, fix it up, put it on the lot, and forget about the lease and the money you say I owe you."

He sat there looking at me.

I added, "When I think of the endless hassles we'll be going through over this—lawyers, court dates, all of that legal stuff—I want to keep it as simple as possible."

He said, "Let's just forget about it."

I stood up and reached out to shake his hand. "Is there anything I should be signing, or can I trust you to take care of all the paperwork?"

"Trust me," he said. And I did. I never heard from them again. Part of the floorboard on the passenger side of our pickup was missing, but it was all ours—free and clear. For the first time in four years I had no debts. When those new staff members decided they wanted the PDI bad enough to kill for it, they got a hell of a lot more than circulation—they walked into the opportunity to meet some business people who had to see cash before the presses rolled. From the attitudes of everyone at the meeting, it appeared that they had developed connections for financial support, possibly from the Teamsters, although I had my doubts about these people getting union support. Regardless of what the future held for the PDI, it was depressing to see people taking over who took those shortcuts.

As we left Iowa City, Shar and I looked back over the past three years. In some respects the PDI had been more demanding than my jailers. One had exacted about as much of my time as the other. Exactly how much money I had raised over the past three years was hard to figure out—we never had a worthwhile accounting system. All I do know is that we never wasted any money—but at the same time I was never able to tap into the kind of money it takes to do what we were doing. The demise of the PDI, though, was directly proportional to the temporary rise of the Church of the New Song. We became overwhelmed by the response of a vocal minority, and for a while, I was as turned on by the response as anyone. I saw the church as a chance to get into the prisons. I sincerely believed, for a while, that the "Truth, Peace, and Freedom" lingo being bandied about was believed by the bandiers. Without a doubt some did believe. But others didn't.

In the process of leaving Iowa City, death threats or no death threats, I picked up a printout of the subscription list.

A month later, Richard Tanner sent me a small bundle of the April 1973 issue of the PDI. That issue consisted of one 8-page section. All copy was set in seven-point type.

The lead story indicated that the federal government's parent behavior-modification project (S.T.A.R.T.) would soon be closed. The story, which was datelined "SPRINGFIELD, MO. PRISON, Federal Prison Colonies," began:

> The Federal Bureau of Prisons, headed by the neo-nazi Commandant, Norman A. Carlson, was dealt a grievous blow in Federal court in a hearing investigating prisoner complaints of gross atrocities. . . . In a week of testimony given by such professional witnesses as Dr. Stephen S. Fox, Ph.D., world renowned professor of neuropsychology at the University of Iowa; Dr. Richard Korn, Ph.D., professor of criminology, University of California; and Dr. Roger Ulrich, Ph.D., the most respected name in the science of behavior modification, the entire system contrived by the federal prisoncrats to violently modify the behavior of federal prisoners was found to be an insidious conspiracy by federal officers acting under the color of federal office to commit and cause to be committed, crimes against humanity and the constitutional welfare of American citizens.

Numerous prisoners testified to beatings and gassings; the illegal use of potent, untested drugs that rendered victims almost dead and wishing they were; the chaining of prisoners to iron cots for long periods of time, where they were forced to lay in their own shit and piss, eating only what they could lick from their faces where the federal guards threw what little food was offered. Long, long lists of blatant atrocities and excuses by the federal prisoncrats of why these crimes against humanity were justified in the United States of America in modern times.

But just as the parent program was being closed down, the article reported, federal behavior-modification forces were regrouping at the new Butner, North Carolina, federal prison. On the state level, at the Marquette (Michigan) Intensive Program Center, a "two-million dollar behavior modification unit has been built" to hold as many as eighty-five "highly disruptive men." Further, in Clinton, New York, the prison's Special Housing Unit 14 had been designed to hold "militants, radicals and natural leaders."

Prison authorities were continually improving their methods of isolating these specially skilled prisoners, including those able to articulate how the criminal justice system is set up to oppress the poor, those whom other prisoners could trust to represent them in conflicts with prison authorities, and jailhouse lawyers. Those methods of isolation included solitary confinement within one prison, and lengthy transfers by bus from one prison to another.

Concerning those prisoners the system set out to destroy, writer John Bennett wrote:

> I'm talking to Cool Hand Luke and his myriad incarnations, mostly the young who play out their defiance on intuition and then vanish, either smashed or dead. . . .The System has a washed-out substitute for everything that's beautiful. The System is a virus in the blood stream of the primal force of life, and the Cool Hand Lukes are the healthiest cells in that blood stream, which is why the System attacks them first. Most of them die before they realize what they're up against.

The tone in PDI articles had, over the past year, become much more dramatic and angry. Our critics described the language and writing styles as inflammatory. What most people did not understand was that many of the prisoners who were being subjected to the tortures of the behavior-modification programs were our friends. Many friends were dying. The anger and frustration felt by the staff increased with each issue. Add that pain to our lack of financial support, which was causing the PDI to face closing down, and the tone became not only understandable but justified.

This might have been a more painful and difficult time for me if it hadn't been for the demands of the Georgeville Community Project. Vegetable gardens were planted and demanded daily care. More people were joining the project.

Chas DuRain, Editorial Artist

One of the most talented cartoonists in the prison press network was Charles DuRain. Chas, as Charles called himself, had been in prison for over twenty years. He was a small fellow, slight of build, in his late forties, who was self-educated as a cartoonist. Ever since his first cartoons arrived at the PDI early in 1972, I had been trying to convince the Kentucky Parole Board to give him a parole date.

In my initial correspondence with Chas, when I first told him I was going to get him his walking papers, he had responded, "Hey, I appreciate all you are doing, but you're wasting your time." His letters continued like that for a long time.

Not until the fall of 1973 was I able to get them to seriously consider releasing him. What they said was that they would agree to release him to Minnesota if no one objected. I got Minnesota to agree. All plans were in place. Then suddenly all plans were cancelled. In a letter from Chas dated September 24, 1973, he told me he hadn't lost hope. "Six months ago I wouldn't have given a plug nickel for my chances, now I'm sure. . . . I have absolute faith in you."

It was then that I called Senator Hubert Humphrey and asked for help. First he called the two Kentucky senators and asked them to help "get the wrinkles ironed out of this parole plan." Then he wrote to the Kentucky Parole Board.

His request prompted immediate action. A letter from Chas dated October 12, 1973, was the first handwritten letter I had ever received from him:

I was transferred suddenly. No typewriters here. Joe, you wouldn't believe this place. Absolutely no locks anywhere! No fences, no guards—nothing like a prison; or at least, nothing like any prison I ever heard of . . . it's now 10:30 P.M.—that's the latest I've been up for 20 years. If I wanted to I could walk straight across the pastures from here to I-65. There's nothing between me and the highway but a three strand barbed-wire fence. But, of course, I won't leave.

While he was waiting, he was presented with the top Penal Press Award by Southern Illinois University. A few weeks later, when Chas arrived in Minnesota, Senator Humphrey was on hand to personally hand him the award.

Another award, this one for special public service, was given by Senator Humphrey to another important PDI contributor. To thank Augie Bergenthal for the help he had given us—he loaned me $15,000 a few months after he had given us the $1,000—we created the award ourselves. Senator Humphrey presented the award to Augie's daughter in Washington, D.C. Augie would remain in prison for another couple of years. Finally, the weight of support for his case from the PDI and the Georgeville Community Project paid off, and he was exonerated and released.

The primary challenge of our Georgeville Project, meanwhile, was to cut expenses. Had the PDI staff moved to Georgeville, in theory we would have been able to raise all our food. The garden was growing more vegetables and fruit than we could use. I had purchased an old used freezer. What we couldn't can, we froze. Our chickens were providing us with a surplus of fresh eggs and meat. When the Georgeville caravan headed for Minneapolis, we would bring along four or five large baskets of eggs. When you ate at the Riverside Cafe, you paid what you could afford. We ate there and paid for our meals with fresh eggs.

Our Charity Begins in Georgeville

Christmas 1973 came and went. The days leading up to it have never been forgotten by me. I look back on that period with many regrets. The project was taking so much of my time that we never really took time to Christmas shop or prepare for the holiday celebration. Sharlane was only a few weeks away from giving birth, and it would have been a perfect time to drop everything, shop for gifts, and settle down for an old-fashioned Christmas.

But we had no money for gifts for ourselves or the folks who were living with us. Storms had me tunneling through snowdrifts to get to our woodpile. One drift beside the house filled an open basement. Pete Wendt and I had installed cement block walls in preparation for adding a greenhouse over the top. I was going to use the building for a pottery works. I had installed a well, piped water to the post office, and added a room to the back of the post office for a bath. With a 5,000-gallon septic tank, we were beginning to live like city folks.

We had decided on a home birth. Sharlane was healthy and strong. She had read everything on the subject, and I had read enough to feel confident that together we could handle the birth. Still, I kept the one local doctor's phone number handy and was grateful that he had promised to be standing by in case we needed help. An intern in obstetrics from the St. Cloud hospital called. He had delivered over six hundred babies, he told us, but he had never seen a home birth. He asked if he could observe. We welcomed his expertise and relaxed, knowing we'd have a doctor close by if we needed one.

Just before Chas arrived in Georgeville, I had bought two more small homes and moved them onto the property. Chas was living and working in one of them. We were sending his fine editorial cartoons out to weekly newspapers and syndication services.

On January 13, in the afternoon, Sharlane told me that the baby would probably be born within the next few hours. We were still heating with wood, but we now had electricity and a phone. I brought the oxygen tank from my welding unit to our upstairs room in the post office to provide Sharlane with additional oxygen during the birth. We were counting on a birthing book authored by Grantly Dick-Read, a British doctor who specialized in obstetrics.

By 6:30 P.M., Sharlane was in labor. The intern hadn't arrived, so I called the doctor. There was no answer. Upstairs, I was alone with Sharlane and Kitty the cat. Downstairs was Sam the dog. Chas was working across the street; the rest of the folks were stuffing wood into stoves to fight the cold and the blizzard that was closing all roads in that section of Minnesota.

The sun by this time had already gone down for the day and it was 30 degrees below zero, but in our room we were warm and cozy. Shar was lying back, supported by a pile of pillows.

Three hours later, three inches of the baby's crown were already there in front of me. Then suddenly progress stopped. Sharlane was working and I was waiting. Occasionally I would turn the valve on the oxygen tank and wave the hose in Sharlane's direction. "Just a little extra oxygen," I would say.

"Don't distract me," she would answer.

After about thirty minutes of looking at the top of the baby's head, I became concerned. We had made such good progress. Now we seemed to be at a standstill.

Just then we heard someone drive up. The intern and a nurse had arrived in a four-wheel-drive pickup and were climbing up the ladder to join us. I explained what had happened and where we were.

The intern looked over my shoulder and said, "Wow! The baby is being born with the caul intact."

He explained that what we had thought was the baby's head was really the caul, or what we knew as the water bag. He had never seen a baby born with the caul intact.

"Do you want me to help?" he asked me.

"Not if it isn't necessary," I answered.

But I welcomed his explanation of how to break the caul using my hemostat. As soon as the caul broke, the water rushed out and the birthing continued. The intern asked about the oxygen tank. I waved some oxygen Sharlane's way.

"Stop it," Sharlane ordered. I did.

Outside the wind was howling. It had been snowing for hours and the wind had turned the snowfall into a blizzard.

"For a while we didn't think we'd make it," the nurse said. "Drifts are building up, and some are all the way across the highway." In addition, she said, the plows hadn't gotten to all the main roads yet; Georgeville was not high on local government's list of priorities.

Sharlane was pushing hard and I was ready. All of a sudden, in a move that happened quickly and smoothly, our baby, our little girl, our Charity Thyra Henrikke, was in my hands.

"This is the first time I have ever seen a baby born pink," the intern said to the nurse, "Look at her. She's pink instead of blue, and she hasn't started breathing yet."

He was kneeling beside me. "Give her a little slap on her butt and she'll start to breathe."

"Not a chance," I answered. I reached for one of her incredibly tiny feet. "This child is going to start her new life with a little tickle." She gave a little start, took a deep breath, and I couldn't do anything except kneel there holding and looking at that amazing little infant. Sharlane reached down and I handed Charity to her. She held her while I tied off the umbilical cord and cut it. Sharlane lay back in the pile of pillows with Charity cuddled up on her breast.

I started taking pictures. The intern and the nurse were right down next to Sharlane looking at Charity.

"She appears to be a perfectly healthy little girl," the intern said. Then he added, "It's very rare that a baby is born with a caul. I've never seen one and I've delivered hundreds of babies. Many cultures consider a child that is born with a caul to be a special child—a child that has been blessed."

Sounds good to me, I thought.

Later that evening, after the intern and nurse were gone, we took a few more pictures. I think there was a bottle of wine, but I'm not certain. We sat around and talked newborn-infant talk. After an hour, Sharlane finally let me hold Charity again while she got up, walked over to the phone, and called her folks in Chicago Heights.

Charity seemed right at home all wrapped up in a warm cotton blanket. I wanted to tell her about her mom. Just talking was good. Holding her on my chest talking must have felt like purring to her. I told her a story while her mom was talking to her grandparents. I didn't have much, but I had stories.

Later I took the oxygen tank downstairs and carried it across the street. When I returned to the room, Shar and I settled down to look the baby over carefully and to give her a gentle bath with a soft cloth and warmed olive oil. Soon Charity was nursing and sleeping and nursing and sleeping; the PDI and the Georgeville Community Project took a backseat to our new addition.

I remember mentioning to Sharlane that no one would believe me when I described how pretty Charity was. Newborns are usually all wrinkly and red and fussy.

A few days later I drove to St. Cloud to register a birth. The folks in the county clerk's office said they couldn't accept it because it wasn't signed by a doctor. I added "Dr." in front of my name and told them if it wasn't registered at once I'd be back with lawyers from the ACLU. It could be that my long hair and huge beard made me appear threatening.

I heard a "Yes sir," turned, and walked.

Prisoner's Death Sparks Protests at Leavenworth

The last part of 1973 and all of 1974 was to be a period filled with tremendous satisfactions and difficult problems. People with felony convictions arrived from the courts with their families, spent the necessary time with us, then moved on to training programs and jobs.

As spring approached, visitors drifted in off Highway 55. It wasn't hard to determine which visitors were workers and which weren't. Usually they would arrive on foot, introduce themselves, and get a drink of water. Workers would look around, see a task that needed doing—like gardening or weeding or repairing vehicles—and pitch right in. Those who weren't working within the hour were allowed to stay for one meal and then were sent on their way.

The PDI, meanwhile, was being published regularly from Iowa City. Issues were small, usually 8 or 12 pages. A one-page *CREATION: The Arts in Prison* was still being edited by Jeanne Schneller, who would work on the PDI until her nursing career eventually took her away to serve the poor living in the volatile Far East and in Third World countries.

Merilea was heading up special projects. In that position, she had gained permission for the PDI to reprint *The Jailhouse Lawyer's Manual*, by Brian Glick and the Prison Law Collective in San Francisco. Although that book was written for California prisoners, with minor modifications it provided prisoners in any state with the information they needed to "fight mistreatment or bad conditions" in federal court without an attorney.

John Price, a prisoner at the Atlanta federal prison when I spoke to the first mass meeting of the Church of the New Song, was in charge of prisoner affairs.

For all practical purposes, the PDI was now a Church of the New Song publication. It was clear, though, that Bob Copeland was firmly in the editor's chair and doing a great job without interference.

With each passing month, I felt we were closer to resuming responsibility for the PDI. Our Harris press and the two Linotype machines were restored and ready to operate. Although our money from the foundation had been approved and we were now receiving around $2,500 a month, we were housing, feeding, and caring for a population that numbered from eight to twenty people. Their needs became a forced priority over personal salaries. Still, I felt what others described as "insane optimism." I still believed that at least one level of government would one day realize not only that our project was saving them money by keeping people out of prison, but also that our programs were contributing to the betterment of society by keeping people out of trouble. Sooner or later, I was positive, the government would reward our successful programs with at least a partial subsidy.

The September 1973 PDI had an aerial photo of the Oklahoma State Pen being burned to the ground. The riot began at 2:30 P.M. on Friday, July 27, when a prisoner grabbed a microphone and announced over the PA system, "This is a revolution!" The story was written by George Knox, our associate editor in the federal prison at El Reno, Oklahoma, where some of the riot participants were quickly sent. Again and again, he and other PDI associate editors had provided informative articles on existing or impending problems at McAlester prisons. These articles were always sent to the wardens. The wardens never listened. In this particular instance, not listening was going to cost the taxpayers of Oklahoma about $30 million.

Another article reported grim news from Leavenworth.

According to the article, in the early morning of July 29, prisoner DellaRocca was brought to Leavenworth on his way to Danbury, Connecticut, from the medical center prison in Springfield, Missouri. When he arrived at Leavenworth, he was so weak he had to be moved from the marshal's car to a prison cell in a wheelchair.

DellaRocca had been labeled a malingerer while he was at Springfield. At Leavenworth, when he complained of pain to my old boss, he was stripped naked and placed in a hospital isolation cell on the concrete floor with no bedding. A bowl of food was placed in his cell. When a prisoner nurse was caught helping him eat, a guard ordered him to "Get out of there! This bastard can feed himself if he wants to eat." Three on-duty physician's assistants ignored DellaRocca's pleas for medical help. A medical technical assistant named Anderson was one of the few who tried to help.

At 9 A.M. my old boss, the chief surgeon, stated, "It is my opinion that there isn't a damn thing wrong with that man. Let him stay where he is and I will have him transferred back to Danbury in a few days. Personally I don't think there's a damn thing wrong with that fellow, either mentally or physically."

The next day, a serious argument took place between prison nurses and a physician's assistant over the need to bathe DellaRocca. The prisoners prevailed. While they were giving DellaRocca a bath, he stated that he was being murdered and didn't know what he could do or who he could turn to for help. Then he became incoherent and lost consciousness. He was returned to the concrete floor of the cell. By afternoon he was comatose and appeared to be paralyzed except for slight movement in his left arm.

Early on July 31, when he appeared to be dying, DellaRocca was quickly moved from the concrete floor of the strip cell to a cell with a bed. A few minutes later he was dead. Without consulting DellaRocca's family, the doctor performed an autopsy. All of DellaRocca's medical records were gathered together and given to the doctor to ensure that nothing was in them that would reflect unfavorably on the prison hospital or the staff.

No one is certain exactly how the protest started—although it is known that the "sanitization" of DellaRocca's records was an immediate provocation—and I'm not positive how a guard died during the protest, but suddenly, two days after DellaRocca died, prisoners in the dining hall were throwing trays, cups, and anything else that could be airborne. Windows shattered and guards were hit. William Hurst, who was in the prison laundry with Armando Miramon, ordered four guards to sit down. "You are hostages," he told them. "Be quiet, don't cause any problems, and you will not be hurt."

Then Hurst called Warden Daggett and asked him if he was ready to listen to the grievances. At first Daggett was belligerent, but when he learned that four guards were in the laundry he agreed.

The list of thirteen demands that were submitted to the warden were the exact same reasonable demands the prisoners had been trying to get Daggett to look at for many months. They included

- an end to racist policies now in effect;
- freedom of religion for all prisoners;
- an end to arbitrary lockup of all prisoners, and the right to due process at all disciplinary hearings, counsel, and the right to cross-examine and confront witnesses;
- more minority-group guards;
- reorganization of the mechanical (medical) staff within the walls, including psychiatric staff. Three prisoners had died through medical neglect during the previous nine months;
- an end to discrimination by the parole board. Only 1 percent of prisoners were being paroled from the Leavenworth Federal Prison Camp; none were being paroled from behind the walls;
- the right to confidential correspondence with attorneys, the courts, and the press;
- an end to the ban on political books;
- an end to exploitation of prison factory workers;
- the return to all prisoners of the interest on their savings;
- an investigation of federal district court Judge Stanley, who constantly denied petitions for redress under law;
- better food and an end to cutbacks on food allotments; and
- abolition of the hole.

Hurst, who wrote the PDI article with Miramon and Associate Editor John Alkes, agreed to release the hostages as soon as Daggett met with a committee of prisoners in the presence of members of the press. Daggett consented to that arrangement. Committee members—three Chicanos, three blacks, and three whites—were chosen by their fellow prisoners. They included Jesse Lopez, Juan Fernandez, George Santiago, Dennis Kniss, Alvin Jasper, Frank Harris, Robert Butcher, Odell Bennett, and Jack Abbott.

At the end of the meeting, Daggett promised that no reprisals would be taken against committee members if the hostages were released unharmed. Although the hostages were brought in unharmed, news media were forbidden to take pictures of them because two of the guards had been so frightened they lost control of their bowels.

As soon as the press left the room, the nine committee members were taken to Building 63, Leavenworth's "hole," stripped, and locked in solitary cells, along with Bill Hurst, Armando Miramon, and fifty other prisoners.

As soon as the rest of the prison was secured, the goon squad went to work on the prisoners in solitary. Many of them were clubbed into unconsciousness. Although committee member and negotiator Jesse Lopez was not one of the prisoners who had initiated the riot, he was charged with being its leader.

When Associate Warden A. W. Putnam was called to testify before the House Internal Security Committee that was investigating subversion in the prisons, he said, "Certain literature calls for unconventional warfare because it is, in effect, an attack on the integrity of the prison system." Putnam named the literature he considered the most dangerous: the *Prisoners' Digest International*; *Midnight Special*, from the National Lawyers Guild in San Francisco; and *Outlaw*, from the Prisoners Union in San Francisco.

It is impossible for free-world people to comprehend the courage it takes for a prisoner to write an article critical of a prison administrator, to describe the senseless death of a prisoner, to lay out details of a prison revolt, and then sign the article and request that it be bylined. Reading the reports from John Alkes and the others, I remembered an incident that had happened years before, in the same prison hospital where DellaRocca died, when I was clerking for the chief surgeon. I had read one of his reports, but had been unable to understand it, so I walked down the hall to the medical examination room where he was working on a prisoner. Another prisoner was lying against the wall on a gurney, a collapsible stretcher on wheels.

I told my boss I didn't understand what he meant.

"Come here and I'll show you," he said. He walked over to the prisoner on the gurney and grabbed his left leg. He raised the leg suddenly.

The prisoner's face turned white. The pain must have been excruciating. He clutched at the sides of the gurney, and what started out as a scream ended up a sharp expulsion of breath and a sickening groan.

My boss took his pen and added a notation to the physical exam form as he said, "This describes how far the leg can be raised before the pain is so great the prisoner cannot stand it."

"Why didn't you just tell me?" I said.

"It took less time showing you than explaining it."

The FBI Visits Georgeville

Toward the end of 1973, the FBI made its first appearance in the area. Agents stopped at nearby farms and introduced themselves. After the people had been duly impressed, they were asked questions about the project and about me. Two who were questioned were Pete Wendt and his old friend who farmed nearby. Pete was an old German farmer with roots deep in the grange movement. He was a pro-union activist who had openly fought the packinghouse barons. He was as quick to loan you his farm equipment as he was to shake your hand.

His friend had once chased some government people off his land with his .30-06 and spent a little time in the lockup for it. Both Pete and his friend were hardcore Debs Socialists.

The two men listened to the government's concern about law and order in the prisons, answered what questions they could, and just nodded their agreement to anything the agents said. As soon as the "G-men" (Pete's term to describe all law enforcement officials who were not in uniform) left, the two men drove over and filled me in.

"They seem to think you're not a good old law-and-order man, Joe," said Pete.

His friend, who had a streak of frontier stubbornness and independence that was a yard wide, said, "I didn't give that slicker the time of day."

The next time I was in Belgrade, I made it a point to have a cup of coffee with Henry Roos, who was the town marshal. Henry was the ideal lawman. He believed that he could solve problems in his town better than the county sheriff and the courts over in St. Cloud, and he was right.

One of the fellows in our project was a young Chicano from Chicago named Humberto de la Rosa. Humberto had spent a few years in an Illinois youth prison. When he was arrested, the cops didn't like his name so they changed it to Bill Smith. Illinois had shipped him to Iowa City to work in a shoe repair shop. He couldn't read, write, or count his money, but he knew he was being ripped off—so he walked over to the university and told them he thought some education would help him. The officials sent him to me. He had been living under one of the bridges in downtown Iowa City. He moved into 505 with us, we got his name straightened out, and he became part of the family. When we moved to Georgeville, he was one who moved with us.

One night Humberto was insulted and pushed around by a few "toughs" in Belgrade. He walked the four miles to Georgeville, put some sand in an old sock, grabbed a knife, and walked back to Belgrade. Henry had heard him threaten to come back, so he was watching for him. Before Humberto got to the three fellows, Henry stopped him, sat down and talked to him, and ended up giving him a ride back to Georgeville. Henry liked to head off trouble before it started.

Henry wasn't one to betray a confidence and he didn't talk business much, but I felt he would tell me if something was seriously wrong. As we sat and talked now, he was his usually amiable self, so I figured things were okay as far as our end of the township was concerned. I wasn't worried about raids. The project was clean and Henry knew it. Once, when I discovered a person from the project selling barbiturates, I tossed his belongings into a bag and escorted him to the bus station in Belgrade. On the way into town, he kept running his mouth off about how he wasn't afraid of me because he knew I was a pacifist. I took it for almost four miles, but just short of the bus station I slammed on the brakes, kicked him through the passenger door, and was waiting for him when he hit the ground. Then I kicked his ass about every third step he took for the final block to the bus station. Henry was across the street. When I started back to the van he asked, "What was that all about?"

"If it was something I couldn't handle, you know I'd call ya, Henry."

That fall, Pete Wendt and Henry launched a secret write-in campaign to get me elected Crow River Township constable. The constable is the low man on the law-enforcement ladder. People called him before they called Henry. Henry used him to do the chores he was too busy for. I lost the election by one vote and raised hell with Pete for not telling me what he

Stop the Presses! I Want to Get Off! | 191

was doing so I could have voted for myself. My vote would have given my opponent and me three votes each. Elections for constable in Crow River Township were not high priorities for the voters.

It was the closest I ever came to being elected to public office.

Enter Jerry Teterud and Bud Willard for Iowa and the Feds

In the November 1973 PDI, which was published late in January 1974, there is an announcement of the death of Jackson "Curly" Fee, one of 140 prisoners who took part in a peaceful work stoppage at the Marion (Illinois) federal prison. Eddie Sanchez reported to us that a group of guards entered Curly's cell, beat him severely, and dragged him to the "boxcars" (strip cells). A few days later, Curly wasn't talking or eating. Then, on October 27, he was found dead in his cell. The death was labeled a suicide by hanging. Ignored by prison administrators, guards, and news media was the fact that he was in a strip cell with nothing to hang himself with.

On the masthead of the November issue, a new name appeared as a board member of the National Prison Center. Jerry Teterud had been active with the PDI and the Church of the New Song while he was in the Iowa State Penitentiary. As soon as he was paroled, he joined Steve Fox, Merilea, Bob Copeland, Richard Tanner, Ma Jones, Betty Ebert, William Corrado (see sidebar 8), and Becky Hensley on the PDI and moved in with Steve and Jane Fox over on River Street.

━━━━━━━━━━━━ SIDEBAR 8 ━━━━━━━━━━━━

OUT OF THE UNIVERSITY AND INTO THE PDI'S SCHOOL OF HARD KNOCKS (by Wm. Christopher Corrado)

It was the early spring of 1973.

I was served with papers from the University of Iowa's registrar's office notifying me that I was being expelled for failure to pay tuition and board for the second semester. My father had agreed that I would pay for the first semester and he would pay for the second. But when I had visited home the previous Christmas, he saw that I had let my hair grow collar-length. My hair length had always been a major point of contention between Dad and me, and this time was no different. He was in full-tilt boogie punishing mode. Before I returned to Iowa City after the holiday, I asked Dad if he was going to renege on our agreement about the tuition; I had a feeling he was going to do something awful—and he did. So there I was, packing up belongings and saying goodbye to all of my mates at Hillcrest Dormitory—one of the sites of the more memorable student protests of the antiwar movement just a year before.

I was a psychology major, and during my first semester I had met a very intense, brilliant professor in the department; he became my first major male mentor. Steve Fox's area of expertise included sensory deprivation, and how, when it was used over a prolonged period of time, it could trigger psychosis. Dr. Fox was able to apply the findings of his laboratorial research to one of the most punitively inhumane practices of the modern penal system; in prisoners' terms it was referred to as being thrown "in the hole." Rather than bringing about any meaningful rehabilitation or positive results, it usually contributed to pushing an incarcerated person over the edge of sanity and into a state of psychosis.

Steve Fox was a compelling and engaging man. He possessed an uncanny ability to quickly and accurately assess a person's aptitude and talent, as well as the person's heartbreaks and handicaps. This ability gave him deep insight into what motivated an individual. When I made him aware of my present plight with the university, Steve suggested I meet and get involved with a group of people he knew at a not-for-profit collective off-campus. This grassroots group of very bright college graduates and students, as well as just-released ex-prisoners, lived and worked together advocating for humane reform of the American penal system. Steve was aware that I had worked as an emergency-room technician in Chicago and that I was the oldest sibling in a family of nine kids. He felt that the life skills I had learned in those settings, along with my studies in psychology, would dovetail well with the work of these young, progressive intellectuals and ex-prisoners at the charming classic American Craftsman–style house at 505 South Lucas Street.

The house had been painstakingly purchased and established by another wildly charismatic man of almost legendary lore—Joe Grant. Although I had only met the man a couple of times in passing, he was referenced by virtually all who knew him as a deeply warm, loving, and generous man with a great, creative pioneering spirit and a gift for inspiring groups. Evidently, Joe had been the über-father of this entire organization through his Midwestern grit and a determined spirit. This grassroots organization published a monthly newspaper, *Prisoners' Digest International*—a smart, hip, and beautifully turned-out paper written by and for prisoners. This publication was subscribed to by prisoners at penal institutions in the United States and all over the world. At that time, the PDI, as it was known locally, was looking for a person who could help in their circulation department.

I met with the group and in very short order moved into and became part of the household. Once settled, I met Bob Copeland, a smart-as-they-come journalist graduate from Florida who served as the editor of the paper. Merilea was a delicate and talented former teacher and artist who created marvelous graphics and layout design. Randy Knoper was contributing to the organization as an all-around help and budding writer. His date of birth had been drawn by the Selective Service's infamous lottery draft system, which was then in play. Randy had registered as a conscientious objector to the war in Vietnam and was able to reroute his time in the armed services by working in a not-for-profit organization through Antioch University. Jimmy Crawford was a gangly, ever-smiling, long-haired fourteen-year-old from Cedar Rapids, Iowa. He had come from a troubled home and had had a few scrapes with the jurisprudence system. Jimmy's mother, a longtime friend of Joe's, had asked Joe to take him under his wing to get him away from Cedar Rapids, where he had run into minor problems. He was everyone's younger brother and a great love of the household.

John Price was from New Orleans and had served some hard time on a chain gang in Louisiana and in the Atlanta federal penitentiary. John was of Cajun origin and filled with all of the color and culture one might expect from the Big Easy. Although his personal legacy of pain and suffering was deep, he was a spontaneous, gentle, and loving presence who attracted women like bees to honey. John was our ambassador of good living. Brother Richard Tanner and Sister Becky Hensley were a highly spirited couple cohabitating at the Lucas house. Richard had seen nearly a decade of dark days serving time at the notorious federal joint in Fort Leavenworth. Tall, lanky, and never at a loss for words, Richard was something of an evangelist in his own right. He was fiery and animated and beloved by all. Becky was a terrifically talented writer and thinker who grounded Richard and was able to help direct his energy. She had a strong spirit and was unafraid to speak her mind. She also strummed out some wonderful folk music on her guitar from time to time.

And then I met the first major love of my life . . . Becky Evans. Becky was a young girl from a large family in Iowa City. Becky had emancipated herself from her family of origin at a fairly early age and was a true flower child. I was immediately drawn to her, and we became romantically involved almost overnight. Becky had the countenance of a muse from an Andrew Wyeth painting. Her long, flaxen hair framed a sun-kissed face of high cheekbones and deep blue-and-green feline eyes. She had a lovely figure, an infectious laugh, and yet a demure, unassuming way about her. I was blessed to have been held and cherished by her for a few seasons.

Due to financial difficulties, we were forced to move from the Lucas Street house. We found a rather plain, two-story, light-blue and white wood-framed house on Lynn Street, just south of Burlington Avenue, next to the phone company's building. Although it lacked any of the charm and natural aesthetics of Joe Grant's home on South Lucas, it accommodated the basic needs of the collective for the next few months. There I had the pleasure of meeting some of the most colorful characters I've known in my life. Joanne Jones was a housewife from Muscatine, Iowa, who had been sentenced for writing a bad check for groceries. In fact, the vast majority of those behind prison bars in America had poor or no legal representation; were plagued with poverty, a lack of opportunity, or unemployment; or were simply mentally ill. In spite of Joanne's hard life, she was all heart and laughs and packs of Marlboros. We also took in a fellow named James Auburn, who slept in an RV parked in the driveway. Betty Ebert, a thirty-something woman, came in the spring of 1974 after serving ten years at Bedford Hills Penitentiary for Women in New York. She had been convicted of murder for killing her pimp before he killed her. Betty had also been sexually and physically abused by her father. She was nonetheless extremely bright and engaging. She added an element of fun and sophistication to the group.

Iowa City had become one of the hottest countercultural places of the early 1970s. Known as a hotbed of radically left-leaning scholars and thinkers, the University of Iowa was considered one of the top "public Ivy League" schools in the nation. It was nicknamed the "Berkeley of the Midwest." With a student body of some 23,000 added to the population of some 40,000 local residents, it was a bustling and energetic enclave nestled in the rolling bluffs along the Iowa River. Members of our group (especially the women) managed to attract members of a number of great blues and rock-and-roll bands who toured through the city. The whole Luther Allison Band joined our collective for one dinner. We entertained luminaries like author Chuck Storm of Native American fame. We managed to convince the owners of the C.O.D., a terrific venue for rock-and-roll bands similar to Doug Weston's famous Los Troubadours in Los Angeles, to host a couple of benefits for the PDI collective. I recall feverishly putting out hand-drawn and colored posters of underground comic characters inspired by R. Crumb to advertise the events. Our group loved to dance—and dance we did at the C.O.D. Dancing and music and a few beers during happy hour kept our group alive and vibrant.

Shortly after moving to Lynn Street, we began visiting two of the main correctional facilities in Iowa: the Fort Madison Penitentiary in Fort Madison, and the Boys Reformatory in Anamosa. We had gained the legal right to visit and provide pastoral counseling to inmates by becoming ordained ministers of a newly formed spiritual movement, the Church of the New Song (aka CNS), which had been founded by Harry Theriault, a man who was serving time in solitary confinement in a federal prison in La Tuna, Texas. Harry, a brilliant man, had seized upon his constitutional right to practice his religious beliefs. As such, he had proclaimed himself the Bishop of Tellum, and founded a church that could, in theory, legally assemble its members for services behind the walls of any penal institution in America.

This was a great triumph for prisoners, as they could now legally gather under the roof of their respective prisons for church activities. Our hope was that they would be able to establish a palpable and healthy sense of spiritual solidarity, community, and connectedness with their imprisoned brethren under the auspices of their religion. It also allowed our group to provide much-needed contact with the inmates while serving as liaisons to the outside world. Every Sunday, we made the hours-long, arduous drive to both institutions and provided ministerial services and individual counseling to the inmates. We were often accompanied by their friends, family, and lovers. We met with considerable resistance from the prison wardens and administrators, as they feared we were an incendiary group of radical upstarts who were covertly trying to instigate violent uprisings among prisoners. Although some of the group flagrantly flouted their newly earned ministerial privileges as members of CNS, it soon became apparent to officials and prisoners alike that our intentions were peaceful, educational, and, in the grand scheme of things, quite helpful.

Although our spirits at PDI were strong and we fought the good fight, financial and legal difficulties plagued us, and we eventually had to dissolve and go our separate ways.

Today, as a licensed clinical psychologist practicing in California, I look back at my affiliation with the PDI and CNS as unquestionably the most instructive of all of my many thousands of hours of training and internships on my journey to become a doctor of psychology. The men and women I encountered at 505 South Lucas taught me valuable lessons about how our penal institutions had, over the years, systematically and brutally mangled the lives of inmates. As a psychologist with a grounding in human development, it made me profoundly aware of how child abuse and neglect are virtually the petri dish for spawning future generations of prison inmates. These are the little boys and little girls who will have their spirits stunted, their bodies abused, and their fragile psyches mangled by those who were also abused and neglected themselves and who never learned coping and self-regulation skills from their parents. Moreover, my days with the PDI and CNS ingrained in me a tolerance and compassion for those who had the misfortune of a difficult beginning in this world. My Iowa internship with Joe Grant and the ex-prisoners inspired me to continue to learn more about the human condition and the workings of man's psyche, with a view to helping in at least small, incremental ways to shape a brighter and more tolerant and forgiving world for the future.

FIGURE 16. Betty Ebert (*left*) and Jeanne Schneller (*right*) were invaluable to the daily operation of PDI.

Bud Willard, another CNS member, also joined us after being paroled from Leavenworth.

At the meeting where Teterud was elected to the board, much of the discussion centered around whether the PDI should continue publishing. "As our readers are aware, the Digest has never paid for itself and our dismal financial situation has been a consistent topic of discussion on these pages," wrote one staff member.

At this same meeting, the collective agreed on a list of priorities for the coming year that included "Support and development of projects aimed at the abolition of all institutions, relationships and conditions which imprison people; consciousness raising communications to the people on the level of mass behavior; educational and supportive projects relative to returning the solution of 'crime' problems to the communities where they occur; developing a legal resources center to handle problems of incarcerated persons; providing for the immediate needs of prisoners; seeking spiritual solutions to universal problems."

Of the core PDI staff people, Bob Copeland announced that he was moving to Fort Madison to be the Church of the New Song minister at the Iowa State Penitentiary. Jim Crawford and Ma Jones wanted to continue publishing the PDI. Merilea was willing to work on whatever publication the collective decided to publish. Randall Knoper was willing to stay and work with the others. Had I known at the time that only Merilea, Jim, Ma, and Randall had chosen to continue publishing, I would have invited them to join us in Georgeville. Unfortunately, the collective didn't send us any copies of the November issue.

Years later, when the PDI was history, I picked up copies of the last few issues from the Historical Society of Iowa, with whom I had made arrangements to microfilm each issue. I discovered that the PDI staff, the National Prison Center board, and the local Church of the New Song (the latter group was made up of members of the first two groups) were concerned that I had never resigned from any of my "positions" with the organizations. Perhaps their

COURTESY OF PDI ARCHIVES

FIGURE 17. Jim Crawford, bright youngster from Cedar Rapids, Iowa, became a part of the PDI family when his mom, a close friend of Joe Grant's, sent him to Iowa City to experience a collective's lifestyle and to travel with Joe.

hard feelings were the result of their inability to keep enough money and energy flowing into the organizations. Membership in the Church of the New Song was declining, even as the PDI devoted increasing space to endless litanies and exhortations by the CNS leadership. Fewer prisoners and free-world people were renewing their subscriptions. When the November issue was refused by the warden at Leavenworth and returned to Iowa City, no lawyers filed suits in Kansas on behalf of prison subscribers.

The Last PDI

At the Georgeville Community Project, work continued. I was accepting a few speaking engagements. A group of musicians joined us from California. Their harp player wanted to grow up and play with Willie and the Bumble Bees. Great goal, but he had a ways to go.

We thought less about what was happening in Iowa City as our lives became more oriented to solving our own immediate problems. Still, I can recall discussing with Sharlane what my obligations were to the PDI. We could see that they were going to suspend publication soon. I felt that I had to pick up the equipment and give it another try. My original intention was just to reprint the most important articles from progressive publications, from other prison publications, and from our associate editors who were located in every prison in the country. With a staff of three and a concentrated drive to reestablish ties with my original supporters, national board members, and sources of financial help, I felt I could successfully rebuild the PDI.

Sharlane, on the other hand, questioned the advisability of continuing to develop either the Georgeville Community Project or the PDI. We both felt much satisfaction in what we were doing, but we were living in a depressed area, with average or below average schools.

"Is this where we should be raising Charity?" Shar asked.

I knew the answer.

In March 1974, a package of PDIs arrived. The PDI's fourth excerpt from *The Jailhouse Lawyer's Manual* ended with a simple "(To Be Continued)." It never was. That issue, dated December 1973, was to be the last. In Iowa City there was no money, nor was there enough energy to raise any.

Merilea and Randall, under a headline that read "News from Us—Statements by Two Collective Members," wrote eloquently about what they felt the PDI staff, past and present, had accomplished and learned. Merilea ended her article with a simple drawing of a hand with a finger pointing into the future. It was perfect. She headed for California and art school. Jim Crawford headed for the Northwest and ended up working the fishing boats in Alaska. Ma Jones returned to Clinton. I don't know where Randall went.

There was nothing to decide now. I believed I was the only person who could salvage the PDI. Even though I wasn't in Iowa City at the end, the PDI was as much a part of me as Charity was. I was tired and burned out. Yet I didn't think I could refuse to try to do it all again.

I planned to visit Iowa City during the first week of April to pick up the pieces of the paper. Only a few hours before I was ready to leave Georgeville, Richard Tanner called me to explain why I shouldn't bother to come down. "All of the equipment, files, furniture, everything, has been taken to the Quad Cities [Davenport, Bettendorf, Moline, and Rock Island] by Kime and sold," he said.

Again there was nothing to decide. The decision had been made for us. It was over.

Richard's only mistake was calling from a place where his conversation with me was overheard. He ended up taking a serious beating from Kime and two of his friends. I saw Richard about a month later and he was still in very rough shape, with scars that would remind him of the betrayals for the few brief years he had left.

So much animosity.

The most puzzling development was the loss of my home at 505 South Lucas. 505 served as the home to the PDI, the Church of the New Song, and the staff. The payment was $225 a month, which was what I charged us for rent. For that price we had a three-story, seven-bedroom home, with a complete apartment in the basement that was used as our PDI offices. Back then, a bedroom rented for $125 a month for a student. The basement apartment—kitchen, bath, large room with two small rooms—was worth $400 easily. To have the entire home for $225 a month was a steal. So what could the staff have been thinking to skip those $225 payments for months, lose the house, and move into a smaller home for much more money? It just didn't make sense.

Where it left Sharlane, Charity, and me was seriously out in the cold. Our plans had been to live at 505. It was our home. I'd purchased it with my GI Bill from the Korean War, and it was all we had. With that gone, I was exactly where I had been, economically, when John Eastman picked me up from the Sandstone, Minnesota, prison.

Troublesome times. The only difference in the staff was that many new people had been added while I was in the process of developing a way to survive with our own free-and-clear homes, with land for large gardens and room for farm animals where we could raise our own food and sustain ourselves. We were not that far from a major city; the mail came every day. We had four homes, a 90′ × 60′ two-story brick building, a printing plant, a tractor, a pickup, a half-built pottery works, and three-plus years of valuable connections.

The only accumulation of money had come from expert-testimony fees resulting from lawsuits we had initiated on behalf of prisoners. Steve Fox and Brother John Price had stashed the money in a bank in Wisconsin. When it appeared the government might try to grab it, it was quickly used to buy a large 300-acre farm in northeast Iowa near Decorah. That land was purchased when land prices were at their lowest in Iowa, and the rental of the crop land more than covered the payments. Communia Farm was purchased for the express purpose of providing our prisoner staff members with a place to live when the life of the PDI came to an end. It was purchased with PDI/CNS money, and the deed was signed over to Dr. Steve Fox. Dr. Fox was the only non-prisoner in our collective and a professor at the University of Iowa, with tenure and standing in the community. He was the only person in the collective with resources and a home in Iowa City who we believed we could trust.

Once the PDI closed and there was no PDI voice for the prisoners or the church, no ex-prisoners, at least none associated with the PDI or any of the projects that the PDI birthed, were ever allowed to live at the farm.

Never a Greater Need

Over the next few months, we would all learn how inevitable the closing of the PDI was. Had our own burnout and financial failure not brought us down when it did, the government was standing by with an elaborate plan that they were already developing. It's an ending to the story that I must share with you.

On November 6, 1975, drug arrests were made of Michael Remmers and Fletcher Henderson "Sonny" Lott. Both men were Church of the New Song activists. Lott was, in addition, a political activist and musician and had been a fundraiser for the PDI. Remmers was living with Kay Mesner at the time. Six days after the arrest, on November 12, he was released on bond and returned home.

Exactly one week later, on November 19, odds and ends of drugs—heroin, cocaine, MSD, LSD, marijuana, and a variety of barbiturates—were planted in the home of Jane and Steve Fox. When the house was raided the next day, Jane and Steve, Betty Ebert, Mickey Matyka, Will Corrado, Bud Willard, and Jerry Teterud were arrested on charges of possession. Willard and Teterud were also charged with possession of burglary tools and stolen property that were found at the Fox home along with the drugs.

By this time, the paper had long since folded, but people were still living and talking together, and letters were still arriving from prisoners and others around the country.

As for the garbage bags full of marijuana that a cooperating Johnson County deputy sheriff held up for the news cameras, they turned out to contain only garbage. And no one got excited over the small quantities of actual pot that were found. But because heroin, cocaine, MSD, LSD, and barbiturates were found, the defendants started calling lawyers. The *Iowa City Press-Citizen* reported, on November 20, that "attorneys outnumbered defendants" at the arraignments.

Only the defendants understood just how serious the arrests were, since they knew the drugs had been planted. The perplexing question was, "Who was working with the feds and/or the state?"

A few weeks after he was released on bond, Remmers, depressed and unable to find work, bought a pistol. When Mesner found out about the pistol, she asked him to get rid of it. Remmers gave the pistol to Bud Willard, who took it to Sheriff Gary Hughes. Hughes tested the gun, kept on file bullets fired from the gun, and told Willard, a convicted felon, to return the gun to Remmers, a convicted felon.

During this period, Mesner and Remmers were arguing frequently. It was a touchy situation, and many of Mesner's friends were concerned because Remmers's temper was well known in state and federal prisons. While serving a sentence in the Iowa State Penitentiary, he was attacked by two prisoners who had been hired to kill him. Although they stabbed him nineteen times, Remmers outlasted them; when the fight was over, Remmers took the knives away from the two would-be assassins and killed both of them.

On the night of January 9, 1976, Mesner told Remmers to move out. On that same day, Willard finally returned the gun to Remmers. The next day, Remmers became despondent and angry and murdered Mesner with that same pistol.

As convicted felons, it was against the law for either Willard or Remmers to have a gun in his possession. It also was general knowledge that Remmers was not in complete control of himself.

Ultimately, the drug arrests were resolved with fines. Sonny Lott ended up going to prison for a few months because he was in the wrong place at the wrong time.

Later in the year, Bud Willard sent a letter to the editor of the *Iowa City Press-Citizen*. At the time he was a prisoner again, this time in Illinois. In his letter, which was published on November 9, 1976, he claimed he had been working undercover for the government. "I came up with the double agent plan. I simply convinced the authorities that I would be the best informant they ever had, and give them all the information they needed, if I could be released on my own recognizance. . . . It worked."

Later we would learn that Teterud also was working for the government. In fact, according to my information, they both had been released to come to Iowa City as informants for the government.

Willard went on to tell how Sgt. Bob Carpenter of the Johnson County Sheriff's Department had personally told him: "We've been trying to get all these people for a long time . . . *we were lucky to get them through your arrest* [author's emphasis]."

As much as I disliked Jack Kime, his own actions during this period at least convinced many people that he wasn't working with the law. If he had been, he would have delivered the PDI to me in Minnesota. The government had a long-range plan that was working to destroy independent voices around the country. In the case of the PDI, their plans were not wasted. We were gone before I could reestablish the PDI in Georgeville. If I had moved in and taken the paper back before everything was moved to the Quad Cities, I'm sure we would have been arrested along with the others.

Over the years from the time I started the PDI, I had been warned by a number of people that the PDI was high on the government's hit list. The warnings intensified when we used the PDI to inform the prison world about the Church of the New Song. The last serious warning that I received before the bust, in fall 1975, was from Bob Beecroft, a news correspondent for

Mutual Radio Network in Washington, D.C. He told me that my days were numbered unless I made an occupational change. He then told me who to call for a job that appeared to have been designed for me. I called and was hired to be national program director for Offender Aid and Restoration in Charlottesville, Virginia.

Preparing to close down the Georgeville Community Project, we made 110 gallons of homemade sauerkraut, Charlie and Anne Kukuk turned our hogs into sausage, and we held an auction that had cars parked along the roadside for a mile in four directions. We provided free rides for folks in nearby retirement homes so they could get a free, old-time lunch at an auction. We received letters praising that lunch from many of those seniors, many written in German. All credit for the success of the food I attribute to Annie Kukuk.

Everything at the auction went for a song.

As for the PDI, I occasionally ask myself if it can be done again. There has never been a time in the history of prisons when there was a greater need for a PDI, a greater need for questions to be asked concerning our total disregard for proven methods of humane punishment and rehabilitation.

I do have a fantasy: Through a series of carefully placed classified ads I notify the associate editors, board members, advisors, and, yes, the subscribers—wherever they may be. The response is overwhelming. The directors of the foundations that helped in the past are on the phone: "Glad you're back. How much do you need to get going?" Country Joe McDonald calls: "Sure we'll do another fundraiser." The next call doesn't surprise me. It's Richie Havens: "Let's set up another benefit, shoot some more video, and let prisoners know that they will soon have a voice to the free world!"

I have my own dream desktop on-line operation in my home office, I could cut production costs tremendously . . . and payroll costs wouldn't be that much . . . and . . . the entire run of PDI is available in a digitally searchable format online . . . and . . .

Into the Future:

Rambling Thoughts as I Bring
This Story Up to Date

9 to 5

Leaving the PDI, the commune, and the Georgeville Community Project to reenter the world of 9 to 5 was far more difficult than I imagined it would be.

It didn't take long to learn about job openings. Bob Beecroft, with Mutual Radio in D.C., called me with a description of a job with an organization called Offender Aid and Restoration (OAR) in Charlottesville, Virginia. They flew me to D.C. to meet the board of directors. They knew everything about me. I knew nothing about them. Once again it seemed I had to live with a reputation that I knew what I was doing.

I was hired. An interesting move to Virginia followed. I drove a large rental truck with a Chandler and Price hand-fed press and seventy-five drawers of hand-set type. Sharlane and Charity followed me in an old '53 Volvo I'd traded for the pickup. With me in the cab of the truck were our dog Sam, a cat, a hen with sixteen chicks, and an attitude.

On the last leg of the trip, coming down the Blue Ridge Mountains just west of Charlottesville, the brakes failed on the truck. As the truck picked up speed and pulled away from the other drivers, I glanced back at Sharlane, and as I pulled away I could see this "What are you doing?" look on her face. When I finally came to a stop, the Virginia highway patrolman who had been trying to get my attention asked if I knew how fast I was going. I told him, "The culprit was gravity," and explained to him about the brakes. By the time he finished checking my license on his computer and returned to the truck to hand it back to me, Shar and Charity had caught up. We drove into Charlottesville.

Charlottesville was a few comfortable steps up from the commune. Our home was situated so we could look across a valley at Jefferson's Monticello.

I loved the work, although I was never convinced that a national program director was a position OAR needed. Then, shortly after I arrived, Jay Worrell stepped down as director and joined the board, and a Protestant minister was hired to take over. At the first staff meeting, everyone was asked to stand and bow our heads. The new director began praying. I watched and thought to myself, "WTF!" Another speed bump on the road to employment.

One of the OAR staff members was a hard-working young black woman, with a young daughter a couple of years older than Charity, whose pay was being subsidized by the feds during her year-long training period. When the year ended, the director replaced her with a pretty blond airhead.

There were other problems. Money was tight. Our offices were in a home next door to the old Charlottesville jail where the last execution by hanging in Virginia had taken place. The jail was empty and clean. I checked around and found that we could take over the jail for our offices rent-free. We would look good having our offices in cells, and the move would give us national publicity, I told the other board members. I even had the terminology worked out. No one working to help offenders was operating from a location that afforded us a better perspective on the plight of prisoners.

The response was, "That is absolutely ridiculous."

Two years later they made the move.

I appeared before the board and explained that money was going to get progressively more difficult to raise and that we should consider adding one small element to our volunteer training program to ensure future funding: We must train our volunteers to not only counsel offenders but be exposed to the plight of victims.

Once again the answer was, "That is absolutely ridiculous."

Big mistake on their part as funding slowed.

With Worrell out of the picture, I didn't last two years. When the preacher fired me, it came as no surprise. There were too many conflicts. There was the scene when he fired the black woman. When I told him I would be arriving thirty minutes late for staff meetings because I was not interested in his proselytizing, he asked me what I believed in. I gave him a line from a Woody Guthrie song about "Pie in the sky when we die."

I did not fit in. When he handed me the letter informing me that I had been terminated, he stood there watching me while I read it, tore it up, and tossed it in my trashcan. I told him to change "terminated" to "laid off" and said I would leave in one month. He quickly returned with the changes.

Sharlane and Charity returned to Iowa City, rented a small acreage, moved in, and planted a garden. Sharlane went to work at the Iowa Historical Society. We were home.

For the next election, the Iowa Socialists wanted to run a candidate for governor. There wasn't a member of the Iowa Socialist Party who knew more about the party and the election than I did. I was chosen because I was the only member old enough to run. Plus I had that great John Deere Model B tractor to campaign on. A few heads were turned as I drove around the state, but few checked the box for the Socialist candidate. I didn't come close to the necessary number of votes to establish us as a political party with an automatic spot on future ballots; however, in the district where the veterans' hospital was located in Iowa City, we got 17 percent of the vote.

Georgeville Comrade Has Me Back on the Farm

I moved to a farm in Iowa County. Pete Wendt, my Georgeville neighbor, had been in touch with me and wanted to join me in Iowa. His contribution would be his farm machinery, since he was retired. While waiting for Pete and the farm equipment, we started a large garden on an incredibly fertile chunk of land beside Beaver Creek to grow food for ourselves and the

Catholic Worker houses in Iowa. Every dope grower in the area knew me. I told everyone to stay out of the cornfields, and to make sure that they did, that first year I rented the land to a neighboring farmer who was also an Iowa County deputy sheriff.

When Pete suddenly died, I was advised to take all the correspondence to Minnesota to claim the equipment he had agreed to provide. Pete, sympathetic old Socialist that he was, would have wanted me to do so. I wasn't comfortable with the idea. Someone transplanted some pot in the field when the corn was about three feet tall. The deputy spotted the plants and asked me about them. I said, "It's your decision. Tear 'em up or maybe you should call the cops." That got us a good laugh. He tore them up. Someone re-transplanted them; I was charged with manufacturing. It was a setup. I was prepared for a long fight; however, after a preliminary hearing, the attorney for Iowa County said, "Plead guilty and take a 5, or plead not guilty and we'll convict you on your politics alone and promise you 15." I ended up doing six months in the reformatory circus at Anamosa.

Charity

When Charity began fifth grade, she was introduced to the cello, loved it, and within three months was studying with a professional cellist. Iowa City was a small city—60,000 or so—yet we had four full symphony orchestras.

Charity had advantages. We ate organically, and her childhood education was nourished with progressive politics. Radical poet and educator Chuck Miller taught occasional classes in the living room, and Charity sat in on the discussions. Women were part of our circle of friends—strong, independent women. Until she started school, Charity accompanied me to all demonstrations.

So when one of her teachers mentioned that the nuclear bomb was used to save lives and quickly end the war, she requested that her friend Karen Kubby, Iowa City Council member and a Socialist who believed using the bomb was wrong, be allowed to speak to the class. The school said no. Charity took her case to fifteen of the major dailies with a letter to editors requesting support for her position. I still have bags of mail that poured in. Most was hate mail, but people who had witnessed what happened wrote and praised her for speaking up.

A few months later, the Optimists went into the elementary schools to give out their annual Good Reading Awards. Students who read a number of books and designed a poster and a bookmark got an award. When the local Optimist president came to Longfellow School to personally present the awards, Charity politely refused hers, explaining, "I can't accept an award from any organization that won't accept my mother as a member."

The first I knew about the incident was when a friend from the *Des Moines Register* called a couple of days later and asked if he could interview Charity. I asked him what it was about. He explained. I called Charity to the phone, told her who wanted to talk to her, and asked her why she hadn't told me about refusing the award. She shrugged her shoulders as she reached for the phone and said, "It wasn't that important, Dad."

The *Register* feature was followed by a flurry of limos driving Charity to Des Moines so CBS, NBC, and ABC anchors could interview her for the networks.

When *Ms.* magazine called to say they were sending a writer and photographer to Iowa City, I asked Charity if she was ready to talk to the likes of Gloria Steinem. They came, did the story, and a few months later Charity was a 1984 *Ms.* magazine Woman of the Year. Charity and Sharlane headed for New York City. The *New York Times* ran a picture of Charity with Cyndi Lauper, Geraldine Ferraro, and Gloria Steinem under the headline "She's a Terrific Girl."

The Optimists changed their men-only policy a few months later. Score a win for the kid—for all kids.

Off to Arizona

In the meantime, Sharlane had put together a preservation laboratory in the basement of the Iowa Historical Society. When she saw an ad in the *New York Times* for a librarian to establish a preservation department at Arizona State University, she sent them her resume. A few months later, we moved to Tempe.

I took a job with America West Airlines as a reservation clerk and got fired eighteen months later while trying to unionize the clerks.

During this period, Ken Wachsberger contacted me and asked if I'd contribute a brief bio of the PDI, and I agreed to do so. When the original two-volume set was published in 1993, the *Los Angeles Times* devoted the two-page centerspread of the Sunday Book Review supplement to *Voices from the Underground.* The reviewer said it "comes closer than anything I've yet read to putting the sights, sounds, and texture of the '60s on paper." Unfortunately, the majority of the 2,000 sets were stolen. Fortunately, most of the reference departments at the major university libraries had already gotten copies, but Ken was left high and dry until Michigan State University Press recognized how valuable the histories of these underground newspapers were. All those years of Ken gathering the histories had not been wasted.

And while I'm on the subject of the first *Voices*, I must clear up a problem. Ken invited all of the contributors to submit names of people they wanted to include in a collective dedication at the front of the book. I included family members and Meridel LeSueur. I also included the name of a young man who had been busted for dealing pot. I had gone to Cheyenne, Wyoming, to testify on his behalf, hoping they wouldn't be too hard on him. I'd met him in Anamosa, where he was serving a sentence for multiple drunk-driving charges. He was an amiable guy and became a friend during those few months. After the book was published, I learned that he had been rearrested. He had been dealing cocaine while wearing a wire and entrapping people he was selling drugs to. This time he was selling with his wire turned off to pick up some extra cash. Unfortunately the person he sold to had his wire turned on. Bingo. Scotty Remington had done two things that were unforgivable: entrapped friends simply to stay out of prison, and stolen from his handlers. The last time I spoke to him, he had been offered eight years if he would plead guilty. I told him he would be a fool if he didn't take it. He refused, went to trial, and ended up with 12 years.

Meridel

I was introduced to the writings of Meridel LeSueur by poet Chuck Miller. He was teaching a class on "The Proletarian Writers of the Thirties" at our home in Iowa City. Meridel wrote about the people I was most at home with: farmers, laborers, the poor, and those forced to live on the fringe of society. A short time later I met her, in person, at the University of Minnesota

Law College. Phil Berrigan was scheduled to speak. When I arrived, Meridel was sitting in an area down front that was roped off. Whenever I see that kind of setup, I take a seat in the reserved area. I recognized her from the drawing by her daughter Deborah LeSueur on one of her books. I walked over and introduced myself. I told her about the class in Iowa City, that I loved her books, and that I was impressed with her description of the bank robbery in *The Girl.* "There's no way you could have written that scene if you hadn't been driving the getaway car," I said to her. That got her attention.

As she handed me a slip of paper with her address and phone number scribbled on it, she asked what I was doing the next day.

"Whatever you have in mind."

That meeting developed into a friendship, punctuated with visits to Iowa City for readings and later the *Meridel LeSueur Iowa Tour* video, which I produced. We toured six colleges in Iowa. She packed the house every night. I got as much video as I could. In Murray, Iowa, we sat on the front porch of the house where she had been born in 1900. I found an old hymnal in the house that had been published that same year. Meridel paged through the book. At one point she asked, "Do you remember this song from when you were a kid?" and began singing "I Walk in the Garden Alone." I told her that song happened to be my mother's favorite hymn. Meridel and Peggy were good friends, even though they never met.

Word that Meridel was in town spread. A woman walked up and invited Meridel to join her and nine or ten other women from the town at a café close by. Meridel took a seat at the large table. These meetings happened all week. She relived the Meridel legend every day.

Meridel was born a Warton, but she took the name Le Sueur when her mother remarried Arthur Le Sueur, who had been elected Socialist mayor of Minot, North Dakota, when the North Dakota Non-Partisan League kicked the bankers and lawyers and other professionals out of elected office and replaced them with farmers and laborers. When I learned about that incident from Meridel, I remembered the story, which I related earlier in this history, of my mom, as a young teen, accepting $20 and a ride to the polls from former governor Louis B. Hanna to vote a straight Republican ticket, and then voting the Non-Partisan League ticket instead. The league swept the Republicans and Democrats out of office.

Many years later, when she was in her nineties, Mom would think about the $20 she falsely accepted. "That bothers me to this day," she confessed. "But it doesn't bother me as much as it would have if I had voted Republican."

I read Meridel's *Women in the Breadlines* to Peggy after her eyesight began to fail her. There wasn't a word in the book that Peggy couldn't attest to.

Cuba

When I heard one day in 2005 that Ben Fruehauf was taking a cargo schooner full of pianos to Cuba, I called to ask if I could accompany the pianos to do a documentary. My request was denied. There is no room on the schooner for passengers, Captain Paul Whelan told me. But I lucked out. I learned that the captain and the schooner were stuck down in Saint Maarten (French Antilles) without a crew. I wired him immediately and offered my videographer and myself as a crew. I explained that I had experience, and my photographer had even more. I even had a bilingual woman who could cook. Captain Whelan bought it and flew us to Saint

Maarten, and the next day we were being briefed and preparing to set sail on a 110´ two-masted cargo schooner. I lied about my age since the captain would not hire a crewmember who was over sixty, which was his age. At the time I was seventy-five. We ran into some rough sailing. I managed to stay ahead of the captain, but he was the youngest sixty-year-old I've ever met.

The first leg of the trip, to Tampa Bay, Florida, was much more difficult than one could imagine. The Florida Straits are a notoriously unpredictable area for sailing. We sailed into two storms that lasted for a total of four days. It took us almost two weeks to get to Tampa Bay, where we spent two days loading fifty-five pianos and assorted items necessary to prepare the pianos to use in the colleges. We arrived in Cuba almost fifty years to the month from my last time there. It felt great to be back. After unloading the pianos, we sailed up the coast to the Hemingway Marina and spent the next few weeks visiting friends. There were two well-worn sets of *Voices from the Underground* in the University of Havana library.

(*Pat yourself on the back, Ken Wachsberger.*)

During our last meeting in Cuba, over dinner, I confessed that I was seventy-five. The captain bought me a beer and said I could sail with him anytime.

I was anticipating trouble when I flew from Havana to Miami International. I had two bottles of Russian vodka and a case of Hatuey beer, bags of cameras, and my normal excessive amount of stuff plus ten rolled-up paintings on canvases. At the gate I handed the fellow my passport, which had Cuban approval stamps in the book rather than on pieces of paper that could be discarded so as not to upset the uniforms at customs; he gave it the same look he had given the person in front of me and handed it back. I was relieved. I did not want my passport pulled.

Just before returning, Ben and I were sitting in Havana International Airport talking, and I noticed he was reading a manuscript with the name "Decca" on it. I asked if that was in reference to Jessica Mitford, the writer. He said it was.

I said, "Jessica was on the board of directors of my underground newspaper during the Vietnam War, the *Prisoners' Digest International.*"

"She's my mom," said Ben.

Small world.

Peggy moved to Arizona to live with us, and that was a perfect environment for her. She had always lived in the North Country and had emigrated from Norway. Being able to walk into the back yard and pick an orange fresh off a tree was magic to her.

Our moves were to a series of college towns: Iowa City, Tempe, Madison, Evanston, and Lawrence.

Here in Lawrence, Kansas, where I now live, watching Ken Wachsberger's dream project once again take shape, and recognizing that it is impossible to retell, in the detail I would prefer, the story of the PDI, all the people involved, and all that led up to its birth and followed its death, I am grateful that I had the opportunity to tell as much as I did. The entire PDI should be included, but that's not possible. What is possible is to digitize every issue and place everything online. Watching the reemergence of those voices from the underground is an inspiration. New generations of protestors are taking to the streets around the world under an OCCUPY banner, and there is an excitement on the street that is building.

Finally, the lists of the names of prisoners on recent hunger strikes in California include PDI editors from back in the day; old lifers who became the best jailhouse lawyers, poets, and writers; and activists who, inside or out, are working to end the brutality that is everyday fare in most prisons in the United States.

We all have spaces we must OCCUPY to ensure that someday there will be greater equity for all.

The PDI and CNS Archives

Odds and ends of information continue to be sent to the PDI archives and CNS archives at the Historical Society of Iowa in Iowa City. Any documents, letters, or information about the PDI and/or CNS that you have access to should be sent. Include a letter stating that the material is to be added to the PDI or CNS collections. Legal documents concerning actions over issues of SPEECH and RELIGION are particularly important.

FIGURE 18. Unfinished painting of Becky Evans and daughter Anna by Joe Grant. Becky died quietly at home, in Iowa City, with Anna and friends at her side. Cause of death was cancer. Joe Grant recalls, "She called me and I drove to Iowa City immediately. I arrived a few minutes after she died."

REBECCA LEA EVANS

November 24, 1954–July 20, 2008

Rest In Peace, Dear Heart

Afterword

PAUL WRIGHT

T**he** United States has had prison publications almost as long as it has had prisons. There are two types of prison publications: the "in-house" prison press, which is published and supported by the state while prisoners are the nominal writers and editors, and which is often the de facto press office for the warden; and the independent prison magazines and newsletters written and published by prisoners with no government support, and which are sometimes critical of the prison and jail regime.

Some of the government-run prison magazines have achieved public acclaim beyond the prison walls, such as the *Angolite* in Louisiana and the *Prison Mirror* in Minnesota, in large part because the government allows them to publish in the first place, and because of their longevity in publishing for decades. Prior to the 1990s almost every prison in America boasted an in-house publication. As the prison population exploded in the 1990s and the repression of American prisoners dramatically increased, among the first casualties were the in-house prison publications, the vast majority of which were simply shuttered and closed. The few that remained were often shadows of their former selves, where the weightiest topics discussed were the prison softball teams.

The real story of prisoners and prisons has for the most part been told in the independent prison magazines and newsletters published by prisoners and their supporters inside and out. Today, *Prison Legal News*, which I started while confined in a maximum-security prison in the State of Washington in 1990, is the longest-running prisoners' rights magazine in American history, having been published monthly for twenty-one years. But we were not the first.

Starting in the late 1960s, prisoners and ex-prisoners began to publish their own magazines and have their own voice, unmuzzled by the state, where they could talk about their dreams, their aspirations, and the brutal cesspools of criminality known as the American gulag. *Prisoners' Digest International* was one of these publications. And it enjoyed much distinguished company. Continuing into the 1990s, the best prisoner writing on and about prisons was published in the *Prison Law Monitor*, *California Prisoner*, *Prison News Service*, and many more. The prison press was often a voice of resistance. At the time he was murdered by New York state police during the Attica uprising, political prisoner Sam Melville was publishing a newsletter appropriately called *The Iced Pig*.

PDI was one of the first independent prison publications to give voice to current and former prisoners. Unlike the government-run prison publications, PDI and the free prison press were not the warden's press office and could, and did, tell it like it was. This was a time of social ferment in American history when many other oppressed groups were, for the first time in history, finding their collective voice and publishing journals by and for their members, with the goal of organizing around demands for greater rights and equality, and also educating the mainstream American public about these issues. Like many of these publications, PDI did not have a long life in terms of longevity or issues published. But it had a profound impact.

It has been in the pages of these journals, a tradition that *Prison Legal News* continues to this day, that the daily reality of the American carceral experience is exposed and discussed in the words of current and former prisoners themselves. The sad reality is that as the number of prisoners in the United States reaches the highest numbers, raw and by percentage of the population, known in human history, the prison press as an institution has largely collapsed. When *Prison Legal News* started in 1990, it was a newsletter focused on the State of Washington, one of at least forty other independent prisoners' rights magazines that were publishing at that time. California alone had six!

The decline of the penal press probably does not have any single cause. Rather it has a variety of causes, ranging from violent repression and censorship by the government, to economics, and to the statistical profile of the average American prisoner as a functionally illiterate, mentally ill substance abuser—a tough combination for any publishing industry to overcome. It's hard to pitch publications to a population that cannot read. But the biggest killer of prison publishing has most likely been apathy and lack of hope on the part of prisoners. In the 1970s, prisoners were no richer and no more literate, saner, or less drug-addicted than today. The government was also as or more repressive. But prisoners had hope. Someone once said, "Man can live without justice, and often must, but he cannot live without hope." When Joe Grant first began publishing in 1971, the civil rights movement had experienced heady victories, legal, legislative, and societal. The Vietnam War was raging, but so was a popular student movement against it. The rights of prisoners stood shoulder to shoulder with the rights of women, of gays and lesbians, of students, black people, and the poor. As prisoners saw historic advances being made by black people around the country—especially in the South (and remember, until the early 1980s prisoners were predominately white)—by gays and lesbians, and by youth, they were encouraged that they, too, could have human rights and be treated with a modicum of the dignity and respect to which every human being is entitled. More importantly, they mobilized and organized for those rights. The Attica uprising of 1971 and subsequent massacre gave rise to the modern American prisoners' rights movement, which made great gains and strides in the 1970s.

Looking back today, it is difficult to imagine that less than forty years ago the federal government gave law-enforcement grants to legal aid groups to represent the rights of prisoners; that Ronald Reagan inaugurated conjugal visits for prisoners in California; and that Jerry Brown, on his first go-around as governor, would sign into law the Inmate Bill of Rights.

These achievements were all duly chronicled, organized, and reported on by the prison press of the day. Prisoners had hope.

Prisons and their occupants are reflections of the society from where prisoners come and to which they return. Today, prisoners are just as repressed, beaten down, and demoralized as their counterparts on the outside. Pretty much the only prison news of the past thirty years has been bad news. When I started *Prison Legal News* in 1990, there were a million people in prisons and jails in the USA. As we begin the second decade of the 2000s, there are over 2.5 million captives in a system that grows exponentially larger each year. Prisoners are more restricted, surveilled, censored, and silenced than at any point in the past forty years. It is little wonder that the prison press is a frail skeleton of what it once was. So, too, is American journalism as a whole.

But even in prison, things don't stand still and they don't stay the same. In the 1950s the media and political press were largely silenced by Joe McCarthy and Cold War repression. But they had their predecessors to remember, and a few brave publications like *Monthly Review* and the *Guardian* kept the presses rolling. When the 1960s and 1970s rolled around with their groundswell of change and social movements, people started publishing their own magazines to have their own voice. I hope we will see that day come again. For now, *Prison Legal News* will remember those who came before us, including *Prisoners' Digest International*, and carry the torch for those who will come after us.

About the Authors

Mumia Abu-Jamal is an award-winning journalist and former Black Panther Party member whose books include *We Want Freedom: A Life in the Black Panther Party*, *Jailhouse Lawyers: Prisoners Defending Prisoners vs. the U.S.A.*, and others. He was living on death row in a Pennsylvania prison when he wrote his foreword. He was finally released to the general prison population after twenty-nine years when the Supreme Court rejected the prosecution's request to reinstate the death penalty that the federal appeals court had declared unconstitutional.

Bob Copeland was an editor of PDI from October 1971 until the final issue was published in April 1973. As a Church of the New Song Sealed Revelation Minister, he worked for two years inside the walls of the Iowa State Penitentiary as minister to the Prison Purlieu, Fort Madison, Iowa. In 1976 he helped found a land cooperative in southeast Minnesota, where he lives with his wife in an earth-sheltered home that they designed and built. He often officiates at weddings as a New Song minister.

Wm. Christopher Corrado is a licensed clinical psychologist in California where he has resided for more than thirty years. He counsels and teaches on psycho-spiritual matters and is a seasoned practitioner of sacred magic in the Christian Hermetic tradition. He has been a long-time proponent of the humane treatment of the mentally challenged and the incarcerated.

After spending many years on Maui writing and raising his children, **Warren Dearden** passed away in 1993. He is survived by his daughter, Nimblewill, and his son, Lightnin', who are working to publish several of Warren's novels, including *Children of All Ages* and *A Free Country*, electronically.

Rebecca Hensley is an instructor of sociology at Southeastern Louisiana University and blogs on race relations. Her site is called "Why Am I Not Surprised?"

Steve Levicoff served as director of the Institute on Religion and Law, where he specialized in legal issues impacting religious rights. He holds a Ph.D. in religion and law from the Union Institute, and his books include *Building Bridges: The Prolife Movement and the Peace Movement*, *Christian Counseling and the Law*, and *Street Smarts: A Survival Guide to Personal Evangelism and the Law*.

Merilea is an artist and political activist. Her favorite non-computer medium is intaglio printmaking, a form of etching and/or engraving on zinc or copper plates. A resident of Oakland, California, she worked on the 2010 mayoral campaign of candidate Rebecca Kaplan. Although Kaplan lost by a narrow margin, she retained her seat as council member at large on the Oakland City Council.

Ken Wachsberger is a long-time author and editor and is the founder and publisher of Azenphony Press. He has been a member of the National Writers Union for over a quarter century and is a former national officer. He is the editor of the four-volume Voices from the Underground series, of which this book is the fourth volume. His books, including his first book, the cult classic *Beercans on the Side of the Road: The Story of Henry the Hitchhiker*, are available at his Azenphony Press website.

Paul Wright is the editor and co-founder of *Prison Legal News*, which he started in 1990 while imprisoned in Washington state and which he continues to edit since his release from prison in 2003. The former jailhouse lawyer vice president of the National Lawyers Guild, he has edited three anthologies on mass imprisonment: *The Celling of America: An Inside Look at the US Prison Industry*, *Prison Nation: The Warehousing of America's Poor*, and *Prison Profiteers: Who Makes Money from Mass Incarceration*. His articles have appeared in dozens of publications and he is a regular national speaker on issues related to prisons and the criminal justice system.

Index

Doyle, Eddie, 80, 81

"Dr. Edgar Schein's List of Behavior-Modifying Tactics," 152–53

Drafted into Service at the PDI (Copeland), 95–96

Drumgo, Fleeta, 108

Drummond (cartoonist), 97, 132

Dunbar, Walter, 114

Dunne, John, 113

DuRain, Charles "Chas," 65, 132, 183–84

E

Eads, William R., 92

Eastman, John, 13, 51–55, 84, 197; *The Day Love Died* (film), 55

Ebert, Betty, 191, 193, *195*, 198

Eckholt, Larry, 64

Eclatarians, 139

Egstrom, Norma Deloris. *See* Lee, Peggy

El Reno (Oklahoma) Federal Prison, 149

Eldora (Iowa) Juvenile Detention Center, 88, 124

Eldridge, Stanley, 97

Eli, Frank: *The Riot*, 112

Ellen (poet), Hillcrest School for Girls, Salem, OR, 68

Erickson, Mary Jean, 149

Erlich, Reese, 88

Evans, Anna, 93, *210*

Evans, Rebecca Lea "Becky," *210, 211*; *Penal Digest International*, 62, 69–73, 76, 93; *Penal Digest International* commune, 88; subscription drives, 120; trip to Miami, 84–85; and William Corrado, 193

Eve, Arthur, 113

EXTRA, 5

F

Famous Artists School, New York City, 91

Farnham, James, 62

Fassler, Bob, 21

Federal Bureau of Investigation visit to Georgeville, MN, 189–90

Federal Bureau of Prisons, 45, 145; brainwashing

and behavioral modification, commitment to, 151; destruction of Joe Grant's artwork, 55; increase in behavior-modification in prisons, 182; permission to visit John Wagner, 140; restraining order against Joe Grant, 144; ruling on long hair in prisons, 135

Felien, Eddie, 170; and *Hundred Flowers*, 6, 169; Minneapolis City Council, election to, 169

Fernandez, Juan, 188

Ferraro, Geraldine, 206

Ferretti, Fred, 113, 115

Fessler, Bob, 23

505. See Penal Digest International

Fletcher, Rex, 62, 65, 123; difficulties in adjusting to living outside of prison, 99–103; parole of, 86

Florida State Penitentiary, Raiford, 90, 103

Fortune in Men's Eyes (play), 98

Fortune Society, New York City, 98–99, 113, 173–74

Fox, Jane, 174, 180, 191, 198

Fox, Michael, xvii, xviii

Fox, Stephen "Steve" S., *125, 126,* 174, 191–92; arrest for drug possession, 198; Communia Farm, purchase of, 198; as an expert witness, 172

Freddie (halfway house resident), 105–6

Free Country, A (Dearden), 74

Free Mumia website, xvii

Freeman, George, 98

Freeworld Times, The, 144

French wines, boycott of, 122

Frost, Al, 82, 83, 84

Fruehauf, Ben, 207, 208

Fugitive, The (television series), 53

G

Gabe & Walker's nightclub, Iowa City, IA, 105, 106

Gabriela (Cuban revolutionary), 10–16

Garza, Anne "Annie," 158, 159, 174

Gay Liberation Front, 177

192, 195; *The Sea*, 86–89; visit to La Tuna
Federal Prison, 155–56; visit to Minnesota
Federal Prison at Sandstone, 156
Mesner, Kay, 198, 199
Mezvinsky, Eddie, 68
Mezvinsky, Myra "Mickey," 68, 90
Michigan State University Press, xxii
Mickey, Stephen, 170
Midnight Special, 189
Milani, Joe, 132
Miller, Chuck, 205, 206
Miller, David, 149
Miller, Henry, 56
Miller, O. G., 108
Mills, John V., 108
Milwaukee 14, 172
Minneapolis Star Tribune, 162, 163
Minnesota Federal Prison, Sandstone, 62, 141,
197; incarceration of Joe Grant, 38–40, 43,
50–51
Minnesota State Penitentiary, Stillwater, 62, 97,
111–12
Miramon, Armando, 188, 189
Missouri State Penitentiary, Jefferson City, 62
Mitchell, Dick, 111–12
Mitford, Jessica, 65, 133, 208
Montgomery, Jim, 84
Monthly Review, 215
Moore, Henry, 62
Moore, Winston E., 88
Morgan, Bobby, 148
Mortenson, Stan, 161
Mother Jones, 5
Mullaney, Anthony, 172–73
Murton, Tom, 144–45; *Accomplices to the Crime*,
119; *The Freeworld Times*, 144; superintendent
of the Arkansas Prison System, 119; warden
of Tucker State Prison Farm, AR, 118
Murton Foundation for Criminal Justice, 144
Mutual Radio Network, 112–13, 200, 203
Myers, Richard E. "Dick," Jr., 68, 73
Myrus, Don, 110, 145–46

N

NAACP Legal Defense Fund, 174
Napoleon XIV (Jerry Samuels): "They're Coming
to Take Me Away, Ha Ha" (song), 164
Nation, The, 5
National Catholic Reporter, 172
National Correctional Industries Association,
Inc., 89, 89n4
National Law Office, 113
National Lawyers Guild, xviii, 61, 135; at Attica
Correctional Facility during 1971 riot, 113;
and Oklahoma State Prison for Women at
McAlester, 124; and prison censorship of
Penal Digest International, 103, 169
National Lawyers Guild, San Francisco, 189
National Prison Center, 134, 174, 180, 191;
formation of, 125–26
National Prisoners Coalition, 149
National Writers Union, xvii
Nelson, Bob, 20, 23
Nemnich, Jerry, 65, 68; and *The Interpreter*, 61;
Worth (poem), 65–66
New Era, The, 62
New Jersey State Penitentiary, Trenton, 97
New Radical Left, 102
New Song College, Clinton, IA, 147, 151;
drug counseling service, 156; eviction
proceedings, 156–61
New York Times, xi, 103–4, 113, 206; compared to
Penal Digest International, 104
New Yorker, 171
newspapers, prison. *See* prison publications
Newton, Huey P., 133
Nin, Anaïs, 56
Nixon, Richard, 134
Nolen, W. L., 107, 108
Norgaard, Erik, 62
North Dakota Non-Partisan League, 207
Nunes, Rodney, 150

O

Oakes, Richard, 41, 175
Occupy Wall Street movement, xii

Wyer, Verna, 62

Y

Young Lords, 113

Z

Z Magazine, 5
Zedong, Mao, 107
Zen and the Art of Motorcycle Maintenance
(Pirsig), 169
Zinn, Howard: *Disobedience and Democracy: Nine
Fallacies on Law and Order*, 31; *A People's
History of the United States*, 89, 89n5;
Vietnam: The Logic of Withdrawal, 31